Accommodation Operation Handbook

OrangeBooks Publication

1st Floor, Rajhans Arcade, Mall Road, Kohka, Bhilai, Chhattisgarh - 490020

Website: **www.orangebooks.in**

© Copyright, 2024, Author

All rights reserved. No part of this book may be reproduced, stored in a retrieval system, or transmitted, in any form by any means, electronic, mechanical, magnetic, optical, chemical, manual, photocopying, recording or otherwise, without the prior written consent of its writer.

First Edition, 2024

ISBN: 978-93-6554-557-9

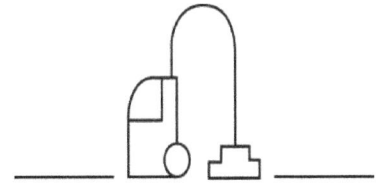

Accommodation Operation Handbook

DR. VIVEK PATHAK

OrangeBooks Publication
www.orangebooks.in

Content

1. Introduction To Hotel Housekeeping 1
2. Role of Housekeeping in Hospitality Industry 4
3. Organization Structure of Housekeeping Department 6
4. Duties And Responsibilities of Housekeeping Staff 8
5. Qualities of Housekeeping Staff 13
6. Types of Rooms 15
7. Daily Routines And Systems of The Housekeeping Department 18
8. The Chamber Maid's Service Room 20
9. Hygienic & Safe Methods of Cleaning 22
10. Daily Cleaning of Rooms 25
11. Standard Room Supplies 32
12. Guest Room Inspection 35
13. Cleaning of Public Areas 40
14. Special Cleaning And Weekly Cleaning 44
15. Composition, Care And Cleaning of Various Surfaces 47
16. Glass & Ceramics-Various Types 52
17. Wood-Various Types And Their Protective Finishes 55
18. Cleaning Equipments 59
19. Cleaning Agent 65
20. First Aid 70
21. Fire Fighting 76
22. Lost And Found Procedure 79
23. Key And Key Controls 81
24. Registers And Formats in Housekeeping 83
25. Interdepartment Relationship 86
26. Hotel Linen 88

27. Linen Room 89
28. Sewing Room 100
29. Uniforms And Protective Clothings 101
30. Fibres And Fabrics 105
31. Laundry 123
32. Stain Removal 134
33. Soft Furnishings 137
34. Pest Control 140
35. Flower Arrangement 144
36. Interior Decoration 150
37. Floor Finishes 160
38. Wall And Wall Coverings 170
39. Carpets 174
40. Lighting 180
41. Planning And Organizing 187
42. Budget 189
43. Emergencies And Dealing With Them 192
44. Environmentally Friendly Processes 196
45. Glossary 198

Introduction To Hotel Housekeeping

The hospitality is a part of larger enterprise known as travel and tourism industry. The travel and tourism is a vast group of business with one goal in common providing necessary and desired products and services to customers and travelers.

Accommodation facilities constitute a vital and fundamental part of tourism supply. Among the important inputs, which flow into the tourism system, is tourism accommodation forming a vital component of tourism superstructure.

Definition:

Hotel is defined by British law as a Place where a bonafide guest receives food and shelter, provided he is in apposition to pay for Band is in a receivable condition. (Rights of admission reserved).

A Hotel may be defined as an establishment whose primary business is providing lodging facilities for the general public and which furnishes one or more of the following services:

Food and Beverage Services.

Room Attendant Services.

Laundry Services.

And use of Furniture and Fixtures.

Growth And Development of Hotel Industry

A Hotel industry is perhaps one of the oldest industries in the world and with establishment of money, sometime in the 6th century B. C came the first real impetus (enterprise) for people to trade and travel. Since prior to that, it was difficult due to lack of standardized medium of exchange. The earliest Inns were ventures by husband and wife who used to provide modest wholesome food, quench thirst (mainly wine) and a large hall to stay for travelers against money. Initially Inns were called "Public Houses or Pubs" and the guests were called "Paying Guest."

These conditions remained for several hundred years. The advent of industrial revolution brought ideas and processes and progress in the business of Inn keeping. The development of railways and ships made travelling more prominent. The industrial revolution also changed travel from social to business travel. There was an urge for quick and clean service because the inns were basically self-service instit"tions.

During the era of 1750 to 1820 the English Inns gained the reputation of being the first in the world and were generally centered around London. In early England public houses were normally called "Inns" or "Taverns". Normally the name Inn was reserved for finer establishments catering to the nobles while the name Taverns was awarded to the houses frequented by common man. In France the establishments were known as "Hotelleries" and the less pretentious houses called "Cabarets". The name hotel is believed to be derived from the word hotelleries around 1760. In America lodging houses were called "Inn" or "Coffee house". By 1800 the USA were the leaders in development of first class hotels.

The real growth of the modern hotels took place in the USA beginning with the opening of the "City Hotel" in 1794 in New York. This was the first building erected for hotel purpose. This period also saw the beginning of chain operations under the guidance of E. M Statlers.

The housekeeping department in a hotel is responsible for cleanliness, maintenance and aesthetic upkeep of the hotel. Just as the name signifies, the role of housekeeping is to keep a clean, comfortable and safe hotel. It is an extension of basic home keeping multiplied into the commercial proportion. Therefore just as we enjoy keeping a sparkling home for ourselves and the guest who visit us, the housekeeping department takes pride in keeping the hotel clean and comfortable so as to create a home away from home.

A hotel survives on the sale of rooms, food and beverage and other minor operating services like laundry, health club, etc. Of these the sale of rooms constitutes a minimum of 50%. In other words, a hotels largest margin of profit comes from room sales as a room once made can be sold over and over again. A good hotel operation ensures optimum room sales to bring about maximum profit

The room sale is dependant on the quality of the room, the decor, the facilities, cleanliness of the room and how safe it is. To make a room appealing to a guest is the duty of the housekeeping, which has to ensure the basic human needs of comfort and security.

What Does A Room Mean To A Guest?

The sale of rooms provides approximately 50% of the total hotel revenue. A room not solpdarotincualar day will lose its opportunity to earn revenue for that day. Because of this feature of rooms, they are referred to as highly perishable commodities.

The Room Means a Boarding To The Guest

D Comfort: Every hotel spends a lot of effort in ensuring the quality of beds, mattresses, channel music, attached bar, etc. These comforts must be regularly maintained and should be properly functioning. It is the housekeeping departments duty to ensure this.

D Safety And Security: The primary device that hotels provide to ensure safety is restricted entry to the room through the door only. Besides this there are double locking systems, strict control of room keys, master keys and safety chain locking systems from within. All electrical wiring in the room should be concealed and no equipments in the room should be faulty.

D Privacy: Room windows are provided with curtains. Superior hotels could have day curtains and heavy night curtains. Windows could normally overlook good scenic view away from the prying eyes of others in the hotel or outside public. The procedure to enter a room is also well defined to ensure guest privacy.

A guest is provided with entertainment, food and beverage; telephone service, etc. in his room. Thus the guest is free to spend his time fulfilling the purpose of his visit, be it a business or holiday. The housekeeping should provide a list of all facilities and a way to avail them.

D Cleanliness And Hygiene: The housekeeping department has got the most important role to play in this respect. Clean and well-maintained areas and equipments create a favorable impression on the guest. Hygiene must be maintained especially in the washrooms, toilets, pool changing room, health club, etc.

D Decor: Colour and design are mood methods whether the guest realizes it or not. The decoration of his room may motivate his like or dislike for the entire operation. Some housekeepers assume the responsibility for the in-house decor and some others enlist the assistance of a professional designer. In both cases the aim is to achieve a balance between beauty and practicality.

A room is very important to a guest and hence he demands the high standards in everything the room stands for.

Important Years in The History of Indian Hotels

- 1897 Indian Hotel Company (I.H.C.) was founded by J. H. Tata. 1903 Taj Bombay was commissioned.

- 1934 Clarks Hotel was purchased by M. S. Oberoi.

- 1966 Oberoi Continental in New Delhi was the first modem luxury hotel to be commissioned in the capital.

- 1973 Oberoi Towers in Bombay was commissioned.

Role of Housekeeping In Hospitality Industry

The housekeeper is the only departmental head that has access to every department The only departmental head who maintains regular relation with other departmental heads and thus obtains an overview of the entire operation. The housekeeping staffs are the eyes and ears of the management The guest indeed forms an instantaneous impression when he walks into the lobby of the hotel which is either enhanced or diminished as he moves from the front office to the elevator and then down the corridor towards the room i.e. approaching with either mild anticipation or otherwise.

When the guest enters a room however all-previous impressions are immediately supplemented by a virtually total response to the room itself. The rooms are the heart of the hotel and unless the decor is appropriate, the air odour free and the furnishing spotlessly clean, the hotel has lost the guest and as well a potential repeat customer forever. The Executive housekeeper and the supervisory team seek out potential employees and train them properly to get maximum output The Executive housekeeper must be constantly in touch with the new products in market and the new cost saving devices and accessories.

Since no hotel wants to room a guest in an unclean room, the housekeeping department must provide the front office with the proper information about the ready rooms in order to meet the anticipated arrivals of the day. The Executive housekeeper is involved in the management planning not only on the day-to-day basis but also in terms of total knowledge of the operation. Housekeeping is that which deals essentially with the cleanliness and all the ancillary services attached to it. Cleanliness is important for health and also for well-being. One can clean by a dirty method but one has to be taught the clean and the right method.

A guest spends more time in his room than he spends in any other part of the hotel. So he can check up the cleanliness if he wishes. Therefore everything should be clean and up to date. The bathroom in particular is the most sensitive place and a dirty toilet or a basin makes a guest feel revolted. An international guest is a fussier one and wants utmost cleanliness everywhere. The decor and good order of maintenance of any hotel also plays a large role in creating a comfortable impression for the guest Decent room supplies and services like the laundry and dry cleaning services, show again that the hotel is considering the guest's comfort and wishing to please him. In most hotels the major part of revenue comes from the rooms. A room empty for one night loses the possible revenue forever. Cleanliness may be a reason for high or low occupancy. This simply shows the importance of cleanliness though lack of furnishing and modernizing can also be a reason for poor occupancy.

Not only the guests get the impression of a hotel through the cleanliness of a room, but also the guests who are invited to attend the functions in a hotel, and the guest who comes to visit a room guest get the impression of the hotel from the cleanliness of the lobby, restaurants, public area, public area toilets; and also from the state of cleanliness of the staff uniform a guest can judge a lot about the hotel; the result of which may be positive or negative. Trade magazines also do monthly assessment of hotels, they mention usually small details:-

> How often the rooms are serviced.

> Whether the guest supplies are according to the standard.

> How many specialty restaurants or coffee shops of bars they have.

The fulfillment of these criteria gives the hotel its desired category. Thus we can see the housekeeping is responsible for overall cleanliness of the establishment and helps the other departments to get more business and earn profit.

Housekeeping being such a large contributor to the profit factor plays a major role as an individual department and has position of its own.

Importance of Housekeeping

1. Housekeeping is a department that deals essentially with cleanliness and all the ancillary services attached to that.

2. Cleanliness is important for health foremost and also for well being. One cannot feel comfortable in an environment that is not clean and well ordered.

3. The hygiene of housekeeping is essential. One can clean by dirty methods, but in our courses we have to stress and demonstrate clean and correct methods. The hygiene factor must always be present.

4. Housekeeping in a hotel provides the accommodation for the guests. A guest spends more time alone in the room than he spends alone in any other part of the hold, therefore he can check on the standards of cleanliness of a room and if he doesn't find it dean then he would loose his confidence in the hotel and change over to another one.

5. The guest linen provided in the room should also be of superior quality and hygienically cleaned as the guest is going to touch it to his body. Dirty linen is unforgiving in any hotel. The pillows and the mattress as well should be checked before letting out the room for the next guest

6. Housekeeping provides second service as per the request of the guest.

7. Other services provided are laundry; dry cleaning, pressing, shoe polishing, valet service, etc.

8. Now days in most hotels, the maximum revenue comes from the sale of rooms, therefore stress must be paid to proper cleanliness of guest rooms and all public areas which are in continuous contact with the guests.

Cleanliness involves health, which is happiness in our life; therefore it's not something to be ignored at our homes as well as at our work place.

Organization Structure of Housekeeping Department

Organization Chart of a Large Hotel:

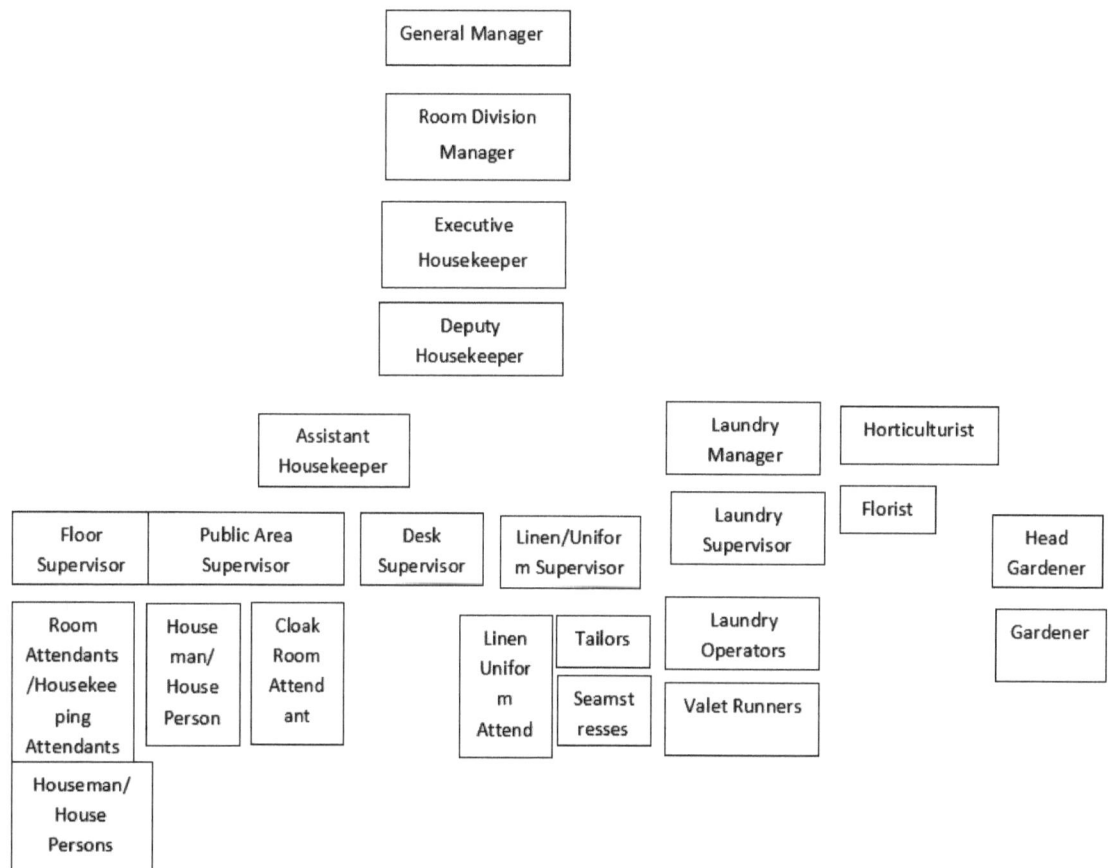

Organization Chart of Medium Hotel

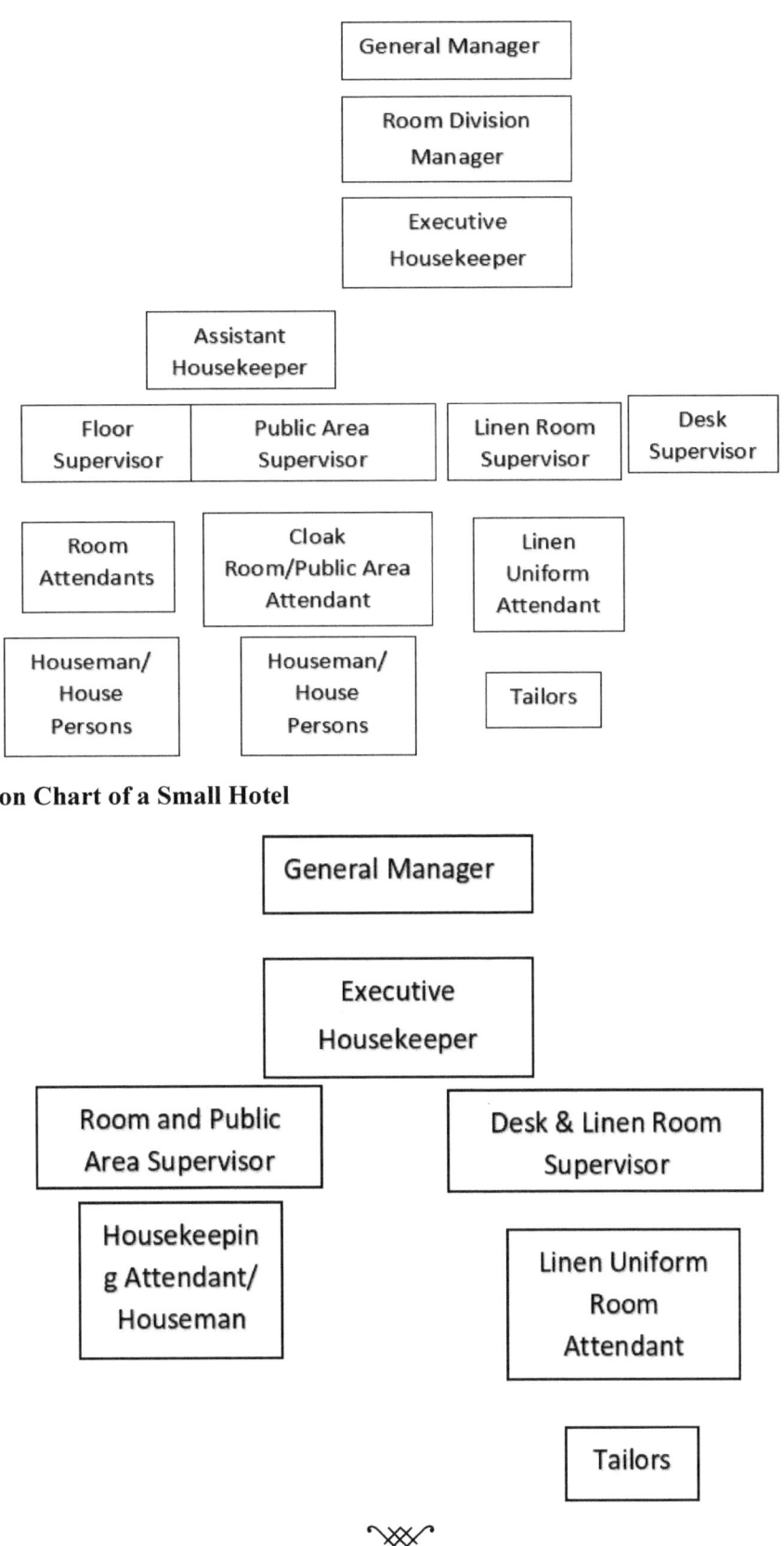

Organization Chart of a Small Hotel

Duties And Responsibilities of Housekeeping Staff

Executive Housekeeper/Director of Accommodation Services/Accommodation Manager

He/she is in charge of the housekeeping department He comes directly under the resident manager in a large hotel. The deputy housekeeper replaces him on his day and time off. His working is mainly administrative which depends on the size of the hotel. In large hotels, his work is more on the management side. In small hotels, his duties would include spot-checking and supervising as well.

His Duties Include The Following:

1. Planning and organizing the department.
2. Planning, organizing and coordinating the work of his staff.
3. Recruiting new staff and inducting them into proper training programmes.
4. Dismissal of staff when they are found unsatisfactory.
5. In small hotels he is expected to supervise while in large hotels he does spot checks (a spot check is a surprise check which helps maintain discipline and the required standard of work amongst staff).
6. Since he forms a link between the management and the staff, he it expected to solve staff grievances and pass on management orders.
7. He is expected to pay courtesy calls to long staying guests.
8. He decides on which rooms to take off for special/ spring cleaning/ renovation, etc.
9. He decides on the type of furniture, decor, linen, and staff requirements in conjunction with the general manager.
10. He is totally responsible for the selection, procurement and control of all the linen and uniforms used in the organization.
11. He is the final authority for the requisitions made for materials like guest supplies, cleaning supplies, cleaning equipments, etc.
12. He prepares the annual housekeeping budget
13. He is responsible for the control of all the housekeeping equipments and supplies.
14. He formulates rules and regulations for his staff and sees that they are followed.
15. He maintains records of contract staff, and those who work on daily wages.

16. He is the signing authority of the department

Deputy Housekeeper

He / She comes next in seniority to the executive housekeeper. Her duties include the following:

1. She takes over on the executive housekeeper's day and time off.
2. She sees to the allocation of work to the staff.
3. She prepares duty roaster for the housekeeping staff and re-schedules them in case of absenteeism.
4. She is required to maintain stock registers.
5. She is in charge of the lost and found department.
6. She checks the proper grooming of staff and settles their disputes and complaints.

Floor Supervisor

She reports to the assistant/deputy housekeeper. Her duties include the following:

1. She inspects each room completed by the room attendant according to the specific room checklist and ensures that they meet the set standards of the hotel.
2. She checks the par stocks of linen, guest supplies and cleaning supplies, cleaning equipments, that is there on her floor and requisitions for the required amount from the stores after the authorization of the executive house keeper.
3. She checks the day-to-day grooming and discipline of the staff under her.
4. She assists the guest in case of information or any medical support
5. She coordinates with the desk supervisor and releases ready rooms and takes departure rooms from her.

Public Area Supervisor

The duties of the public area supervisor include the following:

1. To check all public area and see that the standards of cleanliness is maintained.
2. She removes furniture, curtains, fixtures, etc, which require spot mending, repairs or washing.
3. She checks and controls the working of mechanical equipments and sends them for repairs if required.
4. She checks the working of contract workers in the public area.

Uniform And Linen Supervisor

The uniform and linen supervisor has the flowing duties:

1. He maintains records of linen and uniforms issued and received.
2. He keeps an update of the inventory stock on monthly basis,

3. He deals with any requests or complaints made by the staff or guests of the hotel and passes it on to the laundry department.
4. He checks to the standards of cleanliness and hygiene maintained for all housekeeping linen and staff uniforms.
5. He maintains proper storage place for linen and uniforms.
6. He assigns daily work to the tailors.

Desk Control Supervisor

The desk is the nerve centre for communication with all other departments in the hotel therefore it is of prime importance. It is operated 24 hours so as to provide complete guest satisfaction. The following are the duties of the desk supervisor :

1. Messages are transmitted and received to and from all departments of the hotel including guest calls.
2. Registers like guest call register, attendance register, lost and found register, maintenance/ job order register, log book, etc are maintained here.
3. Filing is a major part of the desk supervisor's job.
4. She should handle all guest complaints and requests promptly.

Cloak Room Attendant

The cloakroom attendant is responsible for the cleanliness and proper maintenance of all the public areas of the hotel. He should ensure that there is always a fresh supply of toilet rolls, soaps, dry clean towels, etc as prescribed by the management. Air fresheners should also be used regularly.

Room Attendant/ Chamber Maid

The room attendants are also known as chambermaids or room boys. And they do the actual cleaning of the entire guest room and toilet/bath area. They are required to clean around 14 -16 rooms a day and the ready

rooms are then checked by the floor supervisor as per the set standards of the hotel. The room attendants are supposed to carry the chambermaid's trolley with them during the cleaning process and refill the trolley at the end of their shift and keep ready for the next day.

Duties And Responsibilities

1. The chambermaid is also called a room attendant. She/he reports to the desk supervisor and is expected to serve 12 - 15 rooms in a day per shift.
2. He is involved in doing daily cleaning of all the guest rooms including the bathrooms allotted to him for the day. This would require a minimum of 20 minutes of cleaning per room, as it involves through cleaning up the mess and resettling and replenishing the supplies of the room and bathroom so as to allow the guest to stay for another day in comfort

3. He is required to keep the chamber maid's service room and the chamber maid's trolley sparkling clean as. it would activate the growth of micro-organisms. Sending soiled linen and garbage to their respected areas as soon as it is brought from the guest rooms. Proper storage of guest linen and supplies under lock and key so that no intruder can remove anything while on the floor.

4. Special cleaning of corridors and public areas is also a part of their duty.

5. Exchange of soiled guest linen for fresh is done by than in small hotels or by the handy men / housemen in case of large hotels as it give more time to the room attendant to service the room properly / thoroughly. The exchange of linen is maintained on the linen exchange slip book, which is kept with the linen supervisor.

6. Listening to guests requests promptly, e.g. refilling of water jug, extra towel / blanket/ toiletries in the room, second service, extra stationery, polishing shoes, etc.

7. Conveying guest complaints to the floor supervisor and solving their queries.

8. Reporting unusual incidences that have occurred or may occur in his section of rooms.

9. In case of lost articles of the guest, the room attendant must hand over the same to the desk control supervisor for further action, and in case the guest has misplaced any of his belongings then he must help the guest find the same.

10. He should keep a track of the guests where-abouts, also checking for scanty baggage, sleep-outs, skipper guests, stay-over guests, etc and inform the same to the desk control supervisor who further informs the front desk.

Horticulturist

Many hotels may contract out the horticulturist work to an outside agency, however a large number of large hotels have a horticulturist section. They maintain a well-grown garden and supply fresh flowers to the hotel as on daily requirement basis. Flowers are largely used by the housekeeping to enhance aesthetically various parts of the hotel. They are used in banquets, guest rooms, restaurants, lobby offices, buffet functions etc. the horticulturist would have to ensure a smooth supply of flowers as well as assist the housekeeping in flower arrangements.

Housemen

These are usually handy men who do the heavy physical work/cleaning required in various areas like the guest rooms, and in public areas. Their job includes heavy duty vacuuming, shifting of furniture, cleaning of windowpanes, brassoing, scrubbing of corridors, etc. They could be employed on daily wages or recruited on contract basis.

S Potters/Pressers

These are people who do the work of stain removal from the clothes. The Pressers do the Job of ironing different types of guest clothing and any emergency stock of housekeeping linen.

Valet/Runner

He is a person who goes from one guest room to another collecting or delivering guest laundry.

Helpers

Helpers are found in a linen and uniform room and they are involved in heavy duty work like transporting soiled linen to laundry, counting of fresh linen, bundling of fresh linen and stacking them on the right rack, etc.

Uniform & Linen Room Attendant

The uniform room supervisor is assisted by the uniform room attendant who is actually dealing with the issuing and receiving of linen and uniforms. His duties are listed below:

1. He is the person who clicks each piece of fresh linen and uniform which has come from the laundry and either gives them to the tailor for repair or stacks them on the storage racks.
2. He is the person who actually does all the physical work.
3. He checks that the amount of linen needed for the up coining shift is ready and waiting for the attendants.
4. He organizes the uniform room, making sure that all employees have clean uniforms available, uniforms, and ascertains that all component parts of each uniform are accounted for.
5. He also checks uniform for tears and stains and overseas uniforms inventory.

Seamstress

The seamstress fabricates a variety of items, from draperies to bed coverings and uniforms, etc. He/She is also responsible for mending and repairing fabric items.

Qualities of Housekeeping Staff

Hotel industry being a service industry, personal projection of its staff reflects and enhances its image and reputation. There are certain qualities, which each h/k staff should possess:

Grooming

This is a quality, which is a must to be possessed by the staff members who are always in guest contact. For example - staffs in public area, room attendants and housemen. Before they start their duty they should make sure that their uniform is crisp, clean and well pressed. It is advisable for the lady staff members to wear light makeup and restrict their jewellery to a minimum. Heavy perfume should be avoided as it may irritate a guest coming in contact with the staff. Hair should be tied nicely and not left loose. High- heeled shoes should be avoided.

Personal Hygiene

Housekeeping staff must always have clean hair, clean cut finger nails, clean hands and feet and should make sure before starting their duty that body odour or mouth odour is not present. This will create bad impression on guest if they notice that people given to service their beds and rooms are dirty, unhygienic and unhealthy. H/keeping staffs must report to the hotel doctor in case of infectious diseases or other illness in case to eliminate any chances of spreading the germs. Carelessness may lead to assault on guest safety.

Honesty

This is the most important quality the housekeeping staff should have. Especially those who have access to the guest room e.g. room attendant or houseman. Quest belongings and other valuables are often found lying here and there in a guest -room and it is easy for the room attendant to smuggle it out. But it is of course personal quality and sense of discipline that checks the temptation of doing so. Any item found this way should be informed; and the management should also reward such staff to motivate them in order that they are not to steal but to win a name and fame for the establishment

Courtesy

A happy guest means good business and as per the sales of the room is concerned the credit goes to the housekeeping staff for update and efficient service. Room attendants, floor supervisors are always in contact with the guest and in case a guest requests some housekeeping service or the other, it must be dealt with politeness and charm. Staffs must show their willingness to render the service asked by guest Complains or request must be listened with patience and staff should restrict their temper even if the guest is asking for an odd service. The guest should be given an impression that they are being taken care of.

Tact & Diplomacy

There are certain rules and policies of the house and it may happen that a guest asked for a service that is beyond and outside management policies. In this case the staff has to be tactful making sure that their action or reaction will not hurt guest feelings.

Eye For Details

This is a very rare quality possessed by highly skilled staffs only, who during their normal work take a note of every thing around and try to better the service on their own without asking or being asked by the supervisors.

Physical Fitness

As most of the housekeeping work is heavy and manual it becomes a must for the staff to be medically fit to cope up with continuous heavy work. The department also has to ensure fatigue reducing environment.

Co-operation & Understanding

It is one of the most important aspects of a good management and is needed to run the establishments smoothly and efficiently. Suppose the house keeper does not co-operate with the front office by making rooms ready within a stipulated time, the Front Office will fall to send the room thus causing loss of revenue and also may be found with irate customer who had a confirm booking.

Types of Rooms

Knowledge of Rooms

The sale of rooms constitutes approx. 50% or more of the total hotel revenue. A 'sale' of room would mean the leasing of the room for occupation for 24 hours at a predetermined cost A room not sold on a particular day has lost its opportunity to cam revenue for that day. Hence rooms arc referred to as highly perishable commodities. The loss of an opportunity to sell a room can also be due to inefficiency of housekeeping in having a room ready when required.

What Does a Room Mean To A Guest?

- It means comfort.
- It means security.
- It means privacy.
- It means convenience.
- It means cleanliness and hygiene.

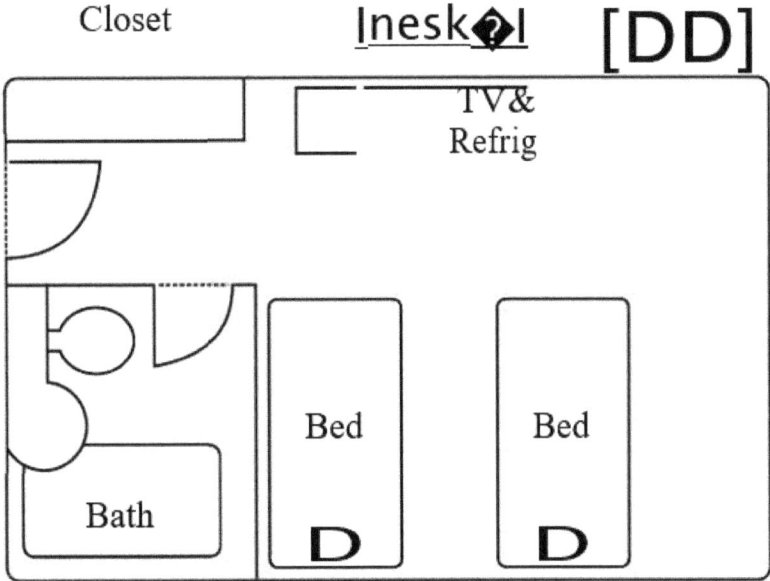

Layout of a Guest Room

Above all, the room is very personal to a guest. Hence he demands the highest standards in everything that the room stands for. Rooms at any time may be occupied (let), vacated (guest has left) or vacant (not occupied last night) and the amount of cleaning given to each room will vary. All rooms require a comfortable, clean and presentable appearance and the work to be done in an occupied room will be enough to maintain this image. In a vacated room all signs of the previous guest have to be removed and the room made ready for a new arrival. A vacant room is one that has not been occupied since the last clean.

Different Types of Rooms Single Room

A room meant for single occupancy having one single bed having two side tables. It is a standard room having a dressing-cum-writing table.

Double Room

A room with one double bed meant for two people but can be sold on single occupancy. It is a standard room having a dressing-cum-writing table.

Twin Room

A room with two single beds meant for two people having only one bedside table between the two beds. It has a dressing-cum-writing table.

Hollywood Twin Room

A room with two single beds and one single headboard meant for two people. If need arises the two beds can be bridged together to make it appear as a double room

Studio Room

A parlour set up with a studio bed, which acts as a sofa during the day and can be converted to a bed during the night.

Parlour

A parlour is a sitting room or a living room not used as a bedroom. The guest is allowed to sit and be comfortable.

Interconnected Room

Two rooms adjacent to each other, having an interconnecting door allowing entry from one room to another, without having to go into the corridor. The interconnecting doors can be opened when require or locked as per the guest request.

Suite

This is a set of rooms consisting of a parlour connecting one or more bed rooms. It has more facilities than a standard room and thus more expensive. The rates of this room is much higher because; the size of the rooms is larger more comforting and has more privacy. It has more facilities like an extra television, a mini fridge, mini bar, etc. Particular decor, and color scheme to suit the theme of the suite. Large and elaborate furniture. It has sitting arrangements separate from the bedding arrangement.

Penthouse Suite

A suite, which has a set of rooms, situated on the top most floors, which have at least one room open to the sky.

Duplexroom

A set of rooms not on the same level, but it is connected by an internal staircase.

Generally, the parlour is at the lower level and the bedrooms are at the upper level.

Executive Room

This is a larger bedroom with a sitting area provided with chairs and usually a sofa.

There is a dressing table as well as a writing table. Newspaper and other business related magazines are also provided.

Efficiency Room

A room that has some sort of kitchen facilities found in motels and residential hotels.

Cabana

Formally a room used for changing purpose was called a cabana. It is a room away from the main building having all basic facilities, mainly situated next to a swimming pool. The decor would not be too luxurious and attractive therefore the rate is less.

Sicoroom

It is a type of room, which has a Murphy bed

All the above-mentioned rooms may be furnished with extra rollaway cots on the demand of she guest at an extra charge. All rooms normally have attached bathrooms. Exceptions would be in hostels where a common bathroom per floor is more economical to the guest and management for the low charges they levy on rooms.

Daily Routines And Systems of The Housekeeping Department

At 7:00 am or 8:00 am when the staff come to work they must first punch their card to prove they are on duty at the timekeeper's office. Then they go to the locker room and change into their uniforms, and then in their uniforms report to work at the housekeeping department (It is usual that they exchange their uniforms on a clean for dirty/ one to one basis, this is done the evening before and left in the locker room cupboards allotted to each staff). Thus they do not waste time in queuing up to collect their uniforms, as it would delay them further.

At the housekeeping department, the work is allocated and the section keys are distributed to the room attendants after taking their signature against it on the key control register. The same is done when the floor master keys are handed over to the floor supervisors. The hotel is divided into sections, which consists of a set number of rooms given to a room attendant to take care of for the day. Normally one prepares the housekeeping day book according to the duty roster.

Housekeeping Day Book

FLOOR	SECTION	NAME OF THE PERSON
I	A	
	B	
	C	
II	A	
	B	
	C	
	D	

Each morning reception sends information to the housekeeping department regarding the occupancy of the hotel, and the anticipated check-outs for the day. Previously one has received a forecast of occupancy. When a computer is in use all information comes through this. The aim is to cover the work according to the occupancy with the staff who is present themselves for work.

If there is a shortage of staff one has to divide out the remaining work among the staff who are present. We call these splitting sections. Room attendants who have vacant rooms are first given the extra rooms, and then sections with no check-outs and then everybody an extra room or two, as required.

The ideally designed housekeeping department has a desk control section which keeps records of all keys that have been issued and received from the concerned staff as well as other relevant details like duty rota schedule, first aid kit, storage of guest supplies and amenities, all important registers like key handling register, guest complaint register, maintenance/job order register, etc. The various keys are stored in the key box and kept under lock and key on a wall near the control desk. It has hook numbered according to the floors and sections of the hotel.

Normally each room attendant is given a work sheet with the list of rooms he is required to service for the day. This includes the vacant, occupied rooms and the anticipated checkouts for the day. This sheet helps the room attendant to know the exact situation of rooms in their sections; therefore it gets easier for them to move directly to the rooms that require their attention. The procedure is that this sheet is clipped on to a clipboard with a pencil and attached on the trolley, the room attendant ticks the rooms they have serviced, so that the floor supervisor can check the completed rooms and release the same to the desk control, which is further released to the front desk/reception. This work sheet is re-entered into the maid's report card and handed over at the end of his shift to the desk control along with the section keys. It is important that any rooms not serviced are noted in the work card and the log is kept for the evening shift staff to do.

At about 2:00 pm every afternoon, every floor supervisor gives a final check on her floor for D.N.D or D/L signs, which exist from the morning. If these signs still exist then she should call the room and inquire if they require daily cleaning now or later in the evening? The supervisor's part of the dialogue should be something like the following:

'Good Afternoon Sir/Madam, this is the housekeeping supervisor speaking. Sorry to disturb you. What time would you like your room to be serviced today please?'

On no account must the room attendant be allowed to telephone the guests. If there is no reply then the supervisor and the room attendant proceeds to the room.

Since all hotels provide their staff with meals on duty therefore no staff must leave the premises until the end of his/her shift. This should be clearly understood by all.

Staff should be cautioned to immediately report any abnormalities to the housekeeping department, e.g. suspicious looking guests/people, abnormal noises or guest behaviors, people loitering in the corridors, etc.

The Chamber Maid's Service Room

Service Room

1. This is where the trolley, linen and guest/ cleaning supplies are stored.

2. The shelves must at all times be kept neat and tidy and clean.

3. Usually the room attendant can empty the soiled linen from all occupied rooms into the laundry bag of the chambermaid trolley.

4. There is water supply provided in the chambermaid service room so as to wash the dirty buckets and mugs and hands. Refilling of water jugs can also be done front here.

5. At the end of each shift, the chambermaid service room should be cleaned and replenished with all supplies and linen for the next day. Shelves should be cleaned daily. Dirty linen and soiled articles should be discarded on the same day, as it would cause, the growth of microorganisms around The trolley should be cleaned as well and all supplies replenished. Lastly the floor should be scrubbed and the room should be left sparklingly clean before the end of the shift of every floor/room attendant.

6. Depending on how many rooms are there on a floor, the room attendants will have to share the chamber maid's service room, during which they must co-operate and take turns in keeping the area clean and fully replenished at all time.

7. Frequently one finds toilet facilities for the housekeeping staff adjacent to the service area and this also must be kept absolutely spotlessly clean. Correct usage of the toilet by ail concerned staff greatly assists being able to keep it clean, and the staff have to be reminded of this.

The Chamber Maid's Trolley

1. The chamber maid's trolley is for convenience and speed so that the room attendant can be able to service rooms at an ease take more time in thoroughly cleaning the room rather than run between floors. The trolley must be kept in an orderly manner at all times. It saves one's feet as one has all the necessities at hand, so there is no need to run constantly back and forth. It helps one to have a fast ordered method of work.

2. There are separate receptacles for dirty linen and garbage and this enables absolute separation of dirty from clean, which is essential and must be strictly adhered to.

3. Normally the top shelf contains all the supplies necessary like note pads, pencil/pen, other stationary, gargle glasses, emery paper, soaps, shampoo sachets, etc.

4. T he first shelf has all bath linen like bath towels, hand towels, face towels, bathmats, etc.

5. The second shelf contains all bed linen like bed sheets, pillow cases/slips, etc.

6. The bottom shelf normally holds cleaning materials and equipments. If there is no bottom shelf then one can store this under the garbage bag and the laundry bag.

7. It is just as easy to keep the trolley tidy, as it is a matter of the organization and its discipline.

8. At the end of one's shift one must clean the trolley and remove all garbage and dirty linen and re-set the trolley for the next clay's shift.

9. When one is servicing a room one parks the trolley outside the door with the open shelves facing towards the room. Since the room attendant should leave the door open always of the room he will find it easy to remove the necessary requirements from the trolley.

10. If the laundry bag or the garbage bag has become full, then the room attendant should empty the same and put another bag for the garbage as well as empty the soiled linen from the laundry bag.

11. After the shift is over, the room attendant should collect all the garbage from the service room and dump it in the garbage room of the hotel so as to prevent odours and germs to spread.

12. Some hotels have linen chutes, this is like a chimney which passes through every floor of the hotel and has it's opening into the laundry room. It has a door and a locking system on each floor through which all soiled linen is disposed off. This saves time for the room attendant to go down with the soiled linen.

13. When a hotel has no chute, the ditty linen has to be collected in trolleys by the housemen and taken to the laundry department The floors are then re-stocked with fresh linen by the housemen who do the transporting through trolleys.

Hygienic & Safe Methods of Cleaning

Principles of Cleaning

The following are the principles of cleaning

1. Removal of superficial dirt is done from higher level to lower level till stretch level.
2. Sweeping with a broom is done before dusting and dusting is done before vacuum cleaning.
3. Bending with stiff knees should be avoided.
4. Where there are alternative methods of cleaning the least harmful ones should be used.
5. 3. Cleaning methods while being efficient should be economical, less time consuming and low in labour and material cost.
6. Perform all processes likely to create dust at an early stage, eg. Emptying ashtrays, sweeping, bed making etc.
7. Worksafetly
8. Start cleaning from the furthest point and move towards the entrance/ exit point.

Methods of Organising Cleaning

The following are the methods of organizing cleaning In a hotel room:

1. Conventional Method of Cleaning

Under this method one room attendant is in charge of cleaning all the rooms in his section. He has no helpers or assistance. He enters a dirty room and leaves it only when it is completely cleaned. A room attendant looks after all the room allotted to him in his section which would sum up to 14-16 rooms a day. All complaints in this section would be his responsibility for the day.

2. Team/Group Cleaning

Group work in housekeeping is gaining favor in many institutions. This includes 3 to 4 employees working simultaneously in an area. Each team member is an expert in a special segment of work. Time is usually an important aspect therefore the presence of a fellow worker would also help in accelerating the work. Team cleaning builds a feeling of fellowship and unity as it creates a feeling of partnership directly related to morale and profit.

3. Block Cleaning

In this case a room attendant may do one task through out a number of rooms and then come back to do the remaining tasks, thus blocking a number of rooms at a time. He would release the rooms all together when they get completed. This kind of cleaning is suitable to establishments where the rooms are likely to remain vacant for a certain time period or the arrival and departure timing of the guest is recorded like in residential hotels, conference hotels etc.

Housekeeping Hygiene

1. To clean hygienically one must not only make things look clean, but also make them as germ-free as possible. One can with a dirty germ-infested rag make something look clean but this is not a correct practice.

2. It is important for a hotel to keep everything as germ-free as possible since germs can cause diseases and hotels naturally wish to offer as safe an environment as possible.

3. Germs or bacteria are microorganisms that can spread very rapidly given ideal conditions of food, warmth and moisture. They require only tiny quantities. Now since one cannot with a naked eye see germs, one must become extremely be aware of the possibilities of their existence and possible spread.

4. Germs themselves cannot move, but they can be transported on currents of air, on fingers, on cloths, and pieces of equipments.

5. From this you can see how important it is that dirty things and clean are not mixed together. The dirty things should always be isolated and disposed off as soon as possible, e.g. in housekeeping, dirty linen must never be touching clean linen and must be sent off to the laundry for washing, and all garbage collected in a garbage bag and kept in an isolated area of the service room later to be disposed to the garbage room.

6. The dirty things should always be isolated and disposed off as soon as possible, e.g. in housekeeping, dirty linen must never be touching clean linen and must be sent off to the laundry for washing, and all garbage collected in a garbage bag and kept in an isolated area of the service room later to be disposed to the garbage room.

7. Clean working methods are of extreme importance; clean the toilet using disinfectants, it is extremely important also to isolate the toilet brush in a plastic bag, which should be changed daily and stored in a disinfectant solution overnight

8. In the same interests of hygiene, the glass cloth should be used for the purpose of cleaning glass only and not used for other purposes; this will help to keep the area clean as well as the cleaning equipments. Always remember to isolate the dirty cleaning cloths from the clean.

9. To use a guest towel for cleaning the toilet area is the most un-hygienic thing done in hotels as this would not only spread the germs of the guest but also dirty the soiled towel.

10. Cleaning cloths and equipments must be used for cleaning purpose only and should not be mis-used. Correct folding of the cleaning cloths during use also helps to reduce mis-using as the required area would be used and it can be used for a maximum number of times. This also helps to cut down the spread of germs and infection.

11. To sanitize one can follow cleaning processes by wiping with disinfectant This is usually done in the case of toilets as an extra precaution. Remember also tooth glasses are washed in baby-sterilizing solution or some hotels use permanganate. However for

normal bath and wash basin cleaning, most hotels use a detergent that contains some disinfectant, this makes it necessary to follow each washing process with a disinfectant process to, which is time consuming in a hotel.

12. Not only must the equipment and methods be as clean as possible, but also the person involved in doing the process. Great care must be taken by every room attendant to remain hygienically clean from the beginning till the end of his shift A guest would not like to see any staff of the hotel in bad shape during servicing his room, etc.

13. People working in hotels have to work hard, often with a lot of physical exertion so personal cleanliness is essential, minimum one shower a day, short and well combed hair, short nails, clean uniform and a pleasant smile. A use of a deodorant could be recommended to persons who perspire frequently.

14. Hygienic personal habits are of great importance:

No spitting

- Cover your mouth if you cough or sneeze then immediately wash your hands. Wash hands after using the lavatory, and after cleaning it also.
- Don't fiddle with your nose. Don't fiddle with your toes.
- Don't play with your hair and don't comb your hair in public.

Daily Cleaning of Rooms

Daily Cleaning of Departure Rooms

Rooms must be cleaned and serviced each day after the departure of a guest.

All rooms should present a fresh pleasing appearance and provide comfortable conditions for those using them.

Daily maintenance removes dirt, accumulation of which is dangerous for health as it forms breeding ground for germs.

Day to day care encourage high standard of work. It allows the time allocated for special cleaning to be spent out to full advantage.

The room attendants should carry the materials required for cleaning namely: duster, cleaning agent, equipment, fresh linen etc. in the trolley. In short a properly stacked trolley.

1. Leuve the front door open; make work sign "no" on the door. The trolley standing in corridor outside the room to be serviced. The order of the work shall be as follows:
2. Ventilation of the room
3. Switch off the air conditioner or heating system.
4. Removal of soiled linen, used crockery and any other rubbish.
5. Airing of bed and making it.
6. Dusting the furniture.
7. Disinfect the telephone mouthpiece, check for dial tone.
8. Sweeping of the carpets and dusting of the surroundings.
9. Cleaning of furnishing arrangements and appearance of the room.
10. Switch on the bathroom light, dry the floor if wet, wipe down the walls, windows with dry dusters, occasionally damp duster is also used.
11. Use detergent for cleaning washbasin and dirty surfaces.
12. Check for plumbing faults like leakage, faulty flushes, and electrical faults and exposed wires.
13. Replace bath linen and also complimentary items namely toilet soap, shampoo.
14. While working around the room check for damages to the furniture's, walls, windows and other fittings.
15. Replace the complimentary items like match boxes stationers. Etc.
16. After final check up draw the curtains place the DND card on the outside knob of the door.

17. Vacuum the floor finish at the door.
18. Give a final check and remove the sign "no".

Daily Cleaning of Occupied Rooms How To Enter a Room

Prior to reporting on a floor the room attendant already knows the status of a room in his given lot of rooms. The room attendant can prioritize rooms to be attended to first on the basis of immediate needs; 'clean my room', and finally occupied rooms. For occupied rooms look whether the room has a 'do not disturb' card on the door knob. If it does then go to the room which does not. Knock at the door firmly with the index finger knuckle announcing clearly 'housekeeping'. When there is no answer, repeat the knock after 10 seconds announcing yourself as before. If there is still no answer, open the door with the floor master key. Push the door again, knock announcing inside the room 'housekeeping'. When there is no reply and one is relatively sure that there is no one in, open the door wide and keep it that way till the entire cleaning cycle in the room is complete.

Room Cleaning Procedure

1. Switch off the room air-conditioner or heating. Draw all curtains and open the windows for airing the room.
2. Remove soiled linen from beds and bath. Shake out the linen to ensure that no guest articles are lost in the folds of the linen. Put the soiled linen in the linen hamper/laundry bag provided on the chambermaid's trolley.
3. Check for maintenance requirements and report the same to the control desk and enter in the room checklist.
4. Contact room service to remove used trays and glasses.
5. Turn the mattress side-to-side on succeeding days followed by end-to-end turning. Smooth out the mattress and air it.
6. If vacuum cleaning is not available, brush the carpet first to enable the dust to settle while doing the next task.
7. Empty all ashtrays and waste paper baskets.
8. Pick up guest clothes and hang in the closet or place in the wardrobe.
9. Clean the bathroom and replenish all the required supplies, (check the method of cleaning a bathroom
10. Collect all loose articles and magazines and other guest papers and stack them neatly on the writing table.
11. Clean all surfaces in single circular motions with a dry cloth. Use a hand dustpan to collect any unwanted matter on the surfaces without lifting dust in the air. Ensure that all surfaces are spotlessly clean. Pay special attention to nooks and corners especially those points that may not obviously be visible to the guest eye.
12. Use a stiff upholstery brush or vacuum cleaner on upholstered furniture arms, back and seats.

13. Replace, if necessary, stationery as prescribed by the management. The number of items must exactly be as per standard.

14. Dust and replace each item on the dresser, bureaus and desks. Special attention must be given to the display of publicity material as prescribed by the management.

15. Clean lamp shades with a clean dry duster. Lift lamps and clean under the base. Replace lamp if damaged and adjust the shade.

16. Disinfect the telephone in the room and the bathroom with Dettol. Wipe balance of the telephone with a damp cloth. Then check phone for the dial tone.

17. Clean mirrors with a dry cloth first then with a damp newspaper to make it sparkling.

18. Dust closet, shelves, hangers and rods. Brush the closet floor. Supply new laundry bags and replace the missing hangers. Replace drawers/shelves with paper liners if required.

19. Dust both the sides of the room doors, headboard, windowsills, inside and outside of the window rails, top of the radiators and air-conditioning units.

20. Close the windows.

21. If vacuum cleaner is available then vacuuming of carpet should be done at this stage as against brushing the carpet as mentioned earlier.

22. Arrange furniture if necessary.

23. Switch on the air-conditioning or heating on the minimum temperature for a departure room and at the same temperature the guest has left has left for an occupied room.

24. Have a last look at the room referring to the checklist for completion of work and exit the room closing the door behind you.

Bathroom Cleaning Procedure Basic Principles

   a. Cleaning activity starts from the ceiling downwards to the floor.

   b. Floors are cleaned from the wall farthest to the door to the exit.

1. Open all windows and exhaust vents.

2. Shake out all soiled bathroom linen, e.g. towels, bathmat, etc and deposit in the linen hamper/laundry bag provided on the chambermaid's trolley.

3. Collect the trash from all the ashtrays, sani bins, and waste paper basket and deposit it into the garbage bag provided on the chambermaid's trolley.

4. Clean the ceiling and air-conditioning vents for cobwebs.

5. Wipe off light bulbs and shades with a dry cloth.

6. Wash the bathtub and surrounding tiles and wipe dry. Wipe the shower curtain from both sides with a wet sponge and ensure that all are free from any watermarks.

7. Clean the mirror, (with a dry cloth then wipe using a wet folded newspaper and then again with a dry cloth).

8. Scrub dry the areas surrounding the bash basin and the counter.

9. Scrub the toilet bowl and bidet using the special brush/ Johnny mop. Ensure that it is dry and spotless inside. Clean the seat, lid and the outside of the toilet bowl and put a disinfectant solution inside.

10. Replenish fresh bath linen and guest supplies as per the number or persons in the room. The following is the requirements for a single guest:

Linen
1. 2 bath towel
2. 2 hand towel
3. 2 face towel
4. 1 bathmat
5. bathrobe

Supplies
1. toilet rolls
2. 1 bathroom tumbler
3. soap dish
4. soaps per guest
5. 1 candle stand with candle and matchbox 1 ashtray with a matchbox
6. shoe mitt / shoe shine slip 1 shower cap
7. disposal bags 1 face tissue box
8. 1 toilet tissue roll
9. 1 waste paper basket
10. Place any advertising material as prescribed by the hotel.
11. Close the windows and vents and lastly clean/wipe dry the floor and close the bathroom door giving a final glance to see if all is in place.
12. Note that in occupied rooms, when cleaning around the washbasin counter, collect all guest belongings onto one side and clean the other aide. Again shift the belongings to the other side and clean the surface they were occupying. Finally replace all belongings as the guest had left them.

Points To Be Kept In Mind When Cleaning An Occupied Room
a. DThe room attendant must follow the method of work that will cause least disturbance to the guest occupying that room.

b. DMust plan her work so that systematic method follows. D Should work at a good speed.

c. DShould work efficiently and clean more areas at a time.

Bed Making
Items Required

1. Bed (Also known as Cot. Baby-cot or Crib is the term used to denote beds for babies)
2. Mattress
3. Mattress Protector
4. Pillows
5. Cushions
6. Bolsters
7. Bed Cover / Bed throw or Runner
8. Bed Sheet - 03 Nos.
    - First Sheet - also known as Bottom Sheet
    - Second Sheet
    - Third Sheet- also known as Top Sheet. Sometimes, Crinkle Sheets are used as Top Sheets.
9. Blanket
10. Pillow Covers

N.B: Generally all the items are already there in the Room. The Guest Room Attendant is only supposed to carry the linen, Bed Sheets and Pillow Covers. But, they must check the condition of the Mattress Protector always, and if required, change it.

Steps of Making The Bed
(Considering All The Soil Linen Have Been Stripped off Properly)

- Pull the Mattress towards the foot side, and straighten the Mattress Protector.
- Take the Bottom Sheet. Judge the middle / centre portion of the sheet and spread it.
- Considering the right side UP in such a manner to ensure that there is even fall on all the sides.
- Tuck the sheet from the head side. Now, make the mitre fold at both the comers. Push the Mattress back to its original position. Now, tuck the sheet from the foot side - make the mitre fold at both the comers. Now, tuck the sides.
- Spread the Second Sheet wrong side up. till the end of the mattress or upto the head board in such a manner that there is even fall on the (hand) sides.
- Now spread the Blanket three to four inches from the end of the second sheet or from the end of the head board, ensuring even fall on the (hand) sides.

- Now. spread the Top Sheet right side up upto the end of the blanket i.e. three to four inches from the end of the second sheet, ensuring even fall on the (hand) sides.

- Now, fold the second sheet once till the end of the blanket and the top sheet, and again refold the entire second sheet & blanket & top sheet once as per the length of the first fold - thus managing a gap of six to eight inches from the head board (for accommodating the pillows). The fold thus obtained is known as the head fold, Tuck the head fold from both the sides.

- Now come to the fool side of the bed. Check all the linen properly so as to ensure there are no lumps or crinkled part in the middle. Now, tuck the fool side of the bed - followed by mitring the comers. Tuck the sides of the bed finally to make it neat and complete.

- Now put the pillows in the pillow covers and arrange on the bed.

N.B: If the Motel provides the accessories such as Cushions, Bolsters, Bed Cover *I* Bed throw or Runner - they are arranged neatly on the bed finally to increase the eye appeal or attractiveness.

Bed Making in An Occupied Room

Figure 9-2 How to make a bed is explained in a timeless classic hooklet, "The Correct said. " The detailed instructions have illustrations to match.

Second Service

It is carried out in an occupied room only when a request to clean the room is made by the guest occupying that particular room. Sometimes, guests have a meeting or a get together functions etc. in the room and he wants his room to be cleaned after the so-called function is over. Only light cleaning is done in such cases.

Method of Second Service

a. Remove empty bottles and other room service equipment from the room. D Pick   rubbish from the floor.

b. Arrange the furniture as required. Dust the room where ever necessary.

c. Check the bathroom floor, make it dry if needed. Flush the toilet bowl and dry the area around the sink.

d. Use air freshener if required.

e. Replace toilet soap, paper & linen if necessary. D   Replenish room stationers if necessary.

f. Replace water tumblers and refill the water flask with fresh water if necessary.

Evening/Turn Down Service

In hotels, normally the bulk of room cleaning should have been done in the morning shift The exception would be rooms with the 'do not disturb' sign. Some rooms are occupied by late night/early morning arrivals by international flights. All rooms therefore require an evening service that mostly involves preparing the room for the guest to sleep for the night and it should be done prior to the guest retiring for the night. In this service, the bed is made for night, the room is cleared and soiled bath linen is replaced Night service is carried out in the following way:

1. Knock at the door and enter the room as per the procedure mentioned earlier.
2. Switch on the lights arid ensure that all the light fixtures are working.
3. Draw the heavy curtains.
4. Hang guest clothes if lying around.
5. Take off the bedcover, fold neatly and store in the wardrobe, either in the topmost shelf or in the lowermost shelf.
6. Fold one comer of the blanket to enable the guest to slide in to the bed.
7. Place the breakfast knob order card along with a chocolate/cookies /sweet as prescribed by the management on the pillow.
8. Remove soiled glasses and bottles if any. Replenish fresh glasses and fill in the water flask with drinking water.
9. Empty and clean ashtrays and waste paper baskets.
10. Replace soiled linen - bed and bath if required.
11. Replenish missing toiletries and other supplies.
12. Set climate control as directed.
13. Turn out all the lights except the night lamp/ passage light as prescribed by the management.
14. Before leaving the room give a final glance then lock the door properly, and proceed to the next room.
15. A job order is filled by the desk control supervisor and issued to the maintenance department

Standard Room Supplies

Guest Room Supplies on The Bed
Mattress, mattress protector, bed sheets, blanket, bedspread, pillows, pillowslips, pillow cover.

On The Bed Side Table
Telephone, intercom directory, telephone directory, scribbling pad, pen/pencil, ashtray, flask of water with two glasses, music panel, Bible and Gita on the lower shelf.

On The Coffee Table
Daily newspaper, ashtray with matchbox, periodical hotel magazines.

Soft Furnishings In The Room
Drape/heavy curtains, sheer/lace curtains, Venetian blinds, cushions, carpet on the floor, sofa covers.

On The Dressing Cum Writing Table
Wall mounted mirror with lamps on either sides, writing folder with necessary stationary like letter heads, envelopes, picture postcards, rules and regulation card, restaurant cards, air / train timetables, pen/pencil, suggestion folder, candle with match box, room service menu card.

In The Drawer
Dutch wife/sewing kit, telephone forms.

On The Entrance Door Knob
DND card, clean my room card, fire exit map

In The Closet / Wardrobe / Cupboard
Clothes hangers, laundry bags, valet bags, dry cleaning slips, laundry slip, extra blanket, collect my laundry card.

Other Items in The Room
Guest room safes, luggage rack, television stand with television, refrigerator / minibar, waste paper basket on the floor.

In The Bathroom
Bathtub, grip bar, shower curtain with rod, W.C / water closet, bidet, washbasin.

On The Wash Basin Counter
Wall mounted mirror with lamps on either sides, Wall mounted telephone, hand towels, face towels, soaps, sh$_{amp}$oo sachet, emery paper, tissue box, tissue rolls, gargle glass, shower cap, ashtray, match box.

Under The Counter
Waste paper/sani-bin

On The Towel Rack

Bath towels/Turkish towels

Below The Bath Tub

Bath mat

Different Amenities Supplied For Different Guests

VIP I	Heads of state, Ministers, High ranking government-delegates, National and International dignitaries, etc	Full bar setup. Large flower arrangement, Large fruit basket, Chocolates, Bathrobe, Slippers, and other personal amenities
VIP II	Companies identified as giving high volume business, Top film personalities, Other well known personalities from the world, Foreign visitors and guests of VIP I	Practical bar, Medium flower arrangement; Medium Sized fruit basket, Chocolates, Bathrobe & Slippers, and Special compliments.
VIP III	Decision makers and influential trade VIP's, Persons from airlines, Travel agents, Hotels, etc	Mineral water, Small flower arrangement. Small fruit basket, Bathrobe, and Slippers.
VIP IV	Certain groups, HWC (handle with care) guests, Repeat guests, etc	Mineral water, Bud vase, Small fruit basket, Cookies

Rules on Guest Floor

Prior to commencing work all housekeeping staff, especially room attendants must follow some floor rules that lend an air of efficiency and least inconvenience to guests. Guests want a feeling of privacy and safety in their rooms and their belongings. To prove this trustworthy on the part of the hotel, the room attendant who has the access to the guest- rooms must observe the following rules:

1. Speech amongst the floor staff must be restricted to the minimum. They should always talk in low tone even when the guests are not in sight
2. Unnecessary movements like running, jumping etc. must be avoided.
3. The passage must always be kept free of equipment, tray & trolleys.
4. The floor telephones must be attended promptly.
5. Room attendants must greet all guests according to the time of the day.
6. Staff must be helpful and readily give required information. Misleading a guest through misinformation must be avoided.
7. Alertness to guest movements is necessary so as to report anything suspicious.
8. Remember the guest is always right. Arguing with the guest is prohibited.

9. It is prohibited to enter a room, which displays D.N.D. sign outside.
10. The door of the room in which attendant is cleaning should be kept wide open always.
11. If the guest returns when the room is being cleaned the room attendant must ask the guest if he/she can continue or come later.
12. On entering a room if the guest is found inside either sleeping or awake, quickly withdraw apologizing if required and shut the door softly.

Guest Room Supplies And Amenties Chart

Guestroom Supplies and Amenities			
Guestroom Supplies	**Guestroom Amenities**	**Bathroom Supplies**	**Bathroom Amenities**
Pillows	Stationery	Wash cloths	Facial soap
Pillow cases	Postcards	Hand towels	Bath soap or shower gel
Sheets	Pens	Bath towels	Shampoo
Blankets	Laundry bags	Bath mats	Moisturizer
Water pitcher	Utility bags	Shower curtains and Liners	Shower cap
Clock	Packets (sachets) of coffee or tea, sugar, and powdered creamer, stir sticks	Toilet tissue	Shoe mitt or shoeshine kit
Radio	Chocolates or mints (provided with turndown service)	Facial tissue	Shoe horn
Glasses		Sanitary bags	Sewing kit
Plastic drinking cups		Waste baskets	Bubble bath
Coffee or Tea maker		Toilet seat band	Hair conditioner
Trays		Hair dryer	Cologne or after-shave
Ice buckets		Makeup mirror	Razor
Hangers		Bathrobe	Amenities container
Ashtrays		Disposable slippers	
Waste baskets		Weighing Scale	
Telephone directories			
Stationery folders			
Ironing board & Iron			
Mattress pad covers			
Television program guide			
Bibles			
Do Not Disturb signs			
Table tent cards			
Fire safety			

Table 9.3: Guestroom Supplies and Amenlites

Guest Room Inspection

Inspection Procedure

The main responsibility of the housekeeping supervisor is to control the standard of work within an area. The main purpose of room inspection is to ensure that the required standard of appearance and cleanliness are being met It also ensures that correct supplies are placed in the correct position and that there are no technical faults in the room.

First impression is the lasting impressions and a clean and tidy room will give a good impression that will lead to return of visitors. The most important quality of a housekeeping staff is an eye for a detail. The management reinforces this quality through training and by bringing into practice the maintaining of a room checklist. As with the cleaning and checking an area must be done in a methodical manner to maintain speed and efficiency.

The following points help us inspect a guest room in the correct manner:

a. Walk in one direction around the room.

b. Check from high to low surfaces in order that no area is missed.

c. Look in, under and behind all fixtures and fittings.

d. Use a checklist, as a measure of control.

e. Check that the room has been prepared to required standards,

f. Note anything that has to be repaired or brought up to the required standard.

g. Follow up notes by taking appropriate corrective action.

h. When satisfied that the room/ given area has been prepared as per the prescribed standards of the hotel, then only may it be returned as vacant for resale to the desk control supervisor so as to be further released to the reception.

i. It is possible to achieve the highest standards if the floor supervisor inspects every room under her control on daily basis, in order to avoid any complaints about accommodation.

j. Quality control can be reinforced by spot-checking by upper management.

Room Area Inspection Report
Main Purpose: To control the standards of work. What To Check?

Furniture:
For checking all furniture, there are some general criteria for inspection that should be followed :

a. Cleanliness - i.e. no dust or stains should be seen.

b. Well polished and painted - i.e. no scratches and watermarks should be seen.

Good & safe condition - i.e. it shouldn't be splintered.

Door hinges & double lock- should work smoothly.

Ensure that drawers and handles are fixed properly.

Ensure all are kept in correct position.

Soft Furnishings:
   a. These include curtains, bedspreads, cushions, upholstery, etc.
   b. Check for clean and stain free surface.
   c. No fading marks.
   d. No tears and frays.
   e. Not shrunk.
   f. Free from creases and arranged neatly.

Architectural Fittings:

These include the ceiling and floors that must be checked for the following:
   a. The condition of plaster, paint or wallpaper.
   b. Remove cobwebs especially from comer.
   c. Sometimes an entire glass window ii replaced by glass door therefore to glass cleaning and finger marks. Check the working of all latches and attachments.
   d. Floors should be clean especially the comers, under and behind the furnitures, beds, etc.
   e. Carpets should be uniform and well fixed onto the sub-floor. It should be free from stains, and dirt, which tend to adhere to its surface.

Electrical Fittings And Fixtures:
   a. They should be clean, properly fixed, and all should he in working condition.

In The Bathroom:
   a. The fittings and fixtures in the bathroom should be clean, polished if retjuiires to give shine and free from cracks.
   b. They should be properly installed and in proper working condition.

For Example:

VANITARY UNIT- check the following Mirror, tiles, tooth/gargle glasses, lights, shaver socket, faucets, wash basin (underside, over flow plug and water hole)

WATER CLOSET- check the following; inside and outside of the bowl, under side of the seat and lid, inside the Strap.

SANI BIN, BATH TUB, & SHOWER- check the following;

Tiles, chrome fittings, soap dish, bath tub (over flow plug faucet and water holes), Faucets, shower heads to be checked for water pressure, temperature and diverter, shower head, towel rack, shower curtain (rail and hooks), bathmat or/and rubber mat DOOR-check the following;

Top of the door, the lock and the hooks.

Key Points To Be Observed While Checking or Observing A Room
Courtesy Towards The Guest is Important:
    a. Check for a 'DND' or 'Please Clean My Room' sign.

    b. Always knock on the door before entering the room.

    c. Always greet the guest in the corridor or in any area he is found.

    d. Do not touch any of the guest belongings.

    e. Be willing to help the guest in case of emergency or providing them with relevant information, etc.

Economy is Important Towards A Guest:
    a. Check AC or heating systems.

    b. Report any damages or repairs as soon as possible.

    c. Switch off unnecessary lights and ensure that taps are closed properly so as to avoid wastage of water and electricity.

    d. Distribute only the prescribed amount of guest supplies.

    e. Take care of not damaging the furniture, fittings and fixtures.

Security Should Always Be Observed:
    a. Close the windows and doors properly.

    b. Take care with keys.

    c. Report suspicious occurrences.

    d. Hand in lost property immediately.

Why is Inspection Important:
1. Housekeeping room report helps a lot in the inspection procedure.

2. An occupied room without any luggage should come into the knowledge of the floor supervisor who in turn informs the Housekeeper. A room with this status implies unauthorized occupancy or a person who can manage to take off without paying the bill because a guest's luggage is the hotel's best security.

3. Yet another occasion which calls for detailed inspection is an occupied room with small and light luggage which once again means, that a guest with intentions of skipping the bill can walk out with it, without anyone doubting about it.

4. A very good knowledge of the allotted rooms helps to detect any damage to the hotel property or if anything is missing. If reported in time in case of departure rooms the compensation for the damaged or the missing article can be acquired from the guest.

5. A clear idea of a day's guest occupancy of a concerned floor can help to inspect any discrepancy in it. By the count of beds used in a particular type of room, or by the no. of cloths and bath linen it can be made out if the room has been sold legitimately or not.

6. Normally no pets are allowed inside a hotel hence a proper inspection will help to find out if any pet has been smuggled into a room by a guest.

7. A close watch must be kept on any person moving on the floors, specially the visitors, and if any suspicious person comes into notice proper action has to be pursued. Any kind of guest misbehavior, causing disturbance to the other guests should be reported for prompt action.

8. Any change of room by any guest must be reported for timely rectification in the h/k occupancy status list.

9. Presence of parasites should be immediately treated with pest control methods.

10. Any arms and ammunition seen in the room should be reported.

The maid's cart is trolley meant to stock a given number of linen items, supplies and equipment required for service for an allotted number of rooms. Each maid after receiving their room assignment should check their supplies against a standard list of items to avoid needless trips. The maid is responsible for the condition, cleanliness and appearance of her cart. The cart is a large fitted conveyance and its lower shelf of the cart is used to carry heavier items like mattresses, bed sheets and night spreads.

The middle and top shelves stack pillowslips and bath linen. In addition the curt may carry cleaning equipment such as feather, brush, dustpan, mops, sponges, dusters, carpet brush or vacuum cleaner, clean scrub bucket, scrub brush on the same end of the maid's cart as the rubbish sack. Also in this cart is carried some cleaning material which include disinfectant: Dettol, de-odoriser, cleaning agents: vim, Sanitizer (sanifresh), liquid soap (teepol). Naphthalene balls, Room fresheners. Polishing material: Basso, wax polish.

Maid's-part/chamber maid's trolley is to be placed along the corridor wall on the same side of the corridor where rooms are being serviced. The cart should be so positioned as to service a minimum of two rooms without much movement. The cart should be light - weight to ensure easy mobility by the maid. Heavy cans also pucker corridor carpets. Maintenance of cart includes oiling of the wheels periodically to ensure smooth movement.

Linen required for I person per day will include :

Night Spreads- 1 for each bed Face towel - 2 for each guest Sheets - 3 for each bed

Hand Towel- 2 for each guest

Pillowcases- I for each pillow (Total 2 pillows per bed) Bath towel - 2 for each bathroom.

Bath Mat- I for each guest.

Codes Related To Housekeeping

0- Occupied. L - luggage but bed unused. OL - Occupied without luggage. V - Vacant. DND - do not disturb. 000-0ut of order. S.B. - Scanty baggage. UR - Under repair. DL- Double lock

Room Check List

Room No.	Occupancy	Telephone	Music TV	Air conditioner	Electricity Plumbing	Linen	Paining Polishing	Carpet Curtain	Furniture	Others
101										
102										
103										
104										
105										
106										
107										
108										
109										
110										

Remarks:

Cleaning of Public Areas

A guest will judge a hotel's level of cleanliness by it's public areas. Housekeeping is responsible for lobbies and the back-of-the-house, kitchens, exterior areas, meeting rooms, pest control and waste removal, etc.

The general classification of a hotel for cleaning would be on the basis of :

Front-of-The-House & Back-of-The-House
The Front-of-The-House Includes
Foyers, lobby, corridors, restaurants, bars, swimming pool, gardens, kids activity center and other areas which come in guest view.

The Back-of-The-House Includes
Kitchen, stewarding, purchase department, trash storage areas, service corridors, staff cafeteria, laundry and housekeeping department, security, HRD, etc.

Cleaning of Corridors/Staircase
The entire cleaning of these areas is carried out when the movement is minimum. Night and early morning are usually the best convenient time. These areas are usually cleaned with mopping cloth attached to a long handle.

The Public Areas Include
The Lobby and entrance just outside the lobby (may be steps or a walk way) the offices one finds in the lobby which is generally Bell-man, Luggage office, Left luggage office. Reception, Information, Cashiers, Telephone & telex room, Front office, Manager's office, Reservation, General Cashier's office.

Banquet Halls, Restaurant & Bars Are Also Classified As Public Areas
Meeting rooms & Banqueting areas come under this heading also.

Shops, Hairdressing Saloons, Health club, other Hotel offices situated at the front of the house such as General Manager's office, Resident Manager's, Room division, Food & Beverage, Sales & Marketing, Controller's office: and any corridors that are found in these areas also are included.

Housekeeping is responsible for the cleaning of all these areas. These areas are very diverse in their wall and floor coverings & furniture & decorative effects and can often be a big challenge to the housekeeping department to keep them in top condition. Because they are the public areas of the hotel and therefore seen by so many people the decor tends to be striking.

Since the public areas tend to be at their quietest at night, it is usual to do the major cleaning of these areas at then. Offices are usually also cleaned at night including offices in the back areas which housekeeping also cleans, e.g. Housekeeping office. Personnel office Purchasing,

Receiving, Food & Beverage control, Accounts, Time keeper likewise Restaurants & Bars are generally cleaned in the night also.

Where one has 24 hour operating Coffee shop this presents certain problems for cleaning. It has to be done in the night when it is at its quietest even if occasionally there are some guests. Banqueting & meeting areas are generally cleaned in the day, however when an early morning function is due then they are prepared in the night or the evening before.

Restaurants have to be cleaned between meals during the day as well as at night.

Each shift has a team of housemen or cleaners for the cleaning of these areas and a supervisor to organize and check their work. In some hotels there is only one supervisor in the evening for rooms and public areas. Naturally the night shift for cleaning these areas is the largest as that is when the bulk of the work is done.

Cleaning of Elevators

The housekeeping department is responsible for the cleanliness of the interior of elevator cars. A thorough cleaning of walls, ceiling and floors should be carried out at least once daily. The volume of traffic may require more frequent cleaning of elevator floors. In cleaning elevator car interiors, the car should be taken to the topmost floor for the cleaning procedure to be carried out. Cleaning and polishing must be done in the early hours of the morning when the guest traffic is low. Particular attention must be paid to recessed lighting troughs, ventilation panels, doorsills and grooves and the area around the operators control panel.

Cleaning of Guest Corridors

A houseman is assigned to do this task and is responsible for the cleanliness of ceilings, walls, and floors. Carpeted floors should be vacuum cleaned daily, tile floors to be brushed, swept clean and then wet mopped. They should also remove stains. Floors tile edges; comers, baseboards and the immediate wall area above are to be inspected to ensure that there are no watermarks. All corridors lighting fixtures are to be cleaned as often as required. It is also the responsibility of a houseman to clean fire extinguisher recesses including glass doors.

Cleaning of Floor Linen Closets

One maid/houseman is assigned daily on a rotating basis to be responsible for each floor linen closet. This procedure is carried out to ensure that the linen closet is kept clean and neat at all times. This assignment includes floor cleaning, dusting and arrangement of shelving and freedom from dishes, silverware, bottles and trash of all kinds.

Cleaning of Lobby Entrance

The lobbies are the areas that require constant vigil, not only because heavy public traffic marks it's passage with trails of footprints, cigarette stubs, and chewing gum wrappers, but also because the appearance of the lobby is all important as it is the are The guest comes in contact with.

Lobby cleaning schedules should be prepared with due regard for the character of the lobby. The particular facilities provided, and the activity and volume of traffic. These schedules must include walls, ceilings and floors, metal work, lighting fixtures and lamps, air handling outlets, planters, windows and draperies, showcases, display boxes, cigar stands, bell captain's office, cloakrooms, etc. the cleaning standard for all marble work and terrazzo floors and stairways are to be separately set forth to ensure that the procedures followed will ensure proper cleanliness without damage to the surface. Aluminum, bronze, stainless steel and cast iron metal work is to be kept highly polished.

Cleaning of Shopping Arcade

The responsibility for cleaning the shops varies in different hotels and is usually dependent upon the type of rental agreement in existence between the hotel and shopkeepers. The housekeeper should check with the management to determine the area or responsibility and the housekeeping procedure necessary for the proper maintenance of these areas. In instances where the responsibility rests with the shops, management has the right and obligation to insists that the cleanliness and order of these shops is at least equal to the standards prescribed for the other areas of the hotel. The types of concessions include casinos, barbers shop and beauty parlors, gifts shops, travel bureaus, offices and showrooms, etc.

Cleaning of Offices

The housekeeping department is responsible for the assignment of personnel for office cleaning. Such cleaning should be scheduled at times when the offices are not in use/service. These cleaning procedures should include desks, chairs and other furniture such as tables and filing cabinets. In order to facilitate this cleaning in good order in office areas, the hotel management requires that office personnel remove all loose papers, file folders, reports, etc from the top of desks and filing cabinets at the close of each working day.

Accounting books, records, purchase orders, invoices, payroll materials, etc must be neatly bundles and labeled. Housekeeping employees should be requisitioned by accounting and auditing department heads, on a regular basis for cleaning these areas.

Cleaning of Swimming Pool

The bottom and sides of a swimming pool must be cleaned daily by pool personnel using standard vacuum cleaning equipment. In hotels, which do not have filtration and water treatment equipment, pools should be emptied not less frequently than once each week and the walls and floors hand scrubbed using wire brushes.

Pool edge tile and overflow gutters should be hand-scrubbed on a continuing schedule so that the total circumference of the pool is completed once every 4 days. All outside terraces including those surrounding swimming pools are to be swept and wet mopped at least once daily depending upon the type of surface. Serrated tiles which have a tendency to accumulate oily films from the bather's feet should be deck- scrubbed using strong detergent solution on a schedule which will maintain the area with it's original colours intact. Cleaners responsible for terrace areas will be responsibly for keeping fungus from growing between tiles. Growth of this nature can be successfully arrested by periodic applications of rock salt.

Employees responsible for swimming pool cleaning should also inspect the diving boards, diving platforms and pool stairs daily to ensure that they are clean and safe. Pool personnel are responsible for all pool site furniture including chairs, lounge tables, sun mats, and garden umbrellas.

Care And Storage of Out-of-Service Furniture

Each hotel possesses relatively large quantities of furniture, which are not always in service. This furniture is most often associated with the food and beverage department and is required for banquets and special functions. Upholstered chairs and sofas, dressers, desks, cribs, etc. usually complete the supply. Because of the large amount of money represented by this furniture and because it's use is usually required on short notice it as important that few simple rules be observed in this care. They are:

1. The storage area should be out of the weather and all in a clean well-ventilated location.

2. No furniture should be placed in the storage area if it requires repair.

3. All furniture should be thoroughly cleaned before being stored.

4. All furniture should be covered during storage.

5. If space limitations require stacking, then this should be done with care and with the provision of adequate padding or other surface guards to prevent spoiling the surfaces.

6. Furniture destined for storage, but which require repair or renovation, should be the subject of a work order, with the work required to be completed prior to placing the furniture in storage.

7. No furniture should be stored in stairwells pr on the service landings.

8. If at all, possible decisions should be made promptly concerning the repair ability of furniture.

Special Cleaning And Weekly Cleaning

Apart from daily cleaning routines and weekly cleaning routine, which you have practiced for room servicing, there ate other cleaning (duties that need to be done on a less frequent basis. E.g. carpet shampooing curtain cleaning, and blanket washing. These duties need to be done in rooms as well as in public areas.

Normally hotels arrange this work in the slackest period of business.

In the rooms one can organize this work in one of two ways. Either one completes all the jobs in a room together, or one does each job at a time. If one has time it is better to put a section or floor of rooms off at Reception and complete all the cleaning work. When time is pressed because of high occupancy, then one does the work, job by job and completes the work in this manner, without putting rooms out of order overnight at all.

Here is a List of The Special Cleaning Tasks To Be Completed in a Room.

Curtain cleaning	laundry or dry cleaning
Bedspread cleaning	laundry or dry cleaning.
Blanket washing	laundry.
Cleaning of mattress/es & turning	Vacuum clean.
Removal of stains	with dry cleaning fluid.

*(Mattresses need to be turned frequently to give even wear. Some hotels mark each end with nos. between 1-12 denoting the Month that end should be at the foot of the bed and uppermost, facing.)

- Wall washing.
- Extremely thorough cleaning of window frame and windows.
- Machine scrubbing of Terrace & balcony.
- Thorough cleaning of all furniture inside out
- Lampshade cleaning (usually done in the dry-cleaning shop.)
- Carpet shampooing.

In The Bathroom

- Wall & ceiling washing.
- Scrubbing of all fittings.
- Scrubbing of floor.

- It is imperative that any necessary maintenance is completed at the same time.

If one is doing all the tasks together one start by stripping the room curtains, bed cloths and all linen. Then one removes to a drawer all the supplies. Remove the lampshades to the dry cleaning unit if it is made of furnishing material.

One Can Then:

1. Wash the walls.
2. Clean mattresses.
3. Clean all furniture.
4. Clean windows and frames.
5. Clean all things in bathroom.
6. Scrub terrace or balcony.
7. Shampoo the carpet
8. Shampoo upholstery.
9. Re-hang curtains.
10. Replace all bedding.
11. Replace all lampshades.
12. Replace supplies in room & bathroom.

A record of the date when all these tasks were completed must be kept in the housekeeping office. This is normally called charting as one has charts per floor or for all rooms. When one organizes this work task by task, it is quite easy for things like blanket and bedspread changing and curtains if one has spares ready and clean. And one can then just go ahead and change, send the dirty to the laundry to be ready as clean for the next day.

It is normal that such a thorough cleaning is carried out once a year at the very least. Good hotels aim for twice a year. Often once as a whole room program in the slapk season and once as tasks when occupancy is high. Some tasks e.g. carpet shampooing; bedspread changing needs to be done oftener. One records all of this on the charts in the office.

Weekly Cleaning

In many hotels there is a weekly schedule worked out to enable all cleaning to be thoroughly covered in the space of one week. It is difficult to do everything in every room every day and in this way with a different extra task to do each day the rooms are kept to a good standard.

The best way to organize this is for the staff to be briefed on the extra task each day and where in the routine they must organize the extra task.

The following is an example list of seven tasks that can be allocated on a daily basis:

Day 1 - Clean baseboards and vacuum clean under beds and all furniture.

Impending on the type of vacuum cleaner you have, one can use a brush attachment for the baseboards & carpet corners, which is very quick. Otherwise wipe with a duster. Carpet corners brush with a stiff hand brush.

Day 2 - High dusting in the room and bathroom and defrost the refrigerator.

The sort of high dusting in the room is wardrobe tops or shelves, hanging lamps and flexes, and high fittings. To de-frost the refrigerator one presses the correct button or puts it off. In some cases the tray beneath the ice-cube maker collects the water as it melts. In some cases there is a pipe going to the back where there is a little container and the water evaporates. One must after wash that container.

Day 3 - Clean the windows

This is usually done with a sponge and water with detergent and one removes with a squeeze. Always wipe the squeeze after each stroke. With practice this is an extremely quick way of window cleaning.

Day 4 - Polish furniture and/or Brass.

This is only in the case of wooden furniture which is still found in many hotels in India. Also one can find brass ornaments e.g. lamp stands etc.

Day 5 - Scrub the bathroom floor and wash baseboards.

Use a scrubbing brush. This once a week treatment keeps the floors in good order.

Wipe with a floor cloth the baseboards.

Day 6 - Scrub the balcony or terrace

Usually a desk scrubber is used for this. That is a scrubbing brush on a long handle. Then one rinse with water and for terrace on ground floor level one can use a floor squeeze to. remove the water. For terraces, stairs and balconies wipe with a floor cloth.

Day 7 - Wipe the tiles in the bathroom the ones that are not surrounding the bath.

In the daily routine one cleans the tiles surrounding the bath. Clean the others with sponge first and cloth to rub up to a shine.

As you can see it is quite a bit of extra work pa day, but it is necessary to keep the rooms to a good standard. The supervisors on each floor must ensure the work is being done each day.

Because each hotel is different, this list must be compiled individually for each property, e.g. some hotels have no balconies or terraces and some have.

Composition, Care And Cleaning of various surfaces

Gold

It is a soft metal found naturally in the earth's crust. It is resistant to acids, alkalis and tarnishing. It could corrode if exposed to mercury.

Gold is used in jewelry, ornaments, decorative finishes, tableware etc.

Silver

It is a soft metal found naturally in the earth as silver salts. It is a white metal unaffected by water, pure air, and foodstuffs. Copper may be added to it to make it harder.

E.g. Sterling silver =(92.5%) silver+ (7.5%) copper

E.P.N.S =nickel+ silver+ an alloy less expensive than sterling.

Tarnishing of silver is due to the action of sulphur from the atmosphere. Tarnish is called silver sulphide and can be removed using

a. Silver Dip

The silver is dipped in thiourea compound, then washed and dried. The liquid is strong therefore use a glass, plastic or earthenware vessel.

b. Polivit

In this case the silver is dipped in a solution of hot soda water, which contains a sheet of aluminum for up to 10 minutes. During this time a chemical exchange of charges takes place and all the tarnish is removed. Remove the silver and wash and then dry and buff using a polishing cloth.

c. Proprietory Brands

In this case the silver is cleaned using branded polishes like silvo, dara, pitambairi etc. which are available in the market Cleaning is easy in which the polish is applied on the required surface then allowed to dry for some time and then removed using waste cotton. A polishing cloth or chamois leather can be used for buffing up the silver item.

d. Burnishing Machine

This machine has highly polished steel balls to which the silver and a detergent solution is added and rotated. The friction causes transfer of charges from the steel balls to the tarnished silver and vise versa. Remove the cleaned silver, wash and dry wipe on a polishing cloth.

Silver can be used for cutlery, hollowware, ornaments, jewellery, tableware, etc. BRASS

This is an alloy of copper and zinc and may be corroded by acids. Tarnishing occurs when brass comes in contact with moist atmosphere so as to form a green verdigris. Heavy abrasives may scratch if used. Brass cleaning can be done using proprietary brands like brasso, pitambari, dara, etc.

Brass is used for making ornaments, decorative finishes, doorknobs, handles, stair case winders, taps, etc.

Enamelling

This method gives a colorful gloss or matt finish to steel or cast-iron pans, signboards, blackboards, etc. molted glass is applied to the surface and sets to form a tough easily cleaned surface. It may eventually crack or scratch and if this happens to cookware then it should not be used.

Plastic Coating

PVC, acrylic and polyester plastics can be used to cover handrails, table and chair legs, broom handle, etc. This is a widely used finish and has the tendency to scratch, which looks unsightly and is difficult to conceal.

Electro Plating

Electroplating is used to deposit metals such as chromium, zinc, tin, silver and gold, on to such surfaces as nickel, brass, steel and copper. The finish is widely used for cutlery, restaurant equipments, cookware, furniture, fixtures and fittings, etc. it is very durable but will eventually be destroyed by chemical metals cleaning like silver dip, and constant friction and repeated exposure to high temperatures.

Galvanising

This does not create a particularly attractive finish but is cheaper and very durable and is used extensively for mop handles, buckets, dustbins, etc. the base metal is coated with a layer of zinc to reduce corrosion.

Anodising

This is an electro-chemical process, which enhances the appearance of aluminum and increases it's resistance to soiling and corrosion. It is used for door and window fittings, etc.

Lacquering

This is usually applied to copper and brass. It is easily applied by painting or spraying and effectively reduces tarnishing to a minimum.

Tinplate

Items such as cheese graters, sieves, wire whisks and copper pans etc may be coated with or dipped in to molten tin as this material has good corrosion resistance, an important fact when an item may be exposed to acid of sulphurous foods and frequent washing.

Copper

It is a hard metal and its properties are similar to brass. Cleaning of copper can be done using an abrasive powder mixed with a grease solvent/acid.

Copper is used for making decorative ornaments, vases, base for kitchen utensils, decorative finishes, etc.

Aluminum

It is resistant to corrosion, and forms a surface layer of aluminum oxide, which resists further attack. It may get attacked by strong alkalis. A protective layer is deposited on the surface of aluminum during manufacture but gets removed if heavy abrasives are used giving white powdery spots. Aluminum can be cleaned using a nylon scourer and hot soap solution, rinse and wipe dry.

Aluminum is used for making window frames, kitchenware, decorative finishes, confectionary equipments, salvers/trays, etc

Chromium

Chromium is the coating on steel/iron or brass. This can become water spotted and greasy but will not tarnish. It may react with alkalis causing surface discoloration. Heavy abrasives will wear off the plate coating of chrome. Besides being coated by chrome, iron/steel can also be coated by zinc, which is called galvanization. Chromium plated items require a little washing and rubbing so as to maintain the shine.

Chromium plated fittings include bathroom fittings like taps, shower head, flush handle, curtain rods, grip bar, etc furniture and decorative finishes, etc.

Stainless Steel

Stainless steel is steel to which 8-25% of chromium is added thus making it corrosion resistant. It is an alloy of iron, chromium and nickel. It is a tough, durable metal usually having a mirror finish. It has good resistance to acids and alkalis and corrosion but silver dips, salt/vinegar mixtures will attack the surface causing discoloration. For cutlery 18/8 S.S is used in which chromium is 18% and nickel is 8%. Black deposits will occur if stainless steel is left in contact with moist aluminum or galvanized surfaces.

Stainless steel is easy to clean. Cooking utensils can be cleaned using hot soapy solution, (for heavy greasy stains a concentrate solution can be used).

Stainless steel is used in Various places like kitchen utensils, work tables, knifes, equipment body like oven, cooking range, closets etc, cutlery, entree, rays/salvers, hollow ware, etc.

Pewter

Pewter is an alloy of tin, copper and antimony. It may tarnish and has little resistance to alkalis, acids and abrasives. Cleaning of pewter can be done using warm detergent solution and a scourer. Wipe dry using a flannelette cloth.

Pewter is used widely used in cutlery, tableware, ornaments etc.

Bronze

It is an alloy of tin and copper and it's properties are similar to brass. Cleaning of bronze can be done using an abrasive powder and a grease solvent for stubborn stains. Bronze can be used for making ornaments, decorative finishes, and furniture finishes, etc.

E.P.N.S

This stands for electro plate nickel silver. EPNS is a layer of nickel and silver plate applied to mild steel or brass. It has good resistance to abrasion, acids and alkalis but the application of metal polishes should be avoided. Warm soapy water along with a soft scourer is used for its cleaning, then wash, rinse and dries, wipe using a clean duster.

EPNS is used for making cutlery, tableware, ornaments, etc.

Metal Furniture

Metals in the form of iron and steel have been used for many years but these and many more owing to their strength and ease of shaping are being used increasingly in modem furniture for the legs and frames of chairs, table frames, etc. other metals require a protective coating and this may be given by anodizing, electroplating or the use of transparent lacquers. Therefore their appearance may be enhanced by daily dusting and wiping with a damp cloth. For example: a table with marble top and metal legs would be hazardous as acid eats into marble and drinks that contain lime juice would harm the marble top, thus a surface protector like a catalyst lacquer should be used to prevent the penetration of and liquid.

Metal Protection

Metals are very strong and may themselves be used to provide protection, such as on the comer of a wall that is vulnerable to banging of trolleys, wheel chairs and cleaning equipments etc. sheets of stainless steel may be placed around light switches, door handles, or on to swing doors which may suffer considerable damage by being opened by people who kick them open (e.g. a waiter carrying a loaded tray) etc.

Metals are also used in the construction of beds, chairs, tables, doors, windows, light fittings, cutlery and cooking and restaurant equipments. Metal surfaces will tarnish, scratch or rust unless protected in some way. The method of protection will depend on the use to which the metal is put.

Various Methods of Protecting Metal Surfaces Painting

Paint is usually applied to steel or wrought iron so as to make it look decorative. Paint prevents the metal from coming into contact with oxygen and moisture, which causes it to rust. The metal must be cleaned thoroughly and all traces of rust must be removed prior to painting. The paint must be applied very thoroughly and kept in good condition.

Enamelling

This method gives a colorful gloss or matt finish to steel or cast-iron pans, signboards, blackboards, etc. molted glass is applied to the surface and sets to form a tough easily cleaned surface. It may eventually crack or scratch and if this happens to cookware then it should not be used.

Plastic Coating

PVC, acrylic and polyester plastics can be used to cover handrails, table and chair legs, broom handle, etc. This is a widely used finish and has the tendency to scratch, which looks unsightly and is difficult to conceal.

Electro Plating

Electroplating is used to deposit metals such as chromium, zinc, tin, silver and gold, on to such surfaces as nickel, brass, steel and copper. The finish is widely used for cutlery, restaurant equipments, cookware, furniture, fixtures and fittings, etc. it is very durable but will eventually be destroyed by chemical metals cleaning like silver dip, and constant friction and repeated exposure to high temperatures.

Galvanising

This does not create a particularly attractive finish but is cheaper and very durable and is used extensively for mop handles, buckets, dustbins, etc. the base metal is coated with a layer of zinc to reduce corrosion.

Anodising

This is an electro-chemical process, which enhances the appearance of aluminum and increases it's resistance to soiling and corrosion. It is used for door and window fittings, etc.

Lacquering

This is usually applied to copper and brass. It is easily applied by painting or spraying and effectively reduces tarnishing to a minimum.

Tinplate

Items such as cheese graters, sieves, wire whisks and copper pans etc may be coated with or dipped in to molten tin as this material has good corrosion resistance, an important fact when an item may be exposed to acid of sulphurous foods and frequent washing.

Glass & Ceramics-Various Types

Glass is a brittle material made from a base of sand, to this another chemical is added in different proportions. The are carefully measured mixtures are fed into a furnace, where it is heated, after which it is led away for shaping, after which it is very carefully cooled. In other words, glass is a mixture of complex silicates formed at high temperature which when cooled is translucent. It is a mixture of sand, sodium/potassium carbonate, calcium carbonate, feldspar, dolomite and cullet (broken glass) which is heated to a temperature between 1300°C - 16000°C.

Glass Can Be Formed By:
- Blowing
- Casting in a mould
- Impressed or cut with an abrasive tool during it's manufacture.

Glass is found in all types of buildings where it is used not only for windows but also for tables, kitchens, furniture, light fittings, mirrors and partitions. To satisfy the demands of these areas of use, glass is made in varying strengths as follows:

a. Lustrous Glass
This is soft enough to enable the outer surface to be cut away into attractive designs. It is very expensive and is used mainly for bowls, drinking glasses, vases, etc which are not in constant use.

b. Borosilicate Glass
This contains borax, which enables the glass to withstand heat. It is therefore used mainly for cookware and is frequently referred to as toughened or flameproof glass.

c. Soda Lime Glass
This contains soda ash and limestone and is much cheaper to produce than lead crystal. It is used for general purpose glassware like tumblers, plates, ashtrays, bottles, ups, shelving windows, pictures and mirrors etc. glass used windows, shelves etc is known as flat glass which is sheet or plate glass.

I. Sheet Glass Is Drawn Continuously From Molten Mass Then Cooled. Sheets Are Manufactured In 1 or 2 ways, either as polished plate or float glass.

II. Plate Glass Is Made From Very Refined Ingredients After Being Rolled And Cooled, It Is Ground and polished. These provide clear, undisturbed vision and are used for shops, windows, minors, and protective coverings for tables.

III. Obscured/Textured Glass Is Required For Bathrooms And Other Places Where Light But Not transparency is required often has a pattern on one side and this is produced when the molten glass flows from the surface between embossed rollers.

IV. Safety Glass Is Glass In Which A Wire Mess Is Incorporated In During The Rolling Process. If broken, the wire mess would prevent the glass from falling to pieces hence used in doors and skylights etc. other forms of safety glass is toughened and laminated glass.

- Laminated glass is made in the form of a sandwich of two thin layers of glass with a filling of vinyl type plastic in the middle. When broken, the glass adheres to the interlayer.

- Toughened glass is made by heating the glass to just below softening point and then rapidly cooled so that a scum is formed which will cause the glass to shatter into tiny fragments.

CERAMICS

This includes bricks, roof tiles, floor tiles, sanitary ware, tableware and wall tiles. They have a base of sand and clay and are extremely porous unless a glass or seal is applied to the outer surface during or after manufacture. The most frequently found ceramic materials are:

a. Earthenware

This is thick, heavy and very porous material, which usually is glazed. It chips easily and must be cleaned, stored and handled with care. It contains a large amount of clay (a large % of organic matter). It is cheap to produce and is used for making mugs, pots, tableware like bowls, vases, ashtrays etc.

b. Fireclay

This includes a small percentage of organic matter together with iron compounds and other pigmenting compounds. It is opaque, off white, porous and used for making sanitary ware.

c. Stoneware

This is similar to earthenware but has a higher stone content. It is fixed at a high temperature giving a stronger material, which is impervious, thus no need for glazing. Some stoneware is oven and flameproof and can be used in the kitchen for cooking.

d. Viterous China

This is also fixed at a temperature higher than that of earthenware. It contains more china clay and quartz and has a higher chip resistance. They are non-porous, strong, heavier and have a standard of appearance mainly used for crockery and sanitary ware.

e. Porcelain

This is an extremely hard, translucent and expensive earthenware containing china clay, stone and feldspar. It is very strong but expensive. Mainly used for tableware.

f. Bone China

This is similar to porcelain but contains more china clay (kaolin) and bone ash. It is fixed at a high temperature than earthenware making it very thin but also strong and 1m pervous. Designs are applied to the outer surface so care should be taken when washing. Bone china is used for making tableware.

g. Bricks And Roof Tiles

This is a mixture of iron compounds, clay and pigments. The porosity and hardness depends on the actual type of tile, as bricks are intended for external use it should be relatively non- porous. A glaze may be applied to decorate bricks and roof tiles.

h. Wall Tiles

Wall tiles are a mixture of china clay, feldspar and flint The body if the tile is opaque and porous but they are usually glazed and may or may not be decorated.

i. Floor Tiles

These are available in various types and grades to suit the type of situation. They are made also with a mixture of clay, feldspar and flint and may or may not be glazed.

Ceramics are basically clayware and during manufacture different proportions of clay, other ingredients and water to form a liquid mixture. After many refining processes, this mixture becomes sufficiently plastic to be shaped into hollow ware or flatware either on a potter's wheel or by mould up. This is then glazed and fixed again. Decoration when necessary is applied, may or may not be glazed.

Wood-Various Types And Their Protective Finishes

Materials in this group of hard surfaces are porous. They are found in all types of establishments and are used for a variety of reasons.

a. Appearance-timber occurs in many colours with an infinite variety of grain patterns

b. Resilience-cork and wood strips

c. Cost - chipboard is a very strong but cheap material to produce

d. Insulation -all these materials will absorb a certain amount of sound and psychologically can create a feeling of warmth and luxury

Porous materials will absorb not only liquids but also dust They are also likely to succumb to fungal attack and pest infestation. They therefore require protection against these problems and regular inspection and maintenance if they are to with stand constant use and retain their appearance.

Wood is frequently used in the construction of upholstered furniture (chairs, beds, etc). When it is covered by upholstered fabrics cleaning staff should be aware of the fact in order to appreciate the need for careful handling of such items.

Solid Wood (Hard or Soft)

Hard wood is a very strong, heavy material used for the construction of :

a. Floors (strip, board, block, par$_{qu}$et, mosaic)

b. Furniture (tables, chairs, chests)

c. Walls (paneling)

d. Light furnishings (lamp shades, picture frames)

e. Kitchen and restaurant ware

It has a more refined grain than softwood and the short fibres make it les likely to splinter. swell or dent. Hardwoods are usually darker than softwoods and include teak, mahogany, oak, walnut, beech, etc. hardwood is expensive and is very often used as a veneer on wood products such as chipboard.

Softwood such as pine, fir are used for the construction of furniture, sub-floors, joists, ceilings, broom handles, etc. where the wood is either covered up or out of public view. Pine has also come into fashion for furniture such as kitchenware, tables, stools, chairs and dressers (i.e. items which at one time were used by servants only). It is easily damaged by li$_{qu}$ids and heavy impact.

Wood Products

These are developed to meet the specific demands of furniture manufactured and to reduce the cost of wooden items. The most widely used woods include :

a. Plywood

b. Chipboard

c. Hard board

d. Block board

PLYWOOD is made by bonding together a number of thin sheets (plies) of wood usually hardwood in such a way that the grain of one sheet is at right angles to those on either side of it Plywood is very strong, it can be bent to any shape during manufacture and may have as many as nine plies edged with beading or lipping. It is used for tables, chairs, desks, etc which need to withstand hard use and is therefore found in schools, colleges and halls of residence. Plywood may be covered with plastic laminated or a hardwood veneer.

CHIPBOARD is used extensively for worktops, wardrobes, chest of drawers, etc and nearly always has a wood veneer or plastic laminate. It is heavy, very strong but flexible. It is made by mixing wood chips with a synthetic resin adhesive.

HARDBOARD is more flexible than chipboard and much thinner. It is made from compressed brown fiberboard, smooth on one side with a mesh texture on the other.

Hard board is used for the backing of wardrobes, the base of drawers, door paneling, picture backings and as a base of floor tiles.

BLOCK BOARD consists of strips of wood between veneers. The inner strips of wood are fairly thick (up to 30 mm) making it a strong material used mainly for shelving and tabletops.

Wood products are mainly always with a plastic laminate or wood veneer and so should be cleaned according to the outer surface. Wood products are not generally used for floor or wall surfaces, although hardboard may be needed as a backing material for wail tiles and panels as it helps overcome any unevenness. All of them will deteriorate if excessive amounts of water are allowed to penetrate into them.

Cork

Cork is used in the form of tiles or strips in varying widths. It is extremely porous and will easily crumble, dent bum and stain. It's porosity, however, means that it also has good insulating properties, which makes it suitable for use on walls and floors and in areas where more dense surfaces would appear very cold, noisy and inhospitable. It is also an ideal material for such items as notice boards and bathmats. Housekeeping staff is likely to encounter cork in varying forms like:

- Natural
- Resin sealed
- Waxed
- Amyl coated

NATURAL CORK is most likely to be found on walls and should be regularly dusted only, preferably with a vacuum cleaner as dust will be easily trapped by the matt surface. Bathmats however should be wiped using the minimum of water. They should be kept standing to dry naturally as quickly as possible. They are not considered very hygienic. Resin sealed, waxed and vinyl coated cork is usually used as floor coverings.

Cane, Wicker And Bamboo

These are the names given to the items of furniture made from thick grasses (bamboo), palms (cane), and willow shoots (wicker). They have similar characteristics to timber products but are generally woven or plaited into chairs, tables, baskets, etc. They are easily damaged if they are not used or stored carefully. Regular cleaning is necessary to avoid a building of inaccessible dust, dirt and grease. Cleaning involves brushing or vacuum cleaning each day and wiping approximately once a week with a solution of warm water and washing soda or a solution made up of 5 ml. borax and 50ml of water. Both methods should be followed by rinsing in a cold saline solution (15 gm of salt in 1 litre of water) to help stiffen the strands. It should be allowed to dry naturally and over wetting should therefore be avoided. Oil or wax polishes may be applied, if desired, to those, which are varnished or painted gloss. Polish should not be used on items used with food.

Protecting Wood Surfaces

Unprotected wood will absorb moisture, which causes the grains to swell and so create gaps into which dirt and germs can fall and become trapped when it dries. Liquids such as coffee and wine, leaves stains on the surface, which is difficult to remove and scratching is difficult to avoid particularly on floors. The following are the most frequently found methods of protection and may be referred to as wood finished.

Cellulose Lacquer

This is fairly durable matt or gloss finish, applied mainly to solid timber furniture during manufacture. Which should be dusted and wiped with a damp cloth. Then dried with a soft one. Cream or spray polish may be applied to give a gloss finish. Heat, water or solvents may cause damage to it.

French Polish

This is used on small decorative items of furniture only as heat, water and solvents easily damage it. Deterioration is caused by light and the atmosphere in general. French polishing is produced by rubbing the solid wooden surface with a solution of shellac (dark red resin) and methylated spirit. It should be polished up well, working in the way of the grain, while dusting should be done on daily basis. If desired a cream, liquid or paste polish may be applied occasionally to remove light soiling and improve the gloss.

Oil

Solid wooden furniture can be given a matt protective finish by rubbing the surface with a mixture of oil (usually linseed oil) and resin. This process gives very little protection although it will help to reduce the absorption or water. Daily dusting is essential as the matt finish does little to repel dust. Marks can be removed by lightly rubbing with very fine steel wool. About twice a year the surface should be rubbed with a mixture of equal quantities of turpentine and raw linseed oil. Proprietary polishes should be avoided.

Paint

This is very widely used on furniture, window frames, door surrounds, skirtings, staircases, etc. unlike most other finishes it can be very colourful. Gloss paint is tougher then matt or silk and will with stand more frequent washing. All painted wood should be dusted daily and wiped with a synthetic detergent solution or solvent each week. Spray or cream polishes can be used to retain the shine on gloss surfaces. Although paint is easily damaged by heat, alkalis and abrasives, it is easy and inexpensive to renew.

Resin

Natural and synthetic resins such as polyesters, melamine's and polyurethanes are used extensively on wooden furniture window frames, door surrounds, skirtings, floors and staircases. The finish may be very glossy or matt and is frequently applied to furniture made

from chipboard. Resin is extremely tough, it will resist heat, water, solvents and abrasives but once damaged by scratching or chipping it is very difficult to repair. Dust should be removed daily and cream or spray polish used on the gloss surfaces after damp wiping. Matt surfaces should be nibbed up occasionally using a mixture of 500 ml of turpentine, 100 ml of boiled linseed oil and 500 ml of vinegar.

Wax(Bees)

This is applied to solid wood furniture or floors. The degree of protection depends on the number of coats of wax, which are applied, and the efficiency with which it is rubbed in. This will also affect the degree of gloss. It provides a very attractive finish exposing the pattern of the wood, but it is easily damaged by heat, water and solvents. Waxed surfaces should be dusted daily, cleaned each week with cream or liquid polish. And when considered necessary nibbed with another coat of wax, which should be allowed to dry before rubbing up well.

Cleaning Equipments

Classification & Types of Cleaning Equipments

Containers- buckets, mugs, basins, dustpans, dustbins, sani bins, spray cans, caddies, chambermaid's trolley.

Mops- Dolly/ thread mop, sponge mop, rubber squeezer.

BROOMS- soft broom, hard/stick broom, ceiling broom.

Brushes- long handle scrubbing/ yard brush, carpet brush, upholstery brush, shoe brush, deck scrubber, coat brush, feather brush, etc

Cleaning Cloths- multi-purpose duster, glass cloth, polishing cloth, chamois leather, waste cotton, surgical cotton, sponge, nylon scourer, floor duster.

Mechanical Cleaning Equipments- box sweeper, vacuum cleaner, scrubbing machines, laundry/washing machine, driers, polishing machines.

Sundry- ladder, stools, gloves, scissors, measuring tape, flit pumps, drying racks, storage racks, weighing scales.

Types of Small Equipment	Purpose	Advantages; Disadvantages
Washable dust mops(l); floor mops and wet mops	clean areas such as floors and walls	+Treated to collect dust (l); efficient; easy to use; −Types are not interchangeable
Synthetic brooms	Sweeping	+ Rinseable clean well; durable − Must be washed carefully
Compartmentalized buckets. Buckets with built-in wringer	Carry supplies Take excess water from mop	Light weight; convenient + More stable than set-ons; − Cannot be used as multipurpose buckets
High dusters	Clean high, hard-to-reach areas	− liarly lightweight; effective in cleaning high areas
Carriers, baskets, caddies	Cany cleaning supplies	+ Lightweight − Different types required for various tasks

Table 9.2: Small Equipment

Steel wool	Cleans by sanding the surface lightly	+ Effective, low-cost − Can be too abrasive for many surfaces
Scrubbing pads	Less-abraidve surface cleaner than steel wool	+ less scratch potential dun stee wool; can be used on more surfaces 1

Spray bottles	Hold fluids dispensed from bulk containers	
Whisk brooms Toilet swabs, johnny mops	Sweep loose dirt Long-handled equipment for cleaning toilet bowl	+ Eliminates risks of cleaning toilet bowls with sponges

Method of Use And Mechanism For Each Type

The smooth functioning of any cleaning operation/organization depends upon the proper selection of cleaning equipment's and process as well. Therefore the W/keeper has to choose the right type of equipment. The proper selection of equipment helps in saving time, effort, money and it also increases the efficiency of the staffs.

Equipments Required For The Removal Of Dust

Dust is airborne loose particles that may settle on any surface. During the removal of dust, the particles should be collected and not merely shifted from place to place. Sweeping, mopping, dusting and suction can do the removal of dust.

Brooms & Brushes

They may be used for removing dust (i.e. for dry work) from a variety of surfaces, floors, walls, upholstery, cloths etc. and may have bristles of animal, vegetable or man-made origin. Cobwebs may be removed as dust from cornices; ceilings and high ledges by the use of wall broom the head of which is soft and the long handle of cane.

Dusting Mops

It consists of a head of various shapes and sizes, made from soft twisted cotton yam or synthetic fibers and attached to a long handle, the synthetic fibers are electrostatic and attract the dust.

Dusters & Mitts

They are used for the collection of dust from hard surfaces, and carpets. It consists of a revolving brush between two small dustpans on four rubber-covered wheels and the worker motivates the brush. It is not as efficient as a vacuum cleaner but it is a useful and quick substitute on occasions.

Vacuum or Suction Cleaner

It removes dust and other loose particles from hard or soft surfaces by suction and some, in addition, have brushes to aid the collection of dust. The dust is collected into a container which, may be enclosed within the body of the machine (i.e. cylindrical and canister model), or on the outside in the form of a bag (i.e. Upright model) other mechanical equipment.

Scrubbing Machine

Used for cleaning large surface areas, these have almost replaced hand scrubbing. It consists of one large or several small revolving brush heads to scrub the floor. Some have automatic detergent dispensers. It can also be used for shampooing carpets, if suitable brushes are used.

Polishing Machines

The functioning is similar but with felt pads, which are put on the brush head to buff the floor, once polish has been applied. To keep the brush free from clogged up polish they must be soaked in white spirit before washing.

Equipment Required For Removal Of Dirt

Dirt is dust or other material which adhere to a surface by means of grease or moisture and its removal require a grease solvent or can be removed by washing, shampooing or scrubbing. A proper amount of friction with the addition of hot water, detergent or abrasive is also required.

Wet Mops or Sponge Mops

These are used for cleaning lightly soiled floors in conjunction with a bucket, hot water and detergent the mop consists of a coarse cotton yarn than a dry mop and a sponge mop is another type of wet mop. Both these mops unless washed well after use, become unhygienic and for safety reasons should not be wrung by hand

Polish Applicator Mops

It usually consists of an oblong head attached to a long handle and when after use gets dirty it gets replaced

Squeezees

They are used to remove excess water from the floor; smaller ones are used for window cleaning.

Cloths

The cloth needed for cleaning or for wet work must be absorbent and have a manageable size so that it can be wrung out by hand easily. There is different type of cloths like:

> Swabs

Made of soft absorbent material and are used for wet work above the floor ie. washing paints, baths, and lavatory bases etc.

> Floor Cloths

Made of coarse cotton cloth and are used for floors and w.c. Pedestals.

> Chamois Leather

These were originally skins of chamois goat, but now they are usually skivers, ie. split skin of sheep or stimulated skin. They are used wet for cleaning windows, mirrors, but they are also used dry as polishing cloths for silver. They should be used when necessary and rubbed when dry to soften them. As they are expensive they are only issued when required for special jobs.

> Scrim

It is loosely woven material, which because of its absorbency and not leaving linnets, is often used instead of chamois leather for cleaning windows and mirrors.

➤ Clothe Duster

Made of checked cotton and yellow flagellate cloth and softer in nature and are used for highly polished surfaces.

➤ Rag

It may be obtained from the linen room or made out of sack. It is used for applying polishing and when dirty is thrown away.

➤ Dust Sheet

They are made of thin cotton material about the size of a single Sheet and may be "discards" from the linen room e.g. thin curtains and bedspreads. They must always be kept clean and are used for covering furniture, stored articles during spring-cleaning.

➤ Hearth Clothe

It must be used to protect the carpet or flooring when a fireplace is being cleaned. But are almost obsolete because most hotels now have a central heating system.

➤ Bucket Cloth Or Splash Mat

It is either made of cloth or can be made of thick rubber or a square piece of carpet, and is used for putting it under the bucket to prevent marking of carpels or polished floor.

➤ Druggets

They are made of coarse linen, fine canvas or clear plastic and may be in form of a carpet square or a runner. They are used to protect the floor during bad weather and during redecoration.

Containers

Buckets or pails are made of plastic these days because they are lighter in weight, much quieter in use, and very much easier to clean than those made of galvanized iron. Polish applicator trays are used when applying liquid polish to a floor with a polish applicator mop.

➤ Spray Bottles

It may be used to apply a fine spray of water or cleaning solutions required.

➤ Dust Pans

They are used for gathering of dust with the help of brush. Formerly they were of metal but now plastic ones are more usual.

➤ Dust Bins

They are made of iron or rubber composition or may be in the form of strong disposable sacks attached to a stand, kept on back stairs or in the maid's service room for collection of refuge and foreign matters.

➤ Sanibins

Small metal or plastic containers with lids kept in toilet for collection of soiled items.

CHAMBERMAID'S CADDY

They were originally made of wood or metal but nowadays are made of plastic. They consist of a box with a handle and a fitted tray, which is divided into several compartments, and are used by maids for carrying small items, e.g. cleaning agents and spray bottles.

TROLLEYS

A trolley is a large fitted conveyance, which holds the chambermaid's box and also has a bag for soiled linen and one for rubbish, shelves on which clean linen, and other accessories are carried. It also has a stop on which the vacuum cleaner can rest.

MOP WRINGER TROLLEY

It is a mopping outfit consisting of a trolley used for mopping large areas in public area. It consist of two bucket one for the fresh water and the other for collecting the soiled water along with a mop and a wringer device

JANITORIAL CART

It is a trolley used for carrying the cleaning equipments and supplies in the public area.

LINEN TROLLEY

Used for carrying linen.

Machines	Materials Handling Equipment	Furniture, Fixtures, Equipment	Tools, Electrical, Mechanical Supplies
Attendants' vacuums	Room attendants' carts	Chairs	Ladders
Wet/dry vacs	Linen carts for clean	Tables	Scaffolds
All-purpose vacs for	linen	Mattresses	Casters
furniture, draperies, and vents	Pick-up carts for soiled	Box springs	Chair glides
Back-pack vacs Space vacs Extraction machines Buffers Scrubbers Burnishers Steam cleaning machines High-pressure sprayers Dry-foam shampoo	linen House attendants' carts Dollies Hand trucks Mobile shelving	Bed frames Headboards Night tables Guestroom desks Armoires Sleeper sofas Televisions Radios Lamps Mirrors Paintings	Extension cords

machines Pile lifters Electric brooms Carpet sweepers Wall washers Glass washers Fogging machines and/ or insecticide sprayers Sewing machines Trash-handling equipment Laundry washer/ extractors Dryers		Decorative accessories Telephones Wall-mounted light fixtures Draperies Blinds Towel bars Toilet tissue holders Make-up mirrors	
Spreader/folder			

Table 9.4: A Capital Equipment Roster

This list is merely an overview of what capital equipment may be required A hotel with its own furniture repair facilities would require many specialty tools. Dry cleaning plants also have their own requisite equipment. In some properties, house attendants would be issued hand tools and required to do some minor repairs. In others, this task would be assigned exclusively to maintenance.

Cleaning Agent

Cleaning Agents

- Solvents
- Abrasives- mild, medium, heavyDetergents
- Soaps DisinfectantsAntiseptic Polishes
- Reagents - acid, alkalis, baseDeodorants
- Bleaches and optical whiteners

Dust being composed of loose particles, is removed comparatively easily by the use of various pieces of equipment However, owing to its adherence to surfaces by means of grease or moisture, requires the use of cleaning agents as well as equipment if if is to be removed efficiently, and knowledge of the different type is important so that deterioration of the surfaces is prevented.

Water

It is the simplest cleaning agent and some forms of dirt will be dissolved by it, but normally unless it is used in conjunction with some other agent, e.g. a detergent, water is not an effective cleaning agent. In fact it does not even wet a surface satisfactorily as its surface tension prevents it from spreading. Hardness in water is another consideration to be borne in mind because hardness in water will have adverse effect on the efficacy of some cleaning agents; e.g. soap and soap based washing powders. It can cause premature aging of fabrics, can cause scale and fur to be deposited in boilers, pipes and domestic appliances. Hand water may he softened by the addition of soda.

Detergents

When used in conjunction with water, these can loosen and remove dirt. They are available in packets and bottles, each one differing only in the mixture of chemical substances The basic ingredient of. any detergent is a surfactant. This is a wetting agent which lowers the surface tension of water and to varying degrees emulsifies the grease and suspend soiling. An important consideration in choosing surfactants for a detergent base is that they should be biodegradable i.e. they should be able to break down in rivers. Ideally a detergent should

- Have good wetting power so that the solution penetrates between the article and the dirt particles.
- Good emulsifying power to break up the grease and enable the soiling to be loosened.
- Good suspending power to prevent redeposit ion of the soiling.
- Be effective in all types of water.

- Be effective over a wide range of temperatures. Be harmless to the article and skin.
- Be easy to be rinsed away.
- Be biodegradable.

Detergents may be of 2 types- soapy and synthetic (soap less) Soapy comes in the form of toilet soap. Liquid synthetic detergents are light duty detergents suitable for washing of hard surfaces and lightly soiled fabrics. Powdered synthetic detergents contain many ingredients and are suitable for heavily soiled surfaces and fabrics.

Synthetic Detergents

They have replaced the use of soap in many cleaning procedures because they are not affected by hard water, have good suspending powers, and do not dry with Smears and most are stable in acidic or alkali media. It is for these reasons that as long as the water containing synthetic detergent remains clean, there is no need to rinse hard surfaces such as walls, floors etc. with clear water. Synthetic detergents are available in liquid and powder forms. The liquid form does not have the ingredients essential in heavy-duty powdered detergent such as oxygen, bleach or alkaline builders. But the powdered form contains all these ingredients. Synthetic detergents can therefore be used for floor washing, baths, basins and fabrics and it may be bought in bulk or in small containers.

Soaps

It is obtained when fat or oil is treated with an alkali and the process is saponification. It is a surfactant and is cheap and effective in soft water. It forms scum in hard water and is difficult to rinse away, and is not effective in acid solutions. Apart from toilet soap, it has been largely superceded by synthetic detergent.

Abrasives

These cleaning agents depend upon their rubbing and scratching action to clean dirt from hard surfaces the extent to which they will rub a surface depends on the nature of the abrasive material and on the size and shape of the particles. They can be classified as follows **FINE ABRASIVES** It includes whiting (filtered chalk), jeweler's rouge (a pink oxide of iron).

Medium Abrasive

It includes scouring powders and paste. Scouring powders are made up of fine particles of minerals generally lime stone or calcite mixed with soap or detergent an alkali to remove grease and little bleach.

Hard Abrasive

This includes sand paper, steel wool etc. Other examples are glass, sand and emery papers, steel wool, nylon web, powdered pumice (light porous variety of lava), feldspar, calcite (limestone) fine ash, precipitated whiting (filtered chalk and jeweler's rouge (a pink oxide of iron) the last two being the finest. Rather than being used alone, abrasives are more frequently used in the form of a finely grounded powder, generally limestone or calcite for e.g. Scouring powders like "vim" or in liquid & cream form.

Toilet Cleansers

They are crystalline, powdered or liquid and they rely on their acid content to clean and keep the W.C Pan hygienic. It again maybe of two types, powder & liquid type. Powdered toilet cleansers consists of a soluble acidic powder, chlorinated bleach, finely ground abrasive to help when a brush is used and a bubble giving substance which helps to spread the active ingredient throughout the water. Liquid toilet cleanser may be diluted solution of hydrochloric acid and should be used with great care because the concentration may cause damage to the surface of the pan to surrounding areas and to the person using it if the liquid is spilt. All these toilet cleansers are designed for cleaning and disinfecting of the lavatories and urinals only and should never in any circumstances be mixed with other cleansers because harmful gases are likely to be produced.

Window Cleansers

It consists of water miscible solvent to which a small quantity of surfactant and possibly an alkali are added to improve the polish if effect of the cleanser. Some also contain fine abrasive. The cleanser is applied with a cleaning rag and rubbed off with a clean soft cloth. Water or water, to which some methylated spirit or vinegar has been added, does the job quite well and much more cheaply but entails more rubbing.

Reagents

The cleaning action is carried out by a chemical reaction.

Acid: Acids are used for the removal of metal stains. Vinegar and lemon are used for the removal of tarnish of copper and brass and of mild water stains on bathtubs, etc. More resistant water stains may be removed with stronger acids such as oxalic acid or hydrochloric acid. This should be only used under strict and experienced supervision so that too much is not used and is carefully applied.

Alkali: Caustic soda and ammonia are alkalis and are used as grease emulsifiers and stain removal agents. Strong alkaline cleaning agents based on caustic soda in flakes or in liquid form are available for the cleaning of blocked drains, and other large industrial equipments. Extreme care is to be taken in their use, as they are very strong materials with high ph values.

Absorbants: These carry out the cleaning action by absorbing the stain or grease e.g. starch, French chalk powders, besan or gram flour, Their constituents vary and many are of vegetable origin. Unlike abrasives they are not manufactured.

Paraffin Oil (Wax like or liquid hydrocarbon mixture used as solvent):

It is also efficient for the cleaning of baths but owing to its smell it is seldom used. Organic solvents usually methylated spirit, white spirit (turpentine substitute) and carbon tetrachloride are grease solvents and are used for the removal of grease and wax from different surfaces. The formers are highly inflammable while carbon tetrachloride is harmful if inhaled and should never be used in a confined space. Aerosol dry cleansers are suitable for use on wallpapers.

Polishes

They do not necessarily clean but produce a shine by providing a smooth surface from which light is reflected evenly. They do this by smoothing out any unevenness on the surface of the articles.

These fall into three types - liquid, paste & cream. These fall into three broad categories - spirit base oil base and water base. Spirit based is used primarily for mirrors, windowpanes, etc. Oil based is used on wood, linoleum and synthetic floorings, leather, tiles, etc. Water is used on sealed floors, rubber and thermoplastic floors.

Polishes may be used only after dirt and dust has been removed from surfaces. It s used in small quantities. Ensure that the correct type of polish is used with the correct method of polishing.

Criteria For a Good Polish

a. It should be non greasy.

b. It should give a good shine easily.

c. It should give a hard dry finish to ensure protection and ease of cleaning.

d. It should not mark easily.

e. It should reduce cost of cleaning and maintenance.

f. It should not smell unpleasant.

Bleaches

They are mainly associated with fabrics and used for the removal of stains of perspiration, urine, etc. Strong solution corrodes and discolors copper, aluminum, silver, and stainless steel. E.g. Of bleaches are chlorine, hydrogen peroxide, bleaching powder, etc. Bleach is used for cleaning purposes, and is generally alkaline stabilized solution of sodium hypo chloride and is useful for stained sinks, W. C. Pans but they should never be mixed with other type of soft toilet cleansers. They whiten and have germicidal properties and great care should be taken to prevent spotting of other surfaces.

Bathroom and all Purpose Cleaners

There are a number of bathroom and all-purpose cleaners in the market today. Bathroom chemical cleaners should never be combined and used together. For e.g. when ammonia and chlorine are mixed together, deadly gases are produced. Training should be given to employees regarding how to use toilet cleaners. All-purpose cleaners can be used to wash walls, scrub floors, clean tubs and showers and wash windows and mirrors. They are concentrated and can be diluted with water to meet different cleaning needs.

Disinfectants, Antiseptics & Deodorants

Disinfectants, antiseptics and deodorants are not strictly cleaning agents but are often used during cleaning organization. They use of disinfectants and antiseptics should be

controlled carefully as many have strong smells and their use often suggests illness or bad drains. Disinfectants kill bacteria, antiseptic prevent bacterial growth, deodorant mask unpleasant smell by combining chemically with the particles forming the smell. With the help of these cleaning agents a housekeeping Department plans out its cleaning program.

Basic Non-recyclable Cleaning Supplies	
Cleaning Supplies	**Purpose**
All-purpose liquid cleaner	Cleans most surfaces
Glass Cleaner	Cleans windows, glass, and mirrors
Furniture oil or polish	Cleans wood
Disinfactant cleaner and / or germicide (some are multipurpose / disinfectant combinations)	Cleans and sanitizes / sterilizes bathrooms, rest rooms, food service areas and other areas where contaminatio is a threat
Cleaners (1) Paste cleaners (2)	(1) Fine ground abrasives for cleaning surfaces such as porcelain sinks (2) Non-abrasive cleaners which require more effort but will not scratch
Drain cleaners	Clean drains
Metal cleaners	Cleans, polishes metal surfaces
Toilet bowl cleaners	Cleans, disinfects ceramic toilet bowls
Tile and grout cleaners	Cleans ceramic tiles or grouts, different cleaners required for marble
Carpet cleaning chemicals, other floor care products	Cleans carpets and floors
Deodorizors, Ionizers	Masks unwanted odours; speciality products remove smoke odours
Protective clothing and biohazard gears	Protects from hazardous materials and body fluids
Pesticides	Dry or wet chemicals to control pests

Table 9.1: Basic Non-Reavalable Cleaning Supplies

First Aid

First-Aid

Illness, accidents and other emergencies to guests and staff unfortunately occur from time to time. In any establishment while the h/keeper, may or may not be an official first - aider, she may become involved. And hence may possess some knowledge of first aid, and it is essential that she should be level headed to have a command over the situation so that it doesn't go out of hand.

In the case if illness a doctor is normally called and after the doctor's visit it is the h/keeper's duty to see that his instructions are followed. In case of emergencies ambulance should be called for hospitalization of the patient.

The First Aid Box

First aid boxes are required to be kept, and made available to all members of the staff and the guest at the time of need. The boxes must be checked regularly to ensure that they do not contain less than the minimum required as per the necessity.

The following requirements must be present in the first-aid box

1. Water proof adhesive dressing
2. Roller bandage
3. Triangular or round bandages
4. Sterilized cotton
5. Sterilizes dressing equipment
6. Clinical thermometer
7. Pair of tweezers
8. Eye bath
9. Sterilizes eye pads.
10. Pressure bandage.
11. Safety pin
12. Scissors
13. Antiseptic cream
14. Antiseptic disinfectant
15. Bi-carbonate of soda
16. Painkillers

17. Calamine lotion
18. Feeding cup
19. Medicine glass
20. Pencil torch
21. Bed pans and urine bottles.

Basic Causes of Accidents

10% Physical	88% Supervisory
I. Physical Hazards a. Mechanical b. Electrical c. Steam d. Chemical	**I. Faulty Instructions** a. None b. Not enforced c. Incomplete d. Erroneous
II. Poor Housekeeping a. Improperly piled b. Congestion	**II. Inability of Employee** a. Inexperience b. Unskilled c. Ignorant d. Poor Judgment
III. Defective Equipment a. Machines b. Tools c. Equipment	**III. Poor Discipline** a. Disobedience of rules b. Interference by others c. Fooling
IV. Unsafe Building Conditions a. Fire protection b. Exits c. Floors	**IV. Unsafe Practice** a. Chance-taking b. Short cuts c. Haste
V. Improper Working Conditions a. Ventilation b. Sanitation c. Light	**V. Lack of Concentration** a. Attention distracted b. Inattention

VI. Improper Planning
  a. Layout of operations
  b. Layout of machinery
  c. Unsafe practices

VII. Improper Dress
  a. No goggles-gloves -masks
  b. Unsuitable-long sleeves-high heels

VI. Mentally Unfit
  a. Fatigue
  b. Excitable
  c. Temper

VIII. Physically Unfit
  a. Defective
  b. Weak
  c. Fatigue

First Aid Causes And Remedies

Shock:

Causes: It may be caused due to a sudden injury or through hemorrhage or through mental stimulus such as bad news.

Remedies: Make the patient lie flat with all constricting clothing loosened, kept warm by covering with a blanket and given nothing by mouth except for the case due to mental stimulus.

Fainting:

Cause: It may be due to shock or excess loss of blood from any part of the Body.

Remedies: The patient should be laid flat and prevented from being crowded so That plenty of fresh air can pass through. And then call for the doctor.

Heart Attack:

Causes: It is due to clotting of blood in the heart and acute chest pain, Breathlessness occurs.

Remedies: The patient should be propped up or allowed to sit forward on a Chair and on no account should be moved till the doctor comes.

Stroke:

Cause: It is associated with high blood pressure and often brings in partial or full paralysis.
Remedies: The patient should be treated as same as for shock.

Concussion:

Cause: It is caused by a blow on the head which may or may not render the patient unconscious.

Remedies: Patient should be treated as it for shock.

Diabetes:

Cause: It is a disease of the pancreas that prevents the body from burning sugar. Even excess of insulin can cause restlessness.

Remedies: The patient should be given some sweet to eat to bring the Sugar level to normal.

Epilepticfits:

Cause: It is a chronic disease that creates convulsions and unconsciousness.

Remedies: Place him flat put something soft under the head loosen His clothes and wait till convulsion ceases.

Convulsion:
Cause: It mostly occurs in babies during teething or due to high Fever. Remedies: The patient should be kept warm with a blanket or given a warm bath.

Asthma:
Cause: It is a chronic disease and results in hard breathing and suffocation. Remedies: In severe cases oxygen is given to the patient.

Poisoning:
Cause: It may due to swallowing, inhaling or injecting.

Remedies: If taken orally the patient must be made to vomit by Feeding salt water or mustard water. or else call a doctor.

Burns and Scalds:
Causes: It may be caused due to direct heat or moist heat. It may be major or minor burns.
Remedies : For minor burns where the skin is not broken the affected part should be immersed in cold water. For major bums proper clean dressing is required. A burning person should always be rolled in a blanket on the ground.

Electric Shock:
Cause: It can be caused due to faulty wires or equipment.

Remedies: The current should be switched off and artificial respiration given if necessary and then a doctor called.

Cut And Abrasions:
Cause: It may be caused due to sharp ends touching the body.

Remedies: The wound should be cleaned with warm water and antiseptic cream and dressed properly.

Nose Bleeding:
Cause: It may be spontaneous or due to blow.

Remedies: The patient should be laid down and the soft part of the nose pinched and to ask the patient to breathe from the mouth.

Fractures And Sprains:
Cause: They are generally caused due to sudden fall giving rise to pain and swelling.

Remedies: In case of fractures movements must be stopped dill such time it is plastered. A sprain should be bandaged using crepe bandage Immersection cool water.

Foreign Body in The Eye:
Cause: It is due to grit or glass or any dirt falling in the eye.

Remedies : The injured eye should not be rubbed. It should be bathed with the aid of the eye bath and the nose blown thoroughly. It may also be removed with the help of the comer of a handkerchief.

Drowning:

Cause: It may be an accident.

Remedies: Restore the person from water, pump out the water from the stomach and give artificial respiration if necessary.

Simple Tips For Preventing Accidents

Figure 3 1: *10 Tips for Preventing Accidents*

A simple, back-to-basics approach to safety procedures can be very effective in minimizing accidents. Veteran executive housekeepers say that monitoring adherence to simple safety procedures can reduce the number of accidents by half.

1. Attendants should wear the proper protective gear, including gloves and protective eyewear. In expensive filter masks can vastly reduce accidents associated with fumes.

2. Attendants should make sure vacuum cords are rolled up when vacuums are not in use. This reduces the danger of tripping over the cord.

3. No employee should run. This presents the dangers of tripping and falling.

4. Wet floor signs should always be used, even if the floor is damp and will dry quickly, Failure to use them endangers both staff and guests.

5. Long hair should be tied back. Generally, no dangling jewelry should be worn. These items can easily be snagged or caught in machinery, thereby posing a hazard.

6. Shoes with nonskid soles should be mandatory safety equipment.

7. Carts, caddies, or baskets-not arms-are the only recommended carrier for supplies.

8. Employees should not place their hands into any area they cannot see, including the area between the seat cushion and the side of the chair, on high shelves, and behind furniture that is near a wall. Items ranging from needles to razor blades and broken glass may fall into crevices. Shattered glass has been found even on high shelves of closets near bathrooms.

9. Two people must be assigned to any task that requires a ladder : one to climb on the ladder, the other to hold the ladder.

10. Glass should never be placed in the trash. It should go in a special container which is impervious to cuts or rips.

Housekeeping Hazard List	
Potential hazard	**Safety instructions**
Exposure to chemical solvents	Material data sheets posted for employee review
	All chemicals usd are clearly marked
	Protective gear used as per manufacturer's instructions
	Aware of first-aid techniques indicated for chemicals used
	Change in skin condition reported immediately to supervisor
Muscle injury	Use proper lifting techniques
	Get help if load is too heavy
	Two people will assist in turning mattresses
Stumbling / Tripping / Slipping	Keep passage-way clear of obstacles
	Put out warning sign while vacuming the floor
	Wipe up all wet spots immediately
	While cleaning bathtubs, put a hand on opposite side
Vacuum shock	Do not vacuum a wet carpet
	Unplug vacuum before working on it
Broken glass-cuts	Sweep up large pieces, do not pick up with hands
	Vcuum up tiny pieces
	Place glass in container in storage room
Infectious waste / Linen bags	Large red bag for bloody linen or any linen with body fluid or waste
Needle control	Put needles in sharp container
	Use gloves and much caution.

Table 13.2: Housekeeping Hazard List

Fire Fighting

As prevention of personal injury is to be taken similarly precautions possible should be taken against fire. Staff should be made aware of such dangers as;

1. Smoking in bed, in such unsafe places as bedding and linens, stores and in areas where cleaning polishes and rags are kept.
2. Using electric light bulbs which are too strong in lamps.
3. Not reporting faulty, electrical equipment, sockets etc.
4. Not unplugging electrical appliances, for example television, heater etc.
5. Leaving camera and magnifying glasses where the sun can catch them.

The Housekeeper Should Make Provision For:

1. Sufficient and suitable ashtrays
2. Suitable waste paper bins.
3. Flame-resistant and non-toxic furnishing materials.
4. Proper storage for cleaning rags, linens, rubbish etc.
5. Low-wattage lamp for children.

It is not always possible to stop fire starting but it should be possible to stop them from spreading and endangering life.

Prevention, control and escape are three things, which requires careful thoughts when considering risk of prevention and bonds scares. A fire certificate is always required for those establishments, which comes under the office act of 1963. Before the fire certificate is issued the fire authority must be satisfied with such requirements as :

1. Means of escape and whether they can be safely used, e.g. unobstructed escape routes.
2. The use of emergency lighting.
3. Clean signs of exit and fire stop doors.
4. Fire fighting equipment of specific type in specified areas.
5. Means of giving warning of fire.
6. Staff-training.
7. Fire practice and appropriate records.
8. Fire detectors (Smoke or heat)
9. Instructions to guest.

The Housekeeper Should See That Her Staffs Are Fully Aware of The Procedure in Case of Fire. The Staff Should Realize The Importance of;

1. Keeping all escape routes clean.
2. Closing fire stop-doors.
3. Reporting faulty spring on doors.
4. Reporting exit signs not lit.
5. Reporting suspected faulty fire equipment.
6. Reporting any missing equipment.
7. Reporting any missing "Instructions to guests"

Fire instructions to the guests should be placed in the rooms where they are most likely to be seen and more detected instruction to the staff may be placed in the floor pantries and in similar places and too should be in several languages. It is essential in public areas and desirable in others that contains and similar hanging materials should be treated and maintained so that they do not readily catch fire.

Fire Emergency
In event of a fire,

a. Operate the nearest fire alarm.
b. Attack fire if there is no personal risk.
c. Close windows.
d. Switch off the electrical appliances.
e. Close doors and report to your immediate supervisor.
f. Carry out instruction, for example rouse guests, make sure rooms are emptied etc.
g. Report to assembly point for roll call.
h. Do not use the lifts.

Fire alarms may be automatically started by heat or smoke detector in the ceilings. These may be connected to a sprinkler system. The standard glass fronted fire alarm is operated by breaking the glass and this sets off the bells, buzzers etc. they may be connected directly to the fire stations if not the operator should call up the fire brigade immediately.

A fire safety program involves fire prevention, detection, notification, control und suppression.

Prevention is clearly linked with maintenance. Any lapse in this field can pose threat to the fire safety of a hotel.

Fire detectors like heat detectors, smoke detectors, and sprinkler systems operate automatically. Heat detectors react to the absolute temperature in a location (fixed temp. detectors). Smoke detectors are of two types-photoelectric detectors triggers when smoke particles either scatter or obscure light. Ionization detectors contains a small amount of radioactive material that establishes a flow of ionized air between charged electrodes in the conductor. Sprinkler system also triggers alarm and also dispenses water for suppression.

Fire Notification Involves :

- Emergency instructions and floor plans
- Building horns and alarms
- Voice alarms and communication system
- Single station smoke detectors (do not serve a building alarm but a local alarm)
- Exit lights (including not exits)

In spite of all efforts there will still be outbreak of fire, and for fire suppression we need sprinklers, standpipes and hose systems, buckets of sands and water, portable extinguishers, and all related equipment (such as fire pumps, emergency generators).

Fire and smoke control equipment includes such items as fire and smoke dampers (limit the spread of fire) in air handling systems, automatic guestroom door closers, alarm-initiated fire and smoke control door closer.

Fire Fighting Equipments

These Include- Buckets of water Easily used but unless checked frequently there may be insufficient waters in them at the time of emergency.

Buckets of sand Useful for smothering small fire and may be used perfectly dry on electrical fire (Never use water).

Hose spread More effective than bucket of water and can extend up to 36 meter.

Fire Extinguishers

Soda acid (conjunction to water) it is used for fire on wood, paper and fabric etc. The colour is red.

Powder colour is blue. Can be used for all risks flammable liquids and gases. Foam colour is cream. It is used for flammable liquids, oils, fats, etc.

Halons colour is green. It is used for flammable and electrical liquids. Fire blankets Used for small fires.

Lost And Found Procedure

'Lost And Found' In the housekeeping refers to those articles inadvertently left or lost by a guest in the hotel. Such articles can range from jewellery, costly electronic goods to simple garments, shoes, foodstuffs, etc.

The housekeeping department of a hotel deals with all the lost & found since most of it comes from the rooms. All types of items that are found in the guestroom or public area should be deposited at the housekeeping dept. as lost property.

Any accommodation establishment must have a policy on lost property, which is also in line with the law. It is the duty of the establishment to protect such articles to a particular time period until they are claimed by the guest. Generally lost and found articles are classified into 2 groups

   a. **Valuable**- The valuable articles generally include all electrical items, important documents, precious metals and stones, large amounts of money, etc.

   b. **Invaluable**-The invaluable articles generally include all items like clothes, bags, shoes, etc.

   c. **Perishable**- The perishable articles generally include all items, which have a shelf life not more than 24 hours or so. This would include foodstuffs, beverages, flowers, etc.

Procedure For Returning/Storing Lost And Found Articles

1. The depositor is required to put the prescribed bag containing the lost articles and clearly indicate in the slip the required information. The slip is made in triplicate, the 1st copy is stapled with the item which is stored, 2nd copy is send to the front office manager for procuring the address of the guest, 3rd copy is retained in the office.

2. Information regarding the item is then transferred to the lost & found register, which is kept in the housekeeper's office for ready reference of the staff in case of any query.

3. Each article is given a serial number which makes it easy to locate it in the storage e.g. ½ would mean 2nd article found in January, i.e., the first digit denotes the month and the second digit denotes the serial no. of the stored article. Description should be clear e.g. just shoes are not enough, the type, the color, material, size etc, that should be mentioned. Finder's name is important for future distribution in future.

4. After collecting the address from the front office department, the housekeeper writes to the guest concerned, informing him about the item left behind. On receiving the confirmation, the article is either sends up to him or retained in the dept. or discarded as per the guest instruction.

5. Whether or not to charge the guest for postal expenses is according to the policy of the establishment. If the guest or his representative collects the article personally, he is made to sign the tag attached to the article. The tag is then filed with relevant details. If it is posted, the executive keeper makes a note of it, collects the tag and writes the name & address of the

guest at the back. Most hotels keep articles for six months and usually valuables are kept for one year.

6. Normally there is a storage room or cupboard for lost & found. This is divided into shelving space and the articles are stored there according to the serial number for every location.

7. Lost & found room is kept locked always and the key is with the desk control supervisor and in her absence it is deposited in a sealed and signed envelope with the front office cashier. The manager on duty can thus return the item to the guest in the absence of the supervisor.

8. The key must be signed in and out in the cashier's register. A file of lost & found queries is also kept in case the articles are found later. This usually records date, name, article lost / found & description and disposal.

9. When the storage time is over, the goods may be returned to the finder. The housekeeper signs all the tags and these acts as a gate-pass for the staff. This system encourages honesty. Some hotels sale unclaimed articles by holding an auction and the money collected is distributed among the staffs. However each company have a slightly different policy on lost & found distribution. Sometimes guest offers a reward to the finder of the valuables and the hotel lets the finder keep them. The hotel can encourage the staff to call up the housekeeping office as soon as an article is found. It is also is sometimes given out to charitable organizations.

LOST & FOUND SLIP

DATE .... SL. NO. ....

NAME OF THE GUEST ....

ADDRESS ....

LOCATION FOUND .... FINDER'S NAME ....

DATE & TIME ....

DESCRIPTION OF THE ARTICLE ....

SIGNATURE OF THE SUPERVISOR

SIGNATURE OF THE RECEIVER ....

DATE ....

SIGNATURE OF THE H/KEEPER

Key And Key Controls

Different keys are issued to different members of the staff according to their job and responsibilities. These are very important for the security, of the guest belongings and hotel property, and keys are issued out at the beginning of a shift, signed for and returned at the end of the shift. The key issue register is maintained for this purpose.

All doors of the guest room in a hotel lock automatically when closed from outside. This means that the door is double locked. Many hotels have chains inside the room, for extra security. Various types of keys are:

Room Keys:
There are different keys for each room issued to a guest and it is important that this key is taken back from the guest when checking out. Normally guest keys have a heavy tag to discourage the guest from removing them from the hotel.

Sub-Master Key:
These are issued to room attendant /chambermaids and normally open doors of a section of room. This key does not open double locked doors and hotel's usually insist that room attendants/chambermaids wear a key belt around the waist so that they are not accidentally misplaced.

Floor Master Key:
These are used by floor-supervisors and opens the doors for one floor. They do not open double locked doors.

General Master Key:
This opens the doors of any rooms of any floor but does not open double locked doors and is carried by Assistant H/Keeper.

Grand Master Key:
It is carried by the Executive H/keeper, and in her absence by the security manager or duty manager. It opens all double locked doors and can even open double locked doors from outside.

Card System:
Electronic card system replaces keys and offer more security as each guest is issued a card with a different program. The card system cuts out the danger of the room being locked in the case of the key getting misplaced. This type of room-locking mechanism uses regular door locks and special plastic cards that act as keys to unlock the doors. The plastic card look like credit card with holes punched in them, some have a magnetic strip. The system uses a computer, which codes the card to lock and unlock doors. If a card is lost or stolen, the procedure for re-keying is quick and inexpensive.

A log can be used to monitor the distribution of master keys. This log should include the date, time, and the name of the person who signed for a particular key. Every time the employee receives or returns a master key, he or she should be required to initial or sign the log. The person issuing the keys should also initial or sign the log for each master key transaction.

Employees issued keys should keep the keys on their persons all the times. Key belts, wristbands, or chains are recommended devices for keeping track of master keys. Room attendants are also responsible for retrieving the guest room key if the guest leaves the key in the room. The key should always be returned back into the custody of the Front Office.

Daily Sign Shket Format For Room Attendants

Daily Sign in Sheet

Date:

Name of Room Attendant	Floor Keys	Time in	Time out

Figure 5.5: The US. Gram Hotel in

Registers And Formats In Housekeeping

Grooming Register

As the name suggests, this register keeps track of the daily grooming of room attendants. Every aspect of their appearance is noted & a remark is made. This register may help in selection of employees of the month.

Sample

EMPLOYEE GROOMING REGISTER							
EMPLOYEE NAME	HAIR	SHAVE	SHOES	PEN	NAME TAG	UNIFORM	NAILS

Key Register

Every room attendant is issued a sub master key for his area at the beginning of his shift. The sub master key can open only certain rooms in a certain section. The room attendant signs for the key when he takes it & then signs again on return at the end of his shift. Each key has a number/code, which is indicated on the register.

Sample

HOUSEKEEPING DEPT. KEY REGISTER					
KEYS	TAKEN BY	TIME	SIGN	TIME RETURNED	SIGN

Missing & Damaged Articles

It is the duty of the room attendant to inform the housekeeping supervisor in case or damaged or missing articles from the room. She will then inform the lobby manager. The situation is dealt with depending upon the value of the article missing or the extent of damage caused according to the hotel policy. It is essential that the housekeeping department maintain a record of the damaged or missing articles. The record shows the date, room no. or location, description of the articles, extent of damage or the value of the missing article. The name of the manager informed is also recorded and logged on it. Steps taken to restore the damaged article are also recorded so that it forms a record as well as a report.

MISSING AND DAMAGED ARTICLES REGISTER

SERIAL OF NO	DATE	ROOM NO. LOCATION	DESCRIPTION OF ARTICLES	EXTENT OF DAMAGE	NAME OF MANAGER	VALUE ARTICLE	REMARKS

Spring Cleaning Register

This refers to thorough cleaning which is carried out once a year. Jobs like washing curtains, bedspreads, shampooing carpets, dry cleaning of expensive rugs etc. In order to carry out this work a set number of rooms are to be blocked at a time.

Sample

Room No.	Painting	Polishing	Lace Curtain Chaning	Heavy Curtain Chaning	Carpet Shampoo	Stone Polishing
101						
102						
103						
104						
105						
106						
107						
108						
109						
110						
111						
112						
113						
114						
115						

GATE PASS

HOTELXYZ	
SERIAL NO.	DATE:
DEPARTMENT:	
PERMIT TO REMOVE FROM THE HOTEL PREMISES THE FOLLOWING:	
LOST & FOUND NO.:	
GUEST NOTE ATTACHED	
SIGNATURE OF EXECUTIVE HOUSEKEEPER:	

Interdepartment Relationship

All the departments of the hotel are required for its effective functioning, and cooperation and teamwork is of great importance. No dept. is isolated they are all interdependent. All the depts. are working towards the satisfaction of the guest. During the course of work the H/keeper comes in contact with practically all the depts. And if the work of all the departmental heads are unhindered and if friction is avoided then a close interdepartmental cooperation can help the establishment to run smoothly.

Front Office

F.O. and h/keeping are both concerned with rooms the former with the letting and the latter with the preparation of the rooms. To do this efficiently there must be a constant exchange of information's between the two depts. The h/keeper relies on the F/0 to let her know on which day's guest are arriving or leaving. When VIP's are expected, special requests have been made for cots, bed-boards or babysitters. This way guest's special requirement may be anticipated and complaints avoided.

To avoid guest being shown into an untidy room the h/keeper should notify the F/0 of "ready rooms" as soon as they are available and when shifting has been completed so the F/0 can transfer the room bill. HK also notifies the F/0 when rooms are "taken off" for redecoration, and again when they are "put on". At certain times of the day the h/keeper will let the F/0 have a control sheet (occupant list, h/keeper's report or vacant room list) so that the F/0 may check the accuracy of the room booking board or chart.

Maintenance

In the course of a day the h/keeper finds many items requiring attention, such as dripping taps, w.c, cisterns not flushing, faulty electrical plugs, broken cords ort the air-conditioner not cooling. These faults should be reported as early as possible. The keeper should cooperate by getting the room doors unlocked promptly when the repair is being done. Agreement has to be reached as to when the maintenance staffs are available for redecoration and told how long this is take. Maintenance should be given rooms ready stripped when renovation is to take place and furniture removed for repair should be labeled. With cooperation jobs get done more quickly. Urgent repairs are normally reported to the maintenance by telephone and if a good relationship exists between the two departments it is more likely that urgent repairs will be dealt with promptly. Unless a room is checked properly before re-sale the h/keeping can't hand it over to the *Flo.* so a close coordination is required.

Food & Beverage

Cooperation here is mainly concerned with linen. While the linen keeper under the supervision of the h/keeper needs to have sufficient stock to meet the demands of the restaurants, the F&B manager should ensure that the time of exchange of linen are respected, and that linen is not misused. The linen room also supplies the clean uniforms.

The h/keeper should be notified of banquets as soon as possible, not only because of the requirements for linen but because in some hotel the h/keeper is responsible for the flowers as well. Cooperation is particularly necessary where there is a floor-waiter service, so that friction does not arise over such trivial matters as waiters not collecting trays from the rooms, waiters leaving trays in the corridor, or causing extra work through careless spills oh the carpets.

Kitchen

The same cooperation is necessary regarding linen as for the restaurant. Here the linen room to the kitchen staff and also the condemned clothe for extra wet work supplies also clean uniform. In addition a happy atmosphere between the chef and the h/keeper, makes one important aspect of staff welfare, i.e. food, much less of a problem as complaints may r be discussed on a more fiendly basis.

Accounts

Wage packets are made up from the information, received from the h/keeper. Regarding hours worked, holidays taken, days lost due to sickness and whether this is accurate and punctual, even this information comes from the h/keeper. It is hoped that the staff of h/keeping dept. will not be kept waiting unnecessarily in the queue for their salary packets. The h/keeper should see that the income tax forms of the new staff, notification of staff leaving and of any accidents, petty cash slips and checked invoices are handed over promptly.

Hall Porter

Cooperation with the head porter is necessary regarding lists for early morning teas and calls, the prompt removal of luggage from the vacated rooms and the willing loan of his staff when house porters are not available. It is helpful if luggage porters tell the h/keeper when room luggage has been vacated.

Security

Cooperation here is mainly concerned with the prevention of fire and theft and to ensure guest privacy security. There are so many security hazards on the floors that liaison is particularly necessary between h/keeping and the security.

Stores

Small hotels where h/keeping doesn't have a personal store has to depend on the general store, which ensures the availability of day-to-day requirements of h/keeping except for linen.

Personnel Department

As personnel dept. deals with the recruitment, undisciplined, grievances, procedures, identity cards for staffs, locker facilities, induction training, warning letters hence h/keeping has to coordinate with the personnel department in connection with the above subjects for it's own staffs.

Purchase Department

The h/keeper has to coordinate with the purchase dept. as this is the dept., which procures various h/keeping supplies such as guest supplies, stationery, linen, cleaning equipment's and agents etc. for the h/keeping staff.

Hotel Linen

Definition of Linen

Linen is the term used for all launderable items. It is also the name given to a certain fibre whose properties are similar to cotton. However, linen in this context means all launderable items like bed and bath linen, table linen, soft furnishings, uniforms, dusters, guest linen, etc.

Classification of Linen

In hotels, generally the term 'house linen' is used, which means the linen used in hotels as opposed to guest's linen and uniforms. This is basically divided into housekeeping linen used in rooms and bathrooms and food and beverage linen used in restaurants, bars and kitchens.

Housekeeping Linen Consists of

1. Single/double sheets
2. Pillowcases
3. Towels- Pool, Turkish/bath, hand, face
4. Bathmats
5. Bathrobes
6. Mattress
7. Mattress protector
8. Curtains - drape/heavy, sheer/light/lace
9. Shower curtains
10. Blankets
11. Bedspreads
12. Dusters/dustsheets

F&B Linen Consists of

1. Table cloths of different sizes Slip cloths/naperons
2. Frillings for banquet tables/buffet skirting Napkins/serviettes
3. Glass cloths Bar runners Tray cloths
4. Kitchen cloths/dusters Oven cloths
5. Again different hotels tend to use a variety of size according to their needs. When purchasing a bed sheet or a blanket, one must keep in mind allowance for shrinkage, tucking in and for folding over the blanket, etc. hence it is important to know the exact size of the item and purchase accordingly.

Linen Room

Linen room is the central dept. for all linen and from it sufficient clean articles in good condition are distributed throughout the establishment. The linen room is a storage place as well as a distribution centre.

There are Basically 2 Types of Linen Rooms;
   a. Centralized
   b. Decentralized

Centralised

In this type of linen room, the linen from all floors is collected and sorted in one central area. The linen keeper has complete control over the linen room. All issues and receipt are made from here. This is good for hotels on different levels or for smaller hotels.

Decentralised

Each floor has it's own par stock and as and when necessary it is replenished from the main linen room. The par is stored in individual pantries. The floor supervisors are responsible for maintaining the par. Hotels with large number of floors use this system. It is also used in resorts areas where the rooms are spread out.

Activities of a Linen Room
   a. Collection of soiled linen
   b. Counting and sorting
   c. Packaging
   d. Dispatch to the laundry
   e. Receiving from the laundry
   f. Checking and sorting
   g. Storing
   h. Distribution to units
   i. Stock taking and maintaining records
   j. Monogramming
   k. Uniforms

Location And Planning

According to their functions linen rooms will vary greatly in size shape and location. However, the location of the linen room-must

- Facilitate easy issue and receipt of linen from floors and departments; therefore it should be situated near the service elevator.

- Facilitate easy flow of linen to and from the laundry, and if it is a contracted out laundry then it should be easily accessible from the outside.

- It should be at a distance from the food production area, as the linen would absorb the odours of food easily.

- It should be close to the housekeeping area and housekeeping office.

Essential Qualities of The Linen Room
These Include The following :

- It should be sufficiently large to carry out all the activities. This will depend on the size of the hotel and exactly what work will be done.

- The doors and aisles should be wide enough to facilitate movements of trolleys.

- It should be adequately lit to be free from glare.

- Walls, ceilings and floors should be easily maintainable.

- It should have a door with a strong lock for security reasons.

- It should have a counter or table type door over which articles / linen and uniforms can be exchanged and prevent the entry of unauthorized people.

In Order To Carry Out The Work Efficiently, The Staff will Require :

- Cupboards, shelves and racks to store linen and uniforms :

    a. Firmly fixed us the weight on them may be considered

    b. Should reach to the ceiling to prevent wastage of space and there should be sufficient space to clean under the last shelf.

    c. Should have slatted shelves to allow free circulation of air.

- A minimum to work tables are required, the surface colour of which should be in contrast to the white linen.

- Bags or baskets for packing soiled linen.

- Sewing machine with necessary attachments for mending and monogramming.

- An electric iron and ironing board or table.

- A suitable table or desk, with drawers for keeping records and books with a telephone.

- Storage space for cleaning equipments

- Trolleys

- Chairs

- Wash basin
- Receiving and issuing counter
- Step ladders to reach high level shelves
- Clothes brush, dustpan and broom, dusters, vacuum cleaner

The hours that the linen room is open will vary. In large hotels the linen room is opened from 6:30 am to 6:30 pm. It is normally opened seven days a week. When closed, the door should always be locked and the key taken to the time office and signed for.

Monogramming

Many hotels have their name embroidered into the linen or their logo, for identification otherwise they mark it themselves with marking ink/marker pens, sew-on-labels, heat-seal machines, embroidery or woven on to the cloth.

Condemned Linen

When an article is found to be sub-standard or badly stained, faded, worn out or mis-shaped it is discarded. This is done only on the authorization of the linen supervisor. As soon it is condemned it is recorded. Depending on the amount of discards, the hotel may decide to dispose the linen by giving it to charity/sell by weight or use to make cut-downs like:

From tom sheets-pillow cases & dust sheets, ironing board covers.

From blankets - oven cloths, ironing board covers.

From table cloths-serviettes, tray cloths, bar runners.

Lenin Discard Record Format

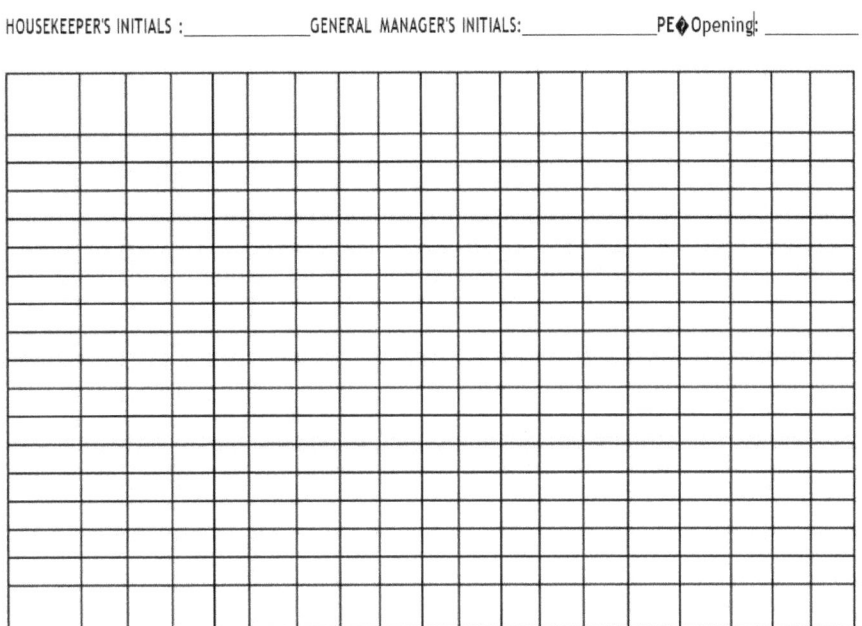

Figure 12.8: The front side of a liner discanl record

Par Stock

Lodging establishments must carry enough linen inventory to ensure that sheets, pillowcases, towels, bathmats, tablecloths, serviettes etc are available when needed. Therefore the amount of linen required to outfit the property at 100% occupancy is defined as 1 PAR. In other words, Par stock is one set of linen, which is required for a single occupancy per room, per day. For example for 1 room, for 1 person, for 1 day the requirement would be:

- Mattress -1
- Mattress protector -1
- Bed sheets -2
- Night sheet -1 Blanket-I Pillow cases -2
- Pillow slips -2 Pillows-2 Turkish towel -2
- Hand towel -2 Face towel-2 Bathmat - 1

In order to speed up the services on the guest floors, par stock of linen are built up on each pantry. Thus the floor staff does not have to make unnecessary trips to the linen room for their requirements. Their daily requirements are provided on the floor level itself. A number of factors go into the setting of "par" which is determined by the establishment after taking the following into consideration:

- Does the hotel have it's own laundry?
- If so, the number of sets can be reduced as the linen would be washed the same day.
- If outside contractors are washing the linen, the delivery period is taken into account.
- How busy is the hotel? What are the peak periods?
- Hot season necessities requires more frequent change of towels.
- How lowering of par would lead to overusing the linen and quicker condemnation etc.
- Output capacity - whether the hotel has a in-house laundry or the laundry is contracted out
- Overall occupancy of the property - i.e. the no. of rooms that the hotel sells in a day.
- The rate of replacement of worn, damaged or stolen linen.
- How many times the linen is changed in the day for a single room.

4-5 times the quantity of linen for re-sheeting is the average amount of linen necessary for most hotels. This means for 100 beds, there should be 400 bed sheets.

100 bed sheets in circulation

100 bed sheets in the floor linen cupboard 100 bed sheets in the linen room

100 bed sheets in the laundry

This allows for only one batch of linen at the laundry at one time, whereas in actual fact there should be 2 or 3 batches. (Occasionally some hotels do not provide the third sheet snooze/crinkle sheet as it is to be laid over the blanket to protect it from overuse, this could save the cost of buying more linen). Thus in some hotels 5-7 times, the quantity of linen is stored.

The par stock for restaurants and bars would depend on the no. of covers served at each meal period and the output frequency of the laundry. For tablecloths and serviettes, a par of 4 is usually maintained. For example;

A restaurant with 70 seats and a turnover of 2.3 for lunch and 1.75 for dinner will need to establish a par of 1,134 serviettes.

Type of Service	No. of seats	Turnover		Par	...tes needed
LUNCH	70	2.3	X	4	644
DINNER	70	1.75	X	4	490

Exchange of Linen
This May Take Place By Soiled Linen Being:

- Directly exchanged for clean over the counter by the chambermaid, runner, waiter or the kitchen porters.

- Listed and bundled, then taken to the linen room at a set time each day and clean linen is collected in exchange of the dirty.

- If dirty linen from the room is to be sent to the linen room then it is sent directly through the linen chute into the linen room.

- Fresh linen for the chambermaid's trolley is collected by each maid after the end of her shift and the trolley is fully sacked with all the requirements before she retires for the day.

Dispatch of Soiled Linen To Laundry

Soiled linen should be sent to the linen room as soon as possible for dispatch to the laundry because to leave it tying about invites misuse, and if in a damp condition, iron mould and mildew can occur, and both these stains need special treatment for their removal. Badly stained items should be sent to the laundry separately from other soiled linen, so that they may receive special attention, which is an added expense.

As far as possible, similar items should be stored together in a common basket and care must be taken that no tapes and comers are left hanging as they may get tom.

The frequency with which a laundry collects and delivers depends largely on the amount of linen being sent, and the time between collection and return of the items may be not more than 48 hours.

Inspection of Linen

When clean laundered linen is brought to the hotel it should be immediately counted and tallied with the number of linen that was dispatched 'shorts' are noted and entered on the next day's laundry list. Ideally after the clean linen has been counted, it is checked for repairs, mending, stains, bad creasing or if it belongs to other hotels, etc. if mending is required then it is stored separately for the in-house tailor/seamstress to mend, if badly stained, then, they are kept separately to be sent back to the laundry, if not then they are stored onto the racks and shelves in correct manners as to follow the system of first in, first out method.

Storage of Linen

During storage, linen must be kept free from dust, but it is inevitable that where linen is being handled, dust will settle therefore all linen should be covered. Linen in constant use may be covered by curtains, which draw across the shelves or stored in cupboards with sliding doors. Less frequently used linen like extra blankets, curtains, upholstery etc. should be covered using dust sheets/condemned sheets. Linen should be used on rotation basis i.e. first in, first out method so that the same linen is not always in circulation. This increases the life. span of the linen. All freshly laundered articles must therefore be put at the bottom. To make counting easy linen should be stacked with the folds outwards and smaller articles like napkins should be placed in bundles of 10.

Purchase / Buying of Linen

It is an economy to buy good quality material for any establishment because of the great use and the frequent launderings to which the linen is subjected. Each type of article should be chosen with regard to the :

- Type of fibre used
- Weave
- Tensile strength
- Washablity
- Colour
- General suitability for the purpose

Linen may be ordered directly from the manufacturer or from a large wholesale store of through a sales representative. It falls expensive if linen is bought in less quantities therefore it is advisable to get the prices and also the samples from various sources before doing the actual purchasing, also purchasing should be always done in bulk as it falls even cheaper. The following points should be kept in touch while purchasing linen :

1. **Obtain Samples And Testfor Quality And The Strength**
   a. Rubbing the material between the hands over dark material and noting the amount of dressing, i.e. starch, which falls on to it, if much falls it denotes a poor quality material.
   b. Looking at the material under a magnifying glass to note the closeness and evenness of the weave.
   c. Noting the firmness of the selvedge and the finish of the machining, especially at the comers.

d. Sending a sample of the material to the laundry to be washed a given number of times, and comparing it with a once-washed sample, to get some idea of the wearing quality.

Samples may also be sent to testing houses to get an idea us to fibre content and count.

2. Buying The Best Quality for The Purpose

a. Buy the best quality at one time as possible in order to get the best price / concession.

b. Buy from a reputed firm, which deals in genuine articles so that in case of any defects or complaints, they would solve your queries.

c. Place orders in good times so that exact requirements can be met particularly regarding size and type required. Most of the large establishments usually go in for the markings on the articles

Linen Inventories

Once proper control of linen has been established, physical inventories should be carried out. The 2 main purpose of physical inventories are :

- To ascertain linen loses.
- To determine the amounts of items needed to bring the stocks to their original pars.

Linen inventories are conducted semi annually or quarterly, but if the loses are severe then it could be taken monthly to determine where and how the loses are taking place. All linen items are segregated and grouped into three categories and inventory of each is carried out on three separate days.

- Linen room which includes linen from guest rooms, chambermaid's trolley, laundry, floor pantries, made-up mobile beddings, and discards etc.
- Uniforms
- F&B linen

Disadvantages of Physical Inventories :

- Time consuming
- Difficult to take as the procedure involves physical counting of all items in the house at a given time.
- No other job can be done, as it is a long process, which takes the whole day.

Method of Taking Linen Inventory

Preferably the counting should be done off-hours, at the end of a normal workday when all guest rooms are made up and no laundering will take place. Usually 2 person teams are formed, in which 1 call out the items and the other writes down the amounts. Sometimes a representative of the controller's office is present to guarantee that the results are accurate. When counting bath linen, distinctions must be made for all sizes.

Count forms should be used at every location and all totals transferred to a master inventory list whose totals will indicate the existing inventory of all items, the loses for the month, and the amount needed to restock the property. The sample inventory form can be summarized as:

Beginning Inventory (of Each Item Counted)

+ Purchases for the month

− Documented discards for the month

= Amounts that should exist

− Current physical inventory (total on hand)

= Loses (shrinkage)

Par stock (of each item counted)

− Total on hand

= Amounts needed

− Amounts on order

= Need to order

The total value of all linen in stock is determined as follows

(Linen in use X it's original price+ 2) + (new linen X market price)= Linen evaluation

Linen Control

Linen control work includes 3 main activities

1. Routine checking that appearance and hygienic standards of linen are maintained
2. Daily flow of stock
3. Statistic presentation and drawing satisfactory result

Hygienic Standards And Appearance of linen is Maintained -

This is done by the daily inspection of both fresh and soiled linen by all staff concerned i.e. all staff using the linen. This however lowers the standards as careless workers either. use the damage article or put it with the soiled linen so that it once again circulates. Also, a lot of time is wasted when there is no stock to change the faulty articles.

When a laundry operates on the premises, the inspection becomes the responsibility of the laundry workers. In case of contracted out laundry, the linen room staff inspect the linen.

Spot checking of linen should be carried out of all areas likely to harbor linen, e.g. outside service lifts, behind bars, maid, service rooms, staff changing rooms, etc. these checks will also highlight any damaged linen which has been discarded by staff, Items which are badly stained or require special treatment by laundry should be sent separately. If inspection is carried out thoroughly on all articles, it means a high standard of linen is maintained and the chance of a guest having a tom or stained bed sheet is less likely and the linen has a longer life. Daily control of linen

This deals with the quantity control of linen sent from floors / departments and dispatched to the laundry. To maintain an initial record of the par stock of linen in each department or floor and also for any subsequent increase in quantity of linen, an indent is made by the person in charge of the dept. of the floor. The top copy of the indent is given to the linen room while the duplicate remains with the floor) dept. concerned. If the extra linen items issued to the floor/dept. as per the indent is returned, the signature of the linen supervisor is obtained on the duplicate copy. This signifies that the extra linen items which are not required daily in the dept/floor have been returned and are no longer the responsibility of the floor/dept.

The daily routine exchange of linen requires no record if the basis of exchange is fresh for soiled and if it is collected by the dept/floor personnel themselves as on the spot counting is undertaken. However, when the linen is sent by chute, room linen control form F&B exchange slip is made out in duplicate. After counting has been done in the presence of the floor supervisor/captain, the amount of soiled linen is entered in and the book is sent down along with the soiled linen. The soiled linen is checked physically by the linen room staff and the amount is tallied with the amount entered on the book. The linen room staff then issues fresh linen on a one-to-one basis. In case the linen room is short of fresh linen at any time, then the linen supervisor enters the balance due on the exchange slip and issues the balance in the next lot. The linen keeper signs and retains the top copy and sends the fresh linen along with the exchange book to the floor/dept. where the floor supervisor/captain on receiving the fresh linen signs.

In case of un in-house laundry, the exchange slip is made in triplicate; the soiled linen is taken directly to the laundry. The laundry supervisor signs, retains the top copy, then the fresh linen is issued from the linen room as mentioned as above. The control of linen room is carried out by

- The daily supervision of the work done by the linen maids
- By the use of the linen room entry book.

This book contains a daily record of the soiled linen brought to the linen room from the floors and depts. and the amount of soiled linen sent to the laundry. There is no duplicate for the record as it is for the reference of the linen room staff only. It is signed and maintained by the linen room supervisor and it helps her to know the day-to-day placements of the linen handled by the staff. It also indicates the reason why the total amount of soiled linen received in a day is not equal to the amount dispatched by the laundry. It also serves a dual purpose of

- Control of quantity and type of item sent to the laundry
- Calculating the laundry charges

Linen is counted when it is sent to the laundry and when received, the amount is checked against the appropriate column of the laundry sheet. The top copy is sent to the laundry, the duplicate is for the accounts dept. and the third copy remains with the linen room. It is signs by the linen room personnel who check the laundry.

When the laundry is off-premises, the laundry charges are paid to the company at regular intervals. This is done by the account dept. only on the authorization of the linen supervisor who submits a statement of the laundry carried out during the stipulated time. When the laundry is on-premises, the laundry charges are not calculated except for guest laundry, as it is dispersed among the other overheads incurred for running the establishment.

The purchase index card is used for entering all stock obtained by the linen room. It is stored in the linen room as part of the reserve stock until it is required for daily use.

Linen Hire

In some parts of the world there is linen hire, where a company rents and launders the linen and returns fresh linen back to the hotel. Because of higher capital cost of equipments and linen, linen hire has become more popular. Owing to the high cost of linen and its upkeep, the hiring of linen from firms offering a linen rental service has become more popular. The firms undertake to supply clean articles in good condition and arrangements are made between the firm and the house regarding the amount of linen required, the frequency of deliveries and the price to be charged. Stocktaking is still normal practice and losses have to be paid for.

Advantages

- It cuts out the heavy initial cost of buying linen.
- No large sum of money is required for replacements; it cuts out the need to order new linen.
- The cost of hiring, which includes laundering, comes from revenue.
- Linen hire charges may be no greater than the combined depreciation and laundering costs.
- Short-term loans are possible for special occasions, eg, banqueting and so there may be less stock and less storage space.
- No repairing of linen on the premises is necessary. Less space is required for the linen room.
- Fewer staff is necessary and therefore there are fewer wages to pay.
- Various sizes of such things as overalls, waiter's jackets and chef's uniforms are available.
- No heavy initial cost of purchasing linen.
- Upkeep of linen, condemning and purchasing of fresh stock is not required.
- No laundering and laundry overheads are eliminated.
- Less space and staff are required for the linen room.
- Linen hire is ideal for seasonal hotels.

Disadvantages

- Little choice regarding quality and style.
- Quality is variable.
- Standards are not always maintained.
- No rags are available from the linen room.

- No renovated articles, e.g. old bed sheets, dust sheets, pillowslips etc are available.

- The contracted price remains the same even when numbers fall over a short period.

- No individuality of the linen items as the hire company has their linen marked with their name, which obviously does not correspond to the identity of the establishment.

- There is limited choice regarding quality and size.

- No makeovers available. In case of bad weather, company strikes, etc the linen will be affected.

- Contract prices and orders will be the same even if the requirement reduces consequently and if the requirement increases the extra stock will be required to be hired at the current prices respective of the contract.

- Standards are not always maintained.

Quantity, Quality And Control of Linen

The quantity of F&B and HK linen required for a hotel will vary as per the set standards of the management of the hotel. There will inevitably come a time when replacements are necessary due to normal wear and tear, excessive wear and tear, loss and lack of proper control. Therefore, training and supervision of staff is essential.

Lack of Control of Linen May Lead to

- Misuse of linen by service staff and housekeeping staff.

- Insufficient care of damp and stained linen, resulting in mildew and the spread of iron mould.

- Carelessness in stripping bed linen, resulting in sheets getting tom by castors.

- Lack of adequate protection during storage, resulting in articles becoming marked and the need for extra laundering.

- Lack of inspection, resulting in tom articles being used and tears becoming worse.

- Insufficient stock and poor rotation, resulting in linen not resting between laundering and the next use.

- Careless handling, resulting in soiling, creasing etc.

- Cupboards and linen room being left unlocked, resulting in loss of linen.

Sewing Room

In all establishments, due to high cost of labour, little hand sewing as well as a great deal of machining is done in the linen room. Extending the life span of the linen is most essential economically and an indirect saving too. "A stitch in time saves nine", therefore any type of linen before and after washing is checked for repairs and immediately given for mending. Thus sewing though a small job would require patience, and time, therefore it is advisable to have one within the hotel. Any emergency alterations, stitching, darning/patching up, repairing flaps of pillow cases, monogramming or hemming can be done at a faster pace. For economy, mending should be carried out before laundering, but dealing with soiled and perhaps wet articles is not pleasant, therefore mending is done when fresh linen arrives from the laundry. Any article not quite up to the standards of the hotel for guest use as well as staff use should be condemned/discarded and later altered into it's smaller versions like table cloths into serviettes and tray cloths, bed sheets into dust sheets and pillow cases, etc. Apart from the above routine work the linen room supervisor can order them to mend on other jobs like:

a. Cutting and stitching the condemned bed sheets in to pillowcases, dusters, etc.

b. Making new curtains or their mending.

c. Mending soft furnishings, upholstery like cushion covers, sheet, covers, etc.

The tailors and cutters are usually men with heavy-duty machines and the women are called the seamstress. These people are specially trained in stitching, mending, darning, machining, and monogramming etc, this saves on the expense to transport the linen to another place for repair and also discourages pilferages, losses during transportation and maintains the identity of the hotel.

Equipments Required in a Sewing Roo
- Sewing machine
- Machine Oil
- Table And Chair
- Needles
- Threads
- Scissors
- Tacking Pins
- Buttons, Hooks, Press Buttons, Zips
- Storage racks for Linen which come for repair
- Waste Basket

Uniforms And Protective Clothings

Uniforms are issued to most people who work in the hospitality industry. Although there are many people who dislike wearing uniforms ofany kind, they do have their advantages. Advantages To The Company

The staff can be easily identified.

Uniforms help to create an atmosphere or set the scene, for example uniforms may be worn either to match the decor or the theme of the outlet.

Uniformed staffs feel a part of the team and their work improves.

Advantages To The Staff

- They save on money to stitch work clothes as well as the laundry expense.

- Staff can get more involved in a messy job if they know that their clothes are the responsibility of the management so they need not clean them personally.

- Staff uniforms not only are impressive but also protective.

- Some uniforms give prestige to the wearer.

Choosing I Selecting Uniforms

When choosing uniforms, it is important to consider the following

1. **Work Environment** - short shelves are more practical for room boys/maids. Some uniforms eg. The headwear of kitchen staff, fulfill an important hygienic function.

2. **Appearance I Style-** while keeping in mind the environment of the establishment, a uniform should be designed in such a way that will look equally good on fat and thin, short and tall people. Well-stitched and fitting garments should be used in public area staff allowing comfort ability during work. They should stay bright and look new even through countless launderings.

3. **Comfort-** comfort in uniforms depends on the right fabric, but even more so on the good fit (tailoring). Staff arc active, hard working people hence they may require to stretch, reach, bend, etc therefore their uniforms should be designed with sample working room so they need not restrict their movements.

4. **Image & Identity-** if we want to create a desirable eye-catching, smart, efficient and professional image for our staff then we have to provide then with the right uniform fit for their status. Emblems, badges, embroidery can be done of the hotel logo and their name department wise. The decor also can be matched with the uniforms and thereby reinforcing the image of the establishment.

5. **Value-** in selection of uniforms, one should seek value, uniforms that look good, comfortable to wear, maintain their appearance even after continuous laundering, economical and cheaper but last long.

6. **Fabric-** after comfort, perhaps fabric selection is the most critical of all factors when purchasing uniforms. Cotton outfits are preferred because they are porous and more absorbent than polyester and cotton blends, however blends are getting more popular because they maintain their look, do not soil and crease easily. Wool is important in cold climate any can only be dry-cleaned thereby proving more expensive.

A List of Rules About Uniforms Written by The Housekeeping Department of The Radisson Hotel

The following standards apply to all employees:

1. Nametags shall be worn at all times.
2. For uniformed employees, uniforms are to be clean and pressed and in good repair.
3. No additional personal wear is to be worn with the uniform, i.e. scarves, sweaters, hats, buttons, or jewellery that would be pinned to the uniform.
4. For non-uniformed employees, tasteful, conservative business clothes are to be worn and must be clean and pressed. No jeans.
5. Shoes shall be clean, polished and in good repair. Tennis shoes and canvas shoes are not allowed.
6. The wearing of jewellery should be of conservative fashion. Excessive jewellery is not allowed.
7. Nose rings or studs will not be worn, in keeping with conservative dress styles, no earrings are to be worn by men.
8. Daily showers and use of deodorants are strongly advised.
9. Fingernails are to be clean and trimmed.
10. No gum chewing is allowed in public guest rooms, etc.
11. Women's make-up should complement normal skin tones and excessive use of make up is not allowed. Women should avoid the use of heavily scented perfumes/colognes and nail polish must complement normal skin tones. Hair should be neat, clean and styled in a conservative fashion.

Moustaches, beards and sideburns should be kept neatly trimmed in a conservative style. No beards are to be grown while working. Otherwise, men's faces are to be clean-shaven. Hair should be neat and styled in a conservative fashion, so as not to extend past the length of the collar of fall into the face when leaning over. Men should avoid the use of heavily scented colognes

Tips on Uniform Selection
Factors That Affect The No.of Sets

When drawing up a uniform budget, consideration should be given to: Staff turnover, Life expectancy of the garment, Seasonal requirements, Anticipated changes that may occur in decor and laundry requirements etc. In general, staff should be provided with at least 2-3 uniforms, depending on the work they are supposed to do. For example kitchen staff, housekeeping room attendants require 4 sets of uniforms, front of the house people do not do hard, tedious jobs therefore they can have 3 sets. When considering the number of sets of uniforms required for staff, the following points should be kept in mind :

1. **Uniform Material-** the life expectancy of a uniform is between 12-18 months, depending on the quality of the material, and the type of job performed during it's use. Hence materials chosen should last for its expected life span.

2. **Nature of The Job-** some jobs in the hotel are very strenuous in nature. Uniforms of utility workers, chefs, stewarding, room attendants, maintenance departments should be durable and hardwearing as it may require laundering every alternate day. While managers, top executives and senior staff in the hierarchy do not require a change daily therefore superior quality material should be used which is appealing to the guest and enhances their image.

3. **Frequency of Laundering-** depending on how often uniforms are sent to the laundry and whether the laundry is in house or contracted out would influence the number of sets of uniforms required.

Issue and Exchange Procedure

In case of new employees uniforms are issued against specific authorization letter received from the personnel department. The employee would be required to sign for the

allotted uniforms and will have to return the same and get the clearance letter from the executive housekeeper, failing which his pay cheque is withheld.

Issue and Exchange Procedure

In case of new employees uniforms are issued against specific authorization letter received from the personnel department. The employee would be required to sign for the allotted uniforms and will have to return the same and get the clearance letter from the executive housekeeper, failing which his pay cheque is withheld.

Exchange Procedure

- For regular employees ensure that they have arrived at the stipulated time.
- Check the uniforms for damages.
- Issue fresh uniform strictly on a one to one basis, ensuring the uniform is for the same staff by checking its label (i.e. Every staff has their uniforms altered as per their size and therefore it should have codes identifying the person).

- If the staff does not want to take the fresh uniform in exchange of the dirty then the linen housekeeper should issue him a uniform slip mentioning the details of exchange. The issue slip should be made in duplicate, one with the employee and the other to be retained in the book. In order to put forward his claim, the employee should produce the slip to the concerned person in the linen room.

- If the uniforms are damaged, they should be mended by the seamstress/tailor before handing them over to the employee so wear, if major damage has taken place then the matter should be informed to the supervisor.

Fibres And Fabrics

Purpose For Using Fabrics

Decorative value	☐	Comfort
Warmth or coolness	☐	Protective qualities
Durability	☐	And for hygienic reasons
Fabrics May Be Subjected To		
❖ A Soiling	❖	Abrasion
❖ Snagging	♦	Creasing

- Fading

The physical and chemical properties of a fibre will contribute to the nature of the fabric e.g. it's:

- Softness
- Durability
- Elasticity
- Lustre
- Resistance to fading, soiling etc.

The properties of the fibres will also determine any treatment, which may be given to the yam or the fabric itself, e.g. dyeing, crease and shrink resistance.

As new fibres and treatments become available so the problem of fading, creasing and wear, and the general maintenance become less troublesome.

The same or different fibres may be fine, thick, fancy, smooth or hairy. Any of these yams may be used in open, close, plain, figured or pile weaves. In this way the appearance and the characteristics of the final fabric are influenced by the type of fibre and the spinning and weaving processes used.

Characteristics of Natural Fibres

Vegetable Fibre	Animal Fibre
1. Strong, with a crisp feel 2. Absorbent 3. Good conductors of heat 4. Non resilient of elastic 5. Stronger wet than dry 6. Affected by mildew if left in a damp condition 7. Mothproof 8. Not harmed by alkalis but lose strength contact with acids	1. Soft 2. Absorbent 3. Poor conductors of heat 4. Resilient and have elasticity & thus it can resist crushing 5. Weaker wet than dry 6. Damaged by heat & disintegrate in sunlight 7. Damaged by alkalis & chlorine bleaches

Types of Fibres

Origin of Fibres			Trade Names	Used in Fabrics For
Natural fibres	Vegetable fibre	Cotton		Bed & table linen
		Linen		Soft ^furnishings, upholatery
Natural fibres	Animal fibre	Wool		Carpets, blankets, soft ^furnishings, upholstery
		Silk		Curtains, wall coverings
Man-made fibres	Regenerated fibres	Viscose	Viloft	
		Modified	Evian, Sarille	Soft furnishing
		viscose	Colvera	Carpets
		Acetate	Dicel, Estron	
		Triacetate	Tricel, Amel	
	Synthetic fibres	Polyamide	Nylon, Enkalon, Celon, Bri-Nova	Bed Linen, blankets, carpets, furnishings
		Polyester	Terylene, Dacron, Trevira	Bed & table linen, net curtains, filllings for pillows & quilts

		Acrylic	Courtelle, Darion, Acrilan, Orion	Blankets, Carpets, upholstery, soft ^furnishings
		Modacrylic	Teklan, Dynel, Verel	Soft ^furnishings, blankets, upholstery
		Polyvinyl	Saran, Movil	Certain, types of upholstery & deck chair coverings
		Polyethylene	Couriene, Polital	Upholsery
		Polypropylene	Cumova, Spunstron	Carpets
		Glass fibre Fibre glass		Curtains, fire blankets

Fibre

It is a basic visible unit from which fabrics are made. Based on their length they can be classified into

Filament & Staple

Filaments are measured in yards, as they are continuous in length. E.g. Monofilament yams are made up of single long strand which is solid and smooth. Silk is an example of filament fibre. Staple fibres are short in length and measure in inches. All natural fibres excluding silk are examples of staple fibre.

Natural fibres are silk, cotton, linen, jute, wool, while man-mads fibres include nylon, rayon, polyester etc.

Properties of Fibre

1. Staple

It is associated with the dimensions of the fibre, i.e. the length and the diameter of the fibre. It is essential that all fibres must be long and fine enough for spinning.

Therefore one can say, the longer the fibre the stronger the yam. Fins filaments like silk will produce fine, smooth uniform fabrics with better draping qualities than coarser fabrics.

2. Strength

The fibre should be strong enough to be spun into yam and ultimately converted into fabrics. In general, natural vegetable fibre is stronger when they are wet while other fabrics like rayon are weaker in that state.

3. Pliability

Pliability is essential to textile fibres so that they may be wrapped one around the other in the formation of the yam. Elasticity is closely related to pliability, in this case it should resist crushing and springing back to its original state.

4. Uniformity

Fibres should be in uniform length and thickness to make a smoother uniform yam to ensure good draping quality.

5. Spinning Quality

In order to have good spinning quality, fibres must possess cohesiveness as this prevents fibre splitting. There are 4 factors important for the fibre to possess cohesiveness,

❖ **Fine-ness of the staple**
- ✓ Nature of the surface of the fibre
- ✓ Pressure through twisting

❖ **Length of the fibre**

1. Absorption of Liquid

The fibre should be able to be bleached or dyed.

2. Comfort

The fibre should be able to absorb moisture as well as give out moisture there by keeping the wearer comfortable and cool.

1. Commercially Available

The fibre should not be too expensive and it should be available in a large quantity at a suitable price in the market.

Animal Fibres

WOOL is obtained from the fur of the sheep but fibers from other animals like horse, camel, llama, goats etc are also used. Wool fibres vary in length from 4.40cm and they also vary in diameter some being finer than others. They have a natural crimp or wave, which gives wool elasticity and resilience enabling it to resist crushing.

SILK is obtained from cocoons spun by the cultivated silkworms in the form of long filaments, which may measure from 274-456m long. A single cocoon may consist of up to 3km of filament. The filaments are smooth and tube like, with no irregularities. Silk is stronger than cotton. The best variety of silk is obtained from moth "BOMBYX MORI". Silkworms of the wild silk moth called "TUSSAH' moth produce wild silk in which the filaments are frequently irregular producing variations in thickness when the silk is woven. Silk material have elegance but due to their expense their use is normally confined to luxury establishments. Silk is a natural fibre, the strongest fibre having the highest tensile strength.

ASBESTOS is a mineral fibre derived from rocks, and the fibres are in silicate form of magnesium. They can be pressed as sheets or yam and fibres. It is quite incombustible and can be used as fire fighting uniforms. They are acid resistant, fire and rust proof. **VEGETABLE Fibres**

COTTON is obtained from cottonseeds and is one of the strongest fibres and the fabric made out of cotton is cheap but durable.

JUTE is a weak fibre and has very little elasticity and weakens when moist. Jute is also used for making twins and sacks and for backing of carpets and linoleum.

KAPOK is derived from seeds of a type of cotton plant found in Java & Sumatra. The fibre is smooth, light & as lot of luster and is often referred to as "cotton silk" & it is mostly used as fillings of cushions and quilts.

RAMIE is very strong with a fine natural luster and is used in high grade furnishing fabrics, especially pile fabrics. Ramie is known as "CHINA GRASS" or "Rhea Grass" and is also known as "glass cloth" and is used as cords or for stitching of canvas cloths.

COIR is husk of coconut. Can be used for mats, doormats and also as stuffing material.

HEMP is obtained from the stem of hemp plant. MANILA hemp is obtained from the leave of the same plant. It can be used to make twines and canvas sacks.

LINEN is obtained from the stem of the flax plant. The length of the fibre, which can be from 500cm to 1m long, enables a fine, strong yam to be spun. The fibres are smooth, straight and almost solid, and these factors account for the chief differences between cotton and linen fabrics. Linen has little resilience (pliability) and creases badly.

Man-Made Fibres

REGENERATED FIBRES (these fibres are retrieved from natural substances, mostly being used is cellulose) like rayon, viscose, evlan, sarille, durafil etc.

SYNTHETIC FIBRES (these fibres are produced by chemical synthesis- built up from basic chemicals) like nylon, Terylene, acrilan, saran, courlene, ulstron etc. These are all created by man from different types of resins and made for convenience. They are long lasting, tear and wear proof and have color competence.

GLASS FIBRES are produced in the form of fine filaments from molten glass. This is non-absorbent resistant to chemicals, fireproof (melting point is 8 1 5°C) and resistant to sunlight. It has very low abrasion resistance and is brittle and is normally used forlightweight curtains like shower curtains and fire blankets.

Characteristics of Natural Fibre Characteristics of Cotton

a. It is non-elastic and hence creases easily.

It conducts heat easily and therefore comfortable to wear as a uniform.

It absorbs water easily and dries faster than other fabrics.

It gets easily damaged by mildew and therefore must be stored under dry conditions.

It weakens and turns yellow after constant exposure to the sunlight.

It gets easily damaged by acids.

Cotton is normally not used on it's own but blended with polyester as it reduces shrinkage and can be used to make table and bed linen, uniforms, bedspreads, soft furnishings, upholstery, dusters etc.

Characteristics of Linen

a. It is very absorbent and a good conductor of heat therefore can be used for uniforms, sheets etc.

It has poor elasticity therefore creases easily and shrinks.

It is very strong when wet and can withstand constant washing and bleaching without getting damaged.

It does not absorb dyes easily

It is very expensive.

To reduce costs, linen can be blended with cotton. Cotton and synthetic blends are stronger, cheaper, lighter and dry faster. Linen can be used for sheets, bedspreads, soft fomishings, upholstery etc.

Characteristics of Wool

a. It is a weak fabric and the weakness increases when it is wet.

Wool is considered to be a warm fabric and a bad conductor of heat.

It is elastic in nature therefore does not crease easily.

It does not spoil easily but retains smell. It gets damaged by alkalis especially chlorine. It also gets damaged by moths, mildew and bacteria.

It turns yellow when exposed to sunlight.

It can be dyed easily.

It is an expensive fabric.

Wool is a thick fabric used for making blankets, carpets, upholstery etc. it is extensively used in carpeting normally blended with nylon.

Characteristics of Silk

a. It is a strong fibre but becomes weak when wet.

It is elastic but tends to crease easily and looses it crease if hung on a hanger.

It is a poor conductor of heat.

It does not shrink and get soiled easily.

It absorbs dyes easily.

Silk can be used in hotels and institutions for decoration purpose like wall hangings, ceiling decor, etc. sometimes guests require personalized valet service for their silk clothing's as they crease if folded and brought to the room.

Characteristics of Man-Made/Artificial Fibre

Characteristics of Rayon

a. It is soft therefore drapes well.

It is a good conductor of heat thus very absorbent and dries faster.

It is not very elastic therefore creases easily.

It resists attack of moths, mildew and bacteria.

It is cheaper than other fabrics, does not soil easily and loose its shape.

It is weakened by prolonged sunlight but does not discolour easily.

All rayon is thermoplastic which means that the fibres melt when they become warm or hot and set hard on cooling.

All fabrics made of 100% rayon are not generally used in hotels, as they are too weak to withstand heat, hardware and constant laundering. Rayon is frequently blended with natural and synthetic fibres so as to resemble cotton blends. E.g. a fabric made from rayon is brocade.

Characterestics of Synthetic Fibre

a. They are non absorbent which makes them easy to launder and dry.

It is smooth which means it can withstand resist soiling.

It is resistant to mildew, bacteria and moths.

It is resistant to sunlight.

Many synthetic fibres are damaged by cigarette burns and get damaged with heat, they do not burn with flames but melt producing poisonous fumes.

Synthetic fibres are extensively used for hotel and institution decor and also for uniforms as they do not fade easily even after frequent washing. They are frequently blended with other fibres to add strength to them. Can be used for making carpets as well. **CONSTRUCTION OF YARN**

SPINNING is the process of drawing out and twisting of a group or bundles of fibres into a continuous thread or yarn of sufficient strength to be woven or knitted into fabrics.

Spinning is of two types :

a. Ring / continuous spinning

Mule / intermittent spinning

Ring/Continuous Spinning

The action of drawing, twisting and winding is continuous and this is called ring spinning. It is a quicker process and has the advantage of reducing operating costs and increased production.

Mule / Intermittent Spinning

The drawing and twisting is stopped while the twisted thread is wound up. This produces a finer and softer yarn with greater evenness and uniformity.

Types of Yarn

Yarn can be classified into:

Simple And Complex / Novelty

Simple yarn: according to the no. of strands they contain such as single, multiple or cable.

Complex/novelty yarn : is usually comprises of a no. of strands / ply of different colour and more irregular than smooth.

Identification of Fibres

Identification of fibres is done through labels, visual inspection and physical tests like burning, tearing and microscopic investigation etc.

Count of Yarn

Measure is hank.

A skein of yarn, 840 yards in length is known as a hank and is the basis of determining the count. If a hank of 840 yards weigh 1 pound, the yarn count is 1 and if 2 hanks weigh 1 pound the yarn count is 2.

Fibre > Yarns Fabrics Comsumers
(Spun) (Knitted) (Bonding/felting) (Finished process)

Construction of Textile Fabrics

A textile fabric is the term used for all kinds of cloth made from fibres or fine filaments by the method of knitting, felting, bonding and weaving.

Knitting

Only one thread is used in this process. The yarn is wound around a needle to form loops, which forms one row. This row of loops is caught by another row of loops and so on till a continuous length of cloth is made.

Felting

This is possible only with fibres, which can stick to one another firmly. When pressure is applied and this forms a cloth, e.g. felted wool,

Bonding

Natural and man-made fibres along with plastic resins are heated and pressed into, sheets of varying thickness. These are called bonded fabrics. They do not crease or shrink, and are mainly used as disposables.

Weaving

Weaving is a method of fabric construction in which two sets of yarn are interwoven/interlaced at right angles. Warp refers to the lengthwise yarns and is stronger than the weft yarns, which is mainly the filling yarn.

Weaving is Done on a Machine Known as The Loom

The main parts of the loom are harness, shuttle, reed, beam/cylinder, picking, battening.

HARNESS

This is a frame consisting of a number of wires known as heddles. Each heddle contains an eye through which one or more warp yams pass. The harness is the up yams pass. The harness is the important part of the loom as it controls the movement of the warp yams upward and downward and this ensures that the correct running of the yam over and below the warp yam to produce the desired pattern in the cloth.

Shuttle

The shuttle holds the filling for the weft yam and is passed backward and forward across the loom.

Reed

It is a frame, which is located directly in front of the harness. This frame pushes forward each time the shuttle passes in between the warp yam and passes back the filling thread in position.

Beam / Cylinder

The beam or cylinder is one in which the warp threads are wrapped in parallel lines and this is placed at the back of the loom, from here the yam passes to the front of the loom where they are attached to the cloth roll. In other words, it is a cylinder like structure on which the warp yams are set parallel to each other before they pass on to the harness.

Picking

Each time the shuttle passes through the shed it throws in the filling yam between the warp yams, this is called picking.

Battening

The filling yam is pushed back and pressed against the previous filling by means of the reed, which is also called batten, and this process is called battening.

Process of Weaving

One of the harnesses raises a certain number of warps and forms a shed through which the shuttle passes. The shuttle carrying the weft yam passes through the shed throwing in the filling yam between the warp yams. This is called picking.

The filling yam is pushed back and pressed against the previous filling by means of a reed also called a batten. This process is called battening. The warp thread is released from the warp beam and the finished cloth is wound around a beam and then finished in front of the loom. Thee operations continue till the desired length of cloth is obtained. SELVEDGE/SELVAGE

In most of the materials the edges, which are known as selvedges, are made with heavier or more closely placed warp yams so that they do not unravel easily.

Count of Cloth (Thread Count)

These are the number of warp and weft yarns in one square inch.

Balance of Cloth

The balance of fabric is determined by the properties of warp yarn to weft yarn. If the number of warp and weft yarns is nearly the same in a square inch the fabric has good balance.

Gray/Greige Goods

This is fabric, which has not been finished or in anyway undergone chemical treatment. TYPES OF WEAVES

Weaves are named according to the system or design followed by interlacing warp and weft yarn. The following are the types of weaves.

1. Plain Weave
2. Twill Weave
3. Satin Weave
4. Figured Weave
5. Pile Weave
6. Cellular Weave PLAIN WEAVE

The weft yarn goes over and under alternate warp threads, as in darning. This is plain weave. Fabrics made in plain weave are normally smooth and their firmness will depend on the number of warp and weft threads per cm, which is on the closeness of the weave. A close weave gives a strong cloth which keeps its shape, but one which tears easily. The weight and the appearance of the plain weave fabrics vary enormously according to the thickness, character and the closeness of the threads, none of which need to be the same for warp and weft yarns.

Chintz, cretonne, scrim and sheeting are fabrics made in a plain weave and form the base of many pile fabrics. Repp is a plain weave fabric where the ribbed effect has been produced by using warp and weft of differing thickness.

It is sometimes refer to as the tabby, home spun or taffeta weave. Variations to the plain weave are: Basket - which looks somewhat like this, i.e. 2 or more filling yarns are interlaced with a corresponding number of warp yarns.

Repp — in this weave yarn of varying thickness are used.

Gingham — in this weave coloured yarns are used.

Twill Weave

The weft threads cross the warp at different intervals in the different rows in a twill weave, so that a series of diagonal lines is produced on the surface of the fabrics. Herringbone patterns are produced by reversing the direction of the twill at regular intervals across the width of the cloth. In a twill weave the threads are normally close together and the finished fabric is firm and hard wearing. Twill sheeting, drill and gabardine are fabrics made in a twill weave.

Satin Weave

This weave differs from the twill weave. In this case there are fewer intersections of the warp and weft threads and the intersections are uniformly distributed. The warp 'floats' over, for example, 4 weft threads and forms the surface of the fabrics, i.e. the fabric is warp faced. The fabric is smooth, usually of dense construction and with an attractive sheen. Owing to the 'floating' threads, it may present little resistance to abrasion and become pulled or snagged. There are many types of furnishing satin made from satin weave like cotton satin, rayon satin etc. A sateen weave is similar to a satin weave but it is the weft threads, which 'float' and the fabric is therefore weft faced.

Figured Weave

These introduce a pattern into the fabric. The pattern maybe introduced by combining two of • the previous mentioned weaves, as in damask, when for table linen warp and weft satin weaves are combined, or the pattern may be introduced by the use of coloured threads additional to the foundation cloth, as in brocade or tapestry. Huckaback and brocatelle are other fabrics woven in a figured weave.

In all these cases, the weaves are produced on a jacquard loom, where each warp thread is controlled individually, the thread as it required is lifted by a harmness, controlled by a series of punched cards corresponding to the pattern to be woven. Fabrics made in figured weaved vary considerably in weight and appearance.

Pile Weave

In a pile weave there are tufts or loops of yam, which stand up from the body of the cloth. The tufts or loops are extra warp or weft threads woven at night angles through the cloth. These extra threads form the pile or surface thickness and they may be cut or uncut. Combining cut and uncut piles can produce patterns. A thick, hardwearing fabric results which has a tendency to 'sprout', snag and collect dust. Velvet is a cut, warp pile fabric, Turkish (terry) toweling is an uncut pile fabric with the pile on both sides of the materials, coquette may be either a cut or uncut pile fabric. Pile fabrics may also be made by tufting, for example candlewick, when the pile needled into an already woven foundation cloth or backing.

Cellular Weave

These weaves give a loosely woven fabric which holds air in the 'cells' between the threads for example cellular blankets.

Originally certain fibres were associated with particular fabrics but this is no longer the case and many fabrics are obtainable in the different natural and man-made fibres. For example, satin was originally always made from silk and made in a satin weave but now cotton, rayon and nylon satins are available.

Fire Resistant Fabrics

Pure wool, glass fibre and modacrylic fabrics are inherently flame retardant. All cotton, linen and most rayon fabrics can have applied finishes which render them flame retardant. Flame resistant fabrics should satisfy BS 3120 and BS 5867 for use of curtains and upholstery coverings in public rooms in all establishments, as well as for bedspreads.

P.S

There are firms, which test samples of fabrics and report on their suitability for fire resistant finishes. Synthetic fibres and wool are generally considered fire retardants. Zippo, a fire retardant finish may be applied to woolen carpets and soft furnishings like curtains, chair covers etc and washed in synthetic detergent at 40°C or may be dry cleaned.

BS 5867 this is the most important specification for flammability of fabrics.

'C' Level of performance is recommended for hotels etc. the fabric is required to be tested twice, once in new condition and again after a cycle of 50 washes.

'B' Level of performance is the usual requirement.

'A' Level of performance is not accepted by the fire officer.

Finishing Process Mechanical Process Bettling

This process produces luster and softness and gives the fabric a firm and leathery feel. It is done for linen and cotton. Bottling was originally done by beating the surface with wooden mallets. But now a machine with a number of steel hammers is used. The fabrics are flattened and the weaves are closed and thus the design and the lustrous effect is produced. Cotton after undergoing this process gets a linen appearance.

Calendering

This is a final process and consists of pressing the material after it has passes through necessary processes. It smoothens out wrinkles as seen and gives a smooth even surface to the fabric. The fabric is passed between very hot and highly polished rollers to increase the luster. This process is repeated several times especially for cotton and linen.

Sanforising

All textile fabrics when made contain certain threads, which are stretched because of it being interlaced with each other. The size of the thread if removed from its fabric will be smaller than when it is inter woven. All that happens when you wash fabrics is that they do not retain their original shape and hence garments made out of fabrics often become smaller than what they were. To get rid of this, a new process called sanforising has been evolved. By this process the manufacturer can now guarantee that the finished product will not shrink or stretch after washing. Briefly, in the process the length is attained by pressing the contracted fabric between a thick cloth and the surface of a steam heated smooth metallic roller as this fabric goes between the cloth and the roller. It is set and smoothened in it's closed up state, thus the fabric does not shrink.

Crinkled/Crepe Material

The creping process is accomplished either by a mechanical or chemical treatment. The mechanical process consists of passing the material between two hot rollers. The rollers have regular indentation at regular intervals, which produces the waved crepe effect on the material. This effect is not very long lasting.

Embossing

By this process, a pattern or a design is embossed on a fabric. This machine consists of two rollers one of them is covered with cloth and the other is engraved with the design. The cloth covering one of the rollers is moistened with soapy water, when the machine operates the impression of the pattern is taken on the covered roller. Then that material is passed through the rollers, which are heated, by steam. As the material is pressed between the two rollers, it passes on the imprint of the design onto the material.

Glazing

This process produces highly glazed finished fabrics. The machine consists of 3 rollers, one of which (the middle one) is covered with cloth. The fabrics are passed between two rollers and then under the third one, which rotates at a great speed giving a high sheen to the fabric.

Napping

This process is used to produce a raised effect on the cloth and to impart to it a soft and pleasing feel. It also covers up defects and renders the fabric warmth because of the spaces created between the raised fibres, which trap and hold air. The fabric is first passed over a revolving cylinder covered with wires. These wires scratch the fabric so as to form a nap. The nap is then clipped to a uniform length or height by passing it through a shearing machine.

Chemical Process

This consists of a process of treating the fabric with chemical agents to change either the appearance or the properties of the cloth.

This is a process, which gives a high degree of lust to cotton with the action of caustic soda. The application of a strong solution of caustic soda makes cotton transparent. The process consists of impregnating the yam or fabric with cold caustic soda solution. Apply under tension to reduce shrinkage and to increase the lust. The process removes twist in the fabric and thus causes the fabric to become smooth and cylindrical which produces a richy effect.

Crease Resistant Finish

This is mostly used for cotton because cotton due to it's natural inelasticity, wrinkles badly. In this process the fabric are treated with a solution of synthetic resin such as phenolformaldehyde & acrylic resins and dries at a high temperature in moist atmosphere. This forms a clear insoluble resin in the fibre, which improves the texture of the fabric. Urea formaldehyde is colorless and can be used for white and light coloured fabrics but phenolformaldehyde being darker in colour is used for dark coloured fabrics only.

Creping

Creping is a chemical process in which the treatment of fabric is done with caustic soda. The soda paste is applied to the fabric in definite design like strips and figures. The parts to which the paste is applied shrinks leaving the other parts unshrunk. Thus the effect of a pluckered or creped material will be produced.

Fire Proof Finish

This is a simple method, which consists of a treatment of boric acid and borax. This however dissolves in water. Another method is the treatment of fabrics with chlorinated compounds such as vinyl chloride or chlorinated rubber and antimony oxide. This solution covers the fabric with a thin non-flammable film, which renders the fabric fire proof.

Dyeing

It can also be called a finishing process as it colours the fabric and also adds to its beauty. Dyeing is a very ancient Indian art, which other countries have learnt. In the early stages, the fabrics were coloured with juices of flowers, fruits, leaves, bark of trees and plants, later on dye stuffs were made from vegetable and mineral sources.

Printing

The designs are either drawn by a brush or stumped onto the material by wooden blocks that were previously carved. A simple method of printing first consisted of dipping the carved block in a paste of colour and then stamping the fabrics with it in a definite pattern. The dye used in printing are the same as those used for dyeing.

Block Printing

This form of printing is practiced even today to gat beautiful designs on fabrics. Blocks from wood are struck together. The design is then carved out on the block to a depth of quarter inch. The fabric to be printed is then stretched on a padded table. If 2 or 3 colours go onto one block a block with one colour on it is printed on the fabric and allowed to dry. Then another block with a second colour is stamped over the same print till the block is completed. This process is separated over the entire fabric surface, which is to be printed.

Machine Printing

A printing machine consists of several copper cylinders, which are engraved with the design to be printed. The number of cylinders will depend upon the number of colours in the print as one roller carries only one colour and the roller is only as wide as the cloth. This form of printing takes very little time but it is the engraving of the design on the cylinder that takes quite a few days.

Other Finishes Given To Fabrics

Water Repellant (E.G. Dril-Sil, Velan)

This is a silicone finish applied to a fabric including carpets, which causes the spillage, eg. Fruit juice, to 'pearl' off the fabric. It is durable to washing but cotton and acetate fabrics show less durability than others.

Oil Repellant (E.G. Scotchgard)

This is a flurochemical finish which gives both oil and water repellency. Stains stand on the surface and can be bottled away. It is expensive but resists laundering and dry cleaning.

Soil Release (E.G. Permalose)

This is an anti-greying finish, which may be applied to fabrics containing polyester.

Crease Resistant And Easy Care (E.G. Calpreta, Bel-O-Fast)

These are resins which prevent creases forming and are applied to cotton, cotton blended with synthetic fibres or viscose fabrics. This can result in loss of strength - tear, tensile and resistance to abrasion. Boiling, bleaching or excessive agitation during washing or spin drying may destroy the finish.

Shrink Resistance (E.G. Sanforising, Rigmel)

The fabric is pre-shrunk for this finish.

Non-Felting For Wool

This is a film of synthetic fibre e.g. nylon, applied for wool to reduce tangling, or the wool may be treated with chemicals to reduce the scaly part of the fibre. This renders the fabric shrink proof and gives a high level of wash ability.

Mothproofing (E.G. Dielmoth, Eulan)

A substance poisonous to moth maggots is applied to the fabric or fibres to obtain a mothproofed finish.

Bacteriostatic Protection (E.G. Actifresh, Durafresh)

This is provided by a chemical, which inhibits the growth of bacteria, which decomposes perspiration.

Characteristics And Uses of Fabrics

Fabric	Fibre	Weave	Appearance	Uses
Baize	All wool	Plain	Surface of cloth is raised and closely cropped, generally green colour	Aprons, storing silver, covering meeting & boardroom tables tables
Brocade	Silk, Cotton, rayon, or synthetic	Figured	Extra weft threads give colour & form pattern	Upholstery, curtains, bedspreads
Candlewick	Cotton, rayon, sarille, triacetate, nylon, courtelle	Plain foundation cloth	Tufted yams are inserted into foundation cloth to give a pattern	Bedspreads, bathmats when made from basorbent fibres

Calico	Cotton	Plain	Thicker than muslin, white, dyed or unbleached	Sheeting, dust covers
Chintz	Cotton	Plain	Printed pattern, glazed finish	Curtains, loose covers and bedspreads
Corduroy	Cotton	Pile (cut)	Cut pile forms lines or cord in warp direction	Upholstery
Cretonne	Cotton, rayon	Plain	Printed pattern, coarser than chintz	Curtains, loose covers
Damask Table	Linen	Figured	Warp & weft faced stain weaves give design & background, self coloured	Table linen
Furnishings	Cotton, linen silk, rayon, polyester & any combination	Figured	Warp sptin & plain waves give better differentiation of design, sometimes further emphasized by different fibres for warp & weft threads, self coloured, great variety of weight	Upholstery, Curtains, loose covers
Denim	Cotton	Plain	Warp dyed, weft undyed, speckled effect	Overalls
Drill	Cotton	Plain	Both warp & weft white or dyed	Overalls
Felt	Wool, Courtelle		Densely matted fibres	To protect tables, carpet
Flannelette	Cotton	Plain	Burshed (teased), fluffiness holds air & fabric is warmer than ordinary cotton fabric	Sometimes for sheets, under blankets
Folkweave	Cotton	Loosely Woven	Coarse coloured yarns in simple designs often with textured or 3D effect	Curtains, bedspreads

Gingham	Cotton	Plain	Check or stripped design	Bathroom curtains, dust sheets
Hessian	Jute	Plain	Fawn coloured but may be dyed	Bed underlays, oven cloths, wall coverings
Huckaback	Lipen, cotton, rayon	Figured	Huckaback weave	Face, hand & continuous roller towels
Moquette	Cotton, wool rayon	Pile	Cut or uncut pile or combination of the two, wool pile on cotton ground is best quality but cotton & rayon piles are hard wearing	Upholstery
Net	Many fibres, polyester best	Open plain	Threads may be twisted or knotted instead of woven, white or coloured	Glass (sheet) curtains
Plush	Cotton, silk man-made	Pile (cut)	Deeper pile than velvet but less closely woven, hard wearing	Upholstery, curtains, loose covers
Repp	Cotton, silk wool, synthetic	Plain	Fine warp & coarser weft gives rib running from selvedge to selvedge, hard wearing	Upholstery, curtains, loose covers
Sateen	Cotton	Stain	Weft faced, smooth	Curtain lining, underside of quilts
Satin	Silk, rayon, cotton, synthetic	Satin	Warp faced, smooth, lustrous, variety of weights, silk originally now cotton satin, rayon satin etc.	Curtains, bedspreads cushion covers
Scrim Tapestry	Linen Wool, cotton, rayon or mixtures	Plain Figured	Lint-free cloth Pattern formed by extra coloured weft threads, closely woven	Window cleaning Upholstery, curtains loose covers
Ticking	Cotton, rayon	Twill, satin	Closely woven stripped or coloured weft threads	Mattress covers, white for enclosing filling for pillows or cushions

Towelling	Cotton	Pile (uncut)	Reversible uncut pile, Turkish (terry weave)	Towels, bathmats
Tweed	Wool	Plains or twill	Heavy fabric, plain or coloured	Upholstery, curtains
Velvet	Silk, cotton rayon, synthetic	Pile (cut)	Warp pile, great variety in weight	Upholstery, curtains, cushions
Velveteen	Cotton, rayon mercerized cotton	Pile (cut)	Weft pile is generally shorter than velvet	Upholstery, Curtains, cushions
Wild Silk	Silk from Silkworm of wild moth	Generally plain	Filaments are irregular in thickness & produce slubs in the fabrics, expensive, hard wearing	Curtains, wall coverings

Laundry

Laundry can be described as a place where washing and finishing of clothes and washable articles are done. There are the following options open to most of the establishments :

On-Site / in-House / on-Premise Laundry

The linen is owned by the establishment and laundered on the premises itself, the advantage being quality control and a high standard of linen can be obtained. Other advantages are :

- No losses, or shorts can occur.
- Less stock required, as the cycle is quicker.
- Can cover emergency requirements.
- Is a capital asset to the establishment.

Disadvantages Being:

- The initial capital investment is great.
- Higher labor costs.
- Technical expertise of special management is required.
- High cost on maintenance, repairs and overheads.

Off-Site / Off-Premise / Contracted Out Laundry

When an establishment owns the linen but sends it out to a private laundry company to be cleared, it is said to be 'contracted out'. The main advantages are :

- No capital outlay.
- Little technical expertise is required.
- Labour costs are saved.

Disadvantage Being:

- Less control over the standards of linen coming after being washed.
- Delivery and collection delays.
- Higher stocks required as it takes longer time for the whole process.
- Losses may occur.
- Extra costs for special treatments.

The Main Purpose of Laundering Linen And Uniforms is to :

- Remove stains and odour from the linen.
- To increase the life span of the linen.
- To wash and clean the clothes.
- To increase the re-use value of the linen.
- To prevent growth of microorganisms.
- To improve the appearance of the linen and make it look presentable.

Important Planning Considerations For An on-Premise Laundry:

1. **Maximum Output That The Laundry Would Be Expected To Handle** - depending upon number of guest rooms and number covers in food and beverage outlets one can get an idea of what the routine load of the laundry would be. The laundry should be designed to handle maximum output for peak periods.

2. **Space** - this would depend on laundry needs, amount of equipment, some properties may allocate extra space in case of growth.

3. **Equipment** - the type and quality of equipment required will depend upon the amount of items to be laundered.

4. **Valet Service** - valet service will require dry cleaning equipments and separate work area for valet staff.

5. **Size of The Property** - a small operation does not require a large laundry.

Since linen and laundry are such expensive and interdependent departments. Hence it is expected that both the departmental heads should have workable knowledge of each other's department. The life of each linen or laundered item depends on the texture of the linen and the number of washes it gets from the laundry. A good laundry is of great importance to any establishment in order that:

- Articles are handled carefully.
- Tensile strength of the material is not impaired.
- White material is kept white.
- Stains are removed when requested.
- Materials are not ruined by the use of excessive bleach.
- List is checked carefully so that there are few shortages.
- The work is carried out as speedily as possible.
- Good cooperation is maintained regarding damage and losses.

Every laundry uses a basic cycle of operation. The Cycle includes the following steps:

1. Collecting soiled linens
2. Transporting soiled linen to the laundry.
3. Sorting
4. Loading
5. Washing
6. Extracting
7. Drying
8. Finishing
9. Folding
10. Storing
11. Transferring linen to use areas

Layout of a Laundry Department

Layout of a Small Laundry Department
The Agents Used in Laundry

A laundry's chemical seeds depends mainly on the types of linens it uses and the soiling conditions encountered.

Water is the major cleaning agent used in the laundry process. 2-5 gallons of water are used for every pound of dry laundry. Drinking water may not always be safe for washing as it contains minerals, which stain or wear linens. Other chemicals can be added to water to help it clean better.

Detergent in which synthetic detergent is effective on oil and grease. Synthetic detergents consist of surfactants that aid soil removal and act as antibacterial agents and fabric softeners. Builders or alkalis are often added to synthetic detergents to soften water and remove oils and grease.

Soaps such as built soaps are used on heavily soiled fabrics. They are another kind of detergents. Neutral or pure soaps contain no alkalis and are used for lightly soiled items. Built soaps contain alkalis and are used for heavily soiled articles. Soaps are destroyed by sours.

Bleaches cause strong chemical reactions that, if not carefully controlled, can damage fabrics. Used properly bleaches can remove stains, kill bacteria, and whiten fabrics. There are two types oxygen bleach and chlorine bleach, Chlorine bleach can be used with any washable colorfast fibre. Oxygen is milder than chlorine and safer for most of the fabric types.

Fabric brighteners keep fabrics looking new and colors close to their original shade. These chemicals are often pre-mixed with detergents and soap.

Alkalis or alkaline builders help detergent lather better and keep stains suspended in the wash water after they have loosened and lifted from the fabric. They help neutralize acidic stains.

Antichlors are sometimes used in rinsing to ensure that all the chlorine in the bleach has been removed.

Mildewcides prevent the growth of bacteria and fungus on the linen for up to 30 days. Sours are mild acid used to neutralize any residual alkalinity in fabrics after washing and rinsing which can cause yellowing and fading of fabrics.

Fabric softeners make fabrics more supple and easier to finish, and are added to wash cycle along with sours. They can reduce flatwork ironing, speed up extraction, reduce drying time, and reduce static electricity in the fabrics. Too much softener, will decrease a fabrics absorbency.

Starches give linen a crisp appearance that stands up during the items use. It is added to the wash cycle in the final step.

Laundry can either be done by hand or be machines. However there are 3 distinct stages involved in the washing of l inen.

1. Pre-Wash
2. Actual Wash
3. Finishing

Every laundry uses a basic cycle of operation. This cycle includes the following steps: PRE-WASH

a. Collecting Sorted Linen

Room attendants should strip linens from beds and bath areas and put them directly into the soiled linen hampers / laundry bags placed on the maid's cart. Items should never be piled on the floor where they can be walked on and soiled further or damaged. F&B linen is also placed in hampers for delivery to the laundry. Stained linen should be knotted in one comer to help in sorting.

Transporting Soiled Linen To The Laundry

Large hotels have a laundry chute which runs through the entire height of the building down to the laundry soil sort area. Linen is either hand carried or carted to the laundry. Dragging of linen should be avoided, as this can be a safety hazard for staff who could trip over trailing items. Linen carts should also be free of protrusions that could snag of tear the items. In case of an off-site laundry marking should be done before transporting.

Sorting

A soil sort area should be large enough to store a day's worth of laundry without slowing down other activities in the laundry. The articles are sorted out according to the following categories :

- ❖ Degree of sorting - stained, heavily, soiled, medium and lightly soled articles are separated.
- ❖ Colour and dye fasteners

Fibre Type

- ❖ Linen that needs repair in mended before washing except in the case of heavily soiled articles.
- ❖ Monogramming must be carried out, before washing in order to control pilferage and help in identification.
- ❖ Condemned or discarded linen is sorted out and cut-down before washing.

'Light linen' this linen has after continuous use lost it's lusture and has become worn out. It can no longer be used for VIP's. However being still in good condition and in one piece and not torn it is used for houseguests or for staff members staying in the hotels. It is stacked and washed separately. It differs from condemned linen in that it is not torn. However, it is not in standard condition.

- ❖ Removal of all fancy articles and attachments like buttons, buckles, rings, etc. false collars found in shirts must also be removed.
- ❖ Empty out all pockets and check folds.

Weighing And Loading

The articles once sorted are weighed in their dry conditions. This is necessary as each washing machine has specific loading instructions, which have to be followed. If this is not paid attention to, the working of the machinery is adversely affected. Weighing is also useful for measuring the productivity of the laundry workers. The modular system of loading is the simplest. Each item of linen has a known weight. So they are counted into piles to the appropriate total weight, e.g. if a bed sheet is known to weigh 500 grams and the capacity of the machine is 25kgs, then 50 bed sheets are counted out for each compartment. Alternately, bundles of linen can be weighed before putting them into compartments.

Actual Washing

Washing

Whatever the type of machine used, for maximum efficiency it must be operated according to the manufacturer's instructions. Temperatures, washing times and processing chemicals vary according to the type of fabrics being laundered. The following indicates how to determine the proper washing program :

- ❖ **Duration-** heavily soiled linen requires more time than lightly soiled linens. The rate at which soil is removed is not always constant. It is the highest at the commencement of the wash, gradually becomes less as time passes.
- ❖ **Temperature-** generally laundry workers should chose the lowest possible temperature to do the job to save energy. However, some detergents and chemicals work properly only in hot water and some types of soils require higher temperatures. Washing temperatures of some linen are listed below : Sheets and pillow cases - 95°C

Bath linen - 60°C Table linen - 60°C Blankets and bed spreads - 20°C Curtains - 30°C

Kitchen and heavily soiled uniforms, dusters and cleaning cloths - 95 °C Silk, nylon, polyester - 30°C Shirts, jeans - 40°C

- ❖ **Agitation -** this is the scrubbing action of the machine. Too little agitation which is frequently caused by overloading washers leads to in adequate washing, overloading also causes unnecessary wear and tear on equipment. Too much agitation can cause fabric damages.
- ❖ **Chemicals -** What chemicals will do the best job on particular soils and fabrics types will have to be decided.
- ❖ **Water Harness -** Hard water contains salt that mix with soap and synthetic detergents to form a sticky substance called soap curd, which makes items stiff.

- **No. of Wash Cycles** - Several Shorter Washes Are Better Than One Long One. More Soil can be removed with repeated suds and clean water than with one solution in which soil remains in suspension and has a chance to re soil the linen.

Wash Cycle

The typical wash process consists of as many as 9 steps. They are :

- **Flush (1.5 to 3 minutes)** - Flushes dissolve and dilute water-soluble soils to reduce the soil load for the upcoming suds step. Items are generally flushed at medium temperatures at high water levels.

- **Break (4 to 10 minutes - optional)** - A high alkaline break (soil-loosening) product is added, which may be followed by additional flushes. The break cycle is usually at medium temperature and a low water level.

Suds (5 to 8 minutes) - this is actual wash cycle to which detergent is added. Items are agitated in hot water at low water levels.

- Carryover suds or intermediate rinse (2 to 5 minutes) - This rinse cycle re-moves soil and alkalinity to help bleach work more effectively. This cycle rinses linens at the same temperature as the suds cycle.

- Bleach (5 to 8 minutes) - Bleach is added to this hot water, low-Water-level cycle. Bleach kills bacteria, whitens fabrics, and removes stains.

- Rinse (1.5 to 3 minutes) - Two or more rinses at medium temperature and high water levels are used to remove detergent and soil from the linens.

- Intermediate extract (1.5 to 2 minutes optional) - This high-speed spin removes detergent and soil from linens, usually after the first rinse step. This cycle should not be used after a suds step, because it could drive soils back into the fabric. It should not be used on no-iron linens unless the temperature of the wash is below 120 degree F (49 degree centigrade.)

- Sour (softener or starch / sizing (laundry chemicals added to wash cycle to stiffen polyester blends.) (3 to 5 minutes) - Softeners and sours added to condition fabric. The cycle runs at medium temperature and at low water levels. Starches are added to stiffen cotton fabrics; sizing is added for polyester blends. Starching / sizing replaces the sour / softener step.

Extract (2 to 12 minutes) - A high-speed spin removes most of the moisture from the linens. The length of the spin depends on fabric type, extractor capacity, and extractor speed.

a. **Rinsing**

This is done using hot and cold water, which is usually recovered and recycled during the last rinse in order to save water.

b. **Hydro-Extraction**

Extraction removes at least 50% of the water used in the rinsing process and thereby reduces the weight to a minimum to prevent pronounced grease from setting into the fabric. It also reduces the drying time.

Finishing

a. **Drying** - items that we dried generally include towels, washcloths and some no-iron blends. Drying times and temperatures vary considerably for different types of linen. In every care, however, drying should be followed by a cool-down period to prevent the hot linen from being damaged or wrinkled by rapid cooling and handling. After drying, linen should be rapidly removed for folding. If folding is delayed wrinkles will set in.

b. **Ironing** - sheets, pillowcases, tablecloths, napkins, and other flat linen can go directly into the flat work irons. Towels do not need ironing they should emerge from the tumble dryer in a soft and fluffy gnat, where upon they may be folded by and or machines. Guest clothing and uniforms are finished on various steam presses.

c. **Folding** - folding can be done by hand or by machine, whatever the case washing and drying items faster than they can be folded leads to unnecessary wrinkling and resorting. Folding personnel must also in inspect linen, storing those that are to be rinsed and rejected, stained, torn and otherwise unsuitable items. Folding and storing should be done well away from the sorted linen area to avoid resorting clean laundry. This step should also be considered as a quality control step.

d. **Storing** - after folding the items we post-sorted and stacked. Post-sorting separates any linen types and sizes that were missed in pre-sorting. There should be enough storage room for at least one par. Finished items should be allowed to rest on shelves for at least 24 hours after laundering because many types of linen get damaged more easily after washing. Once linen is stored on shelves, yellowing and facing can be spotted easily.

e. Transferring Linen To The Used Areas - Linen Is Usually Transferred To Their use areas via carts or trolleys.

Laundry Equipments

Washing Machine

Most washers are made of stainless steel. They are sized by their capacity; sizes vary from 25 to 1,200 pound capacities. Some machines have separate pockets, which hold several large loads at a time. Some washers called tunnel washers have several chambers; each chamber is used for a particular wash cycle. As soon as the first cycle is finished on the first load of laundry, the wash moves into the second chamber. The laundry attendant can load the first chamber with the next batch.

Washers consist of a motor, inside and outside shells, and 'a casing. Their outside shell is stationary and holds the wash water. The inside shell holds the laundry and is perforated to allow water for various cycles to flow in and out. Of the washers motor rotates either the perforated inner shell (on wash wheel washers) or an agitator (agitator washers). Yet in another type a large drum revolves first in one direction and then in the other to prevent .tangling of articles. Agitation, with hot water at 85 degree C - 94 degree C and suitable detergents (usually synthetic with a small quantity of soap added to act as a lubricant) bring about the cleansing action after which rinsing in several waters take place and all these processes may be automatically controlled. The more sophisticated equipment is controlled by computer, which has automatic detergent and solution dispensing capacities and are programmed electronically. Microprocessor - one of the latest innovations in washers - allow greater control over the washer's function than more conventional automatic models. In this water temperature can be regulated more exactly.

Microprocessors also allow operators more case and flexibility in programming combinations of detergents and solutions for specific fabric types and soil levels. Another new invention is reuse washer. This machine saves energy, sewage, water and chemical costs. A water reuse washer is equipped with insulated storage tanks. Water that can be reused is siphoned into the tanks to maintain the proper temperature and then releases into the proper cycle of the next batch of laundry. Control panels allow laundry operator to make adjustments in the water to be reused to account for soil conditions, water hardness, and fabric type. The control also automatically saves reusable water and discharges water that cannot be reused.

Most laundries soften their water and often a "brightener" is added to keep whites white. Heavily solid articles, e.g. Kitchen dusters, may need a little bleach in the washing water, but it should only be used when really necessary as it weakens the material. Table linen may need a little starch and this is added to the last rinsing water. The clean articles are then passed into a :

Washer Extractor -

It is most usually consisting of horizontal drums which, when washing and rinsing, rotates backwards and forwards, agitating the water and articles inside. To extract water from the laundry the drum spins at a high speed. The articles to be laundered are loaded and removed via 'a door in the front of the machine. When it is necessary to separate the clean and dirty linen, e.g. in hospitals the machine will be fitted with a second door through which clean laundry is removed. A smaller number of machines are made which consists of a vertical drum, the machine being loaded from the top. Loading capacities range from about 5 to 250 kg dry weight and give outputs of clean laundry of between 10 to 600kg dry weight per hour. Machines may be programmed to give a specific number of different wash, rinse and extract cycles or they may be programmed by the user, e.g. using punched cards to give the cycles and conditions selected by the user. Depending on the machine, programmes can be varied to give different wash and rinse temperatures, different degrees of agitation and different wash, rinse and extraction times.

Hydro Extractor -

This whirls the water out of the articles leaving them as a very tightly packed mass, which needs shaking out in a special tumbler. However, there are modem washer extractors with a dry weight capacity of about 2 to 100 kg, which can wash, rinse, hydro-extract and shake out all in the one machine. It consists of a perforated vertical cylinder, which spins at high speed. Water is removed using the centrifugal force principle and heated air is passed through. Air is heated by gas electricity, and steam. The airflow must be unrestricted to ensure the dryer's energy efficiency.

Rotary Washing Machines -

These have largely been replaced by the washer extractor. They consist of a horizontal drum, which rotates during washing and rinsing to agitate the articles inside.

Steam Cabinets And Tunne) Washers -

These are only installed in the largest laundries. They essentially consist of a series of compartments linked together. The laundry is loaded in batches at one end and removed at the other end. Such machines can process approx. 250 to 2000 kg dry weight of linen per hour. It effectively eliminates wrinkles from heavy items such as blankets, bed -spreads, curtains and towels. A steam cabinet is simply a box in which articles are hung and steamed to remove wrinkles. A steam tunnel actually moves articles on hangers through a tunnel, steaming them and removing the wrinkles as they move through.

Tumbler Driers -

It consists of a horizontal perforated cylinder through which hot air is blown. The drum rotates in alternate directions to bring all the articles inside into contact with the air stream and to prevent entanglement. Machine capacity ranges from about 5 to 50 kg of dry weight.

Dry Cleaning Machines -

They are similar in some respect to washer extractors. Solvent is introduced into a horizontal perforated drum, which rotates in alternate directions. The machine will spin dry the articles inside. The solvent is filtered during the extraction stage and reused.

Calendar Press or Ironing Machine -

This very large machine consists of several heated and well-padded rollers which iron the articles as it passes through. Only flat articles are calendared and a large calendar press will be wide enough to take a double sheet. After ironing, the articles are folded either by an automatic electric device or by hand and they are then ready for sorting, packing and sending back to the establishment. Turkish towels are not normally ironed nowadays but tumble dried and folded.

Pressers-

They consist of padded plates, which are heated. The items to be pressed are placed on the lower plate and pressed with the upper one. The principle types are rotary and scissor presses. Presses may be designed for the pressing of a variety of articles or for specific types of garment like shirts, trousers, coats, etc.

Handiron-

They consist of a hand held heated plate. Steam irons include a reservoir of water, which can be used to generate steam. Older irons include up to 5 heat settings. Newer irons usually have 3 settings.

Folder -

The machine does not actually fold the laundry, but holds one end of the item to be folded so that the staff can fold it more easily. Folding machines are now available that virtually eliminate tumble-drying and hand folding. These space saving units dry, iron, fold and often cross fold and stack flat work. Some have microprocessor controls that determine fold points and trigger other related function.

An establishment has the choice of the following laundry services commercial or in-house laundry, linen hire that includes laundry service. None of these can be automatically considered as offering the best and most economical laundry-service. At a commercial laundry a brief outline of the work carried out on white cotton articles are 'as follows:

At the laundry the linen is checked and sorted into groups then a suitable number of weights of similar items are put into a washing machine. The articles are put into hot water and suitable detergents, which bring about the cleaning action, after which rinsing in several water takes place and all these processes may be automatically controlled: Most laundry softens their water and often "brightner" is added to help keep white articles white.

❖ Turkish towels are not normally ironed but tumble dried and folded. Ironing is unnecessary if articles are tumble dried and folded while still warm. This is however not possible at a commercial laundry.

❖ Shaped articles like shirts, waiter's jacket, white coats etc. shall not be ironed through a calendar so that they are dealt with hand presses.

- Blankets are possibly the only woolen articles, which an establishment sends to the laundry and here the problem is to keep it fluffy.

- To do this, blankets should be washed in cold water with suitable mild detergent, avoiding the use of soda and bleach. They are dried on racks or put into a heated machine, which tumbles them dry. Acrylic blankets may be laundered more satisfactorily than woolen ones, there is little tendency to shrink and their finish after tumble-drying is excellent.

- Articles, which lose color, that is color, which run, such as yellow dusters, must be kept separate from other articles during washing and during processing.

- Curtain and bedspreads are probably the main rayon articles sent to the laundry and these need care in Washing as rayon fibres are weak when wet and will not stand up to high temperatures. Owing to the high cost of linen and its upkeep, the hiring of linen, from outside firm offering a linen rental service is becoming more popular. The firms undertake to supply clean articles in good condition.

These Have Certain Advantages as Follows :-

=t>> It cuts out heavy initial cost of buying linens.

=t>> Short-term loans are possible for special occasions, e.g. banqueting etc.

=£> No repair of linen on the premises is necessary.

=#> Fewer staff is needed and therefore there are fewer wages to pay.

=t>> The cost of hiring, which includes laundering, is paid for out of revenue.

The Disadvantages Are

=t>> Little choice regarding quality and style.

=£> Standard not always maintained.

=#> No rags available from the linen room.

=t>> The contract price remains the same even when numbers fall over a short period.

Dry Cleaning

The responsibility for sorting, dispatching, receiving and storing of hotel articles to be dry cleaned may be that of the linen keeper or an assistant housekeeper's on arrival at the cleaners, each article is marked with an identifying tape, checked for special stains and items in the pocket and brushed free of loose dust. Although on certain instance different colored articles may be cleaned successfully together. It is normal to divide the work into a number of classifications such as white, medium; darks so that heavily soiled articles are not cleaned with the lightly soiled ones and the dark colored lint does not-transfer to light colored articles or vice versa.

The prepared items are then washed in a dry cleaning solvent in an enclosed machine in which the washing, extraction and drying are all carried out in the same cage. The solvent, because of its cost; is not wasted but distilled or filtered for re-use. Dry cleaning solvents do not effect textile fibres in the same way as water and so when cleaning some materials the risk of shrinkage; severe creasing, distortion or color movement may be greatly reduced. Because water borne soil and stains can only effectively be removed by the use of water, a controlled amount of water and detergent is introduced in the solvent during some dry cleaning processes known as charged systems.

After the articles have been cleaned in a series of solvent washes, they are spun dried to extract the bulk of the solvent and then dried with warm air. The cleaned articles are hung up to remove the smell and checked for stains and any remaining stains are dealt with before pressing.

Stain Removal

Stain is a spot or mark of discoloration caused on fabrics by the contact and absorption of some foreign substances. Some stains are easily removed by ordinary methods or reagents but there are quite a few which need special treatment. Stains can be classifies as animal, vegetable, grease, dye and mineral stains.

1. Animal Stains

Animal stains are those caused by blood, eggs, milk and meat juices. As these contain protein matter heat must be avoided in removing them, otherwise the protein matter will get fixed in the stain.

2. Vegetable Stains

Vegetable stains include those caused by tea, cocoa, coffee, fruit juices and wine, etc. they are acidic and therefore require alkaline reagents to remove them.

3. Grease Stains

This may be grease spots or some colouring matter fixed with grease. These include butter, curry, oil, paint, varnish and tar stains. In removing them, some grease solvents or an absorbent is first used to dissolve or absorb the grease before the removal of the colouring matter.

4. Dye Stains

This may be acidic or alkaline and so the nature of the stain is ascertained before a specific reagent is used.

5. Mineral Stains

Mineral stains such as ironmould, black ink; certain medicines stains are compounds of a metal and a dye. These are first treated by an acid reagent to act on the metal and then by an alkaline solution to neutralize the acid reagent and act on the dye.

Neither perspiration nor scorch marks fall into any of the above groups. Perspiration has no protein component and therefore cannot fall under the vegetable group even though it is acidic. Scorch is a brown stain caused by a very hot iron and is in a class by itself.

Stain removal process may be carried out in the linen room or in the laundry according to the rules of the establishment. But stain removal itself is an important function because the competence in doing it the best way will enhance the reputation of the establishment. All with as soon as they occur or as soon as possible. If old or heavy, stain requires special treatment with stain removal agents. The use of the agents requires care as they can cause weakening of the fibres, bleeding of dyes, damage to special fabric finishes and some are inflammable while others are poisonous.

There are Five Main Stain Removal Agents
Organic Solvents

A	
D	Benzene Acetone
D	Amyl Acetate
D	Methylated Spirit
D	White Spirit (Turpentine Substitute)
B	
D	Carbon Tetrachloride
D	Perchlorethylene
D	Trichlorothyline
	Acids
D	Oxalic Acid
D	Potassium Acid Oxalate
D	Various Rust Removers
	Alkali
D	Soda
D	Borax
	Bleaches
	A. Oxidising
D	Sodium Hydrochloride
D	Hydrogen Peroxide
D	Sodium Perborate
	B. Reducing
D	Sodium Hydrosulphite
	Enzymes
D	Powdered Pepsin
	To Treat An Unknown Stain
•	Soak In Cold Water.
•	Dry And Use A Grease Solvent.
•	Use An Acid.
•	Use An Alkali.

Stains on colored materials are very difficult to remove as many of the stain removal agents affect dyes. In case of carpets and upholstery, stains are particularly difficult to remove because they have to be dealt with "insitu" and the color, the backing padding may present problem.

Grease absorbers in form of aerosol sprays may prove useful. Stain repellents : fabrics may be treated so as to be made "stain repellant" and this may be achieved by the use of furochemicals, e.g. scotchguard, which will give both water and oil repellency. The stains tens to stand on the surface and can be blotted away (not wiped). And if the stain is absorbed it still can be removed with the solvent cleansers.

For Specific Stains
Points To Be Remembered
'When Removing Stains, it is Worth Remembering The Following:

- ❖ Treat the stains as soon as possible.
- ❖ Consider the fibre of which the fabric is made. i.e. one must know the nature and texture of the fabric especially when chemical reagents and bleaches are to be used.
- ❖ If a colored article, check effect of remover on an unimportant part if possible.
- ❖ Use the weakest methods first.
- ❖ Use a weak solution several times, rather than one strong one.
- ❖ When using a chemical always place the stained area over an absorbent pad of clean cloth.
- ❖ To avoid a "ring" always treats from an area round the stain and work towards the centre.
- ❖ After using a chemical neutralize or rinse well.
- ❖ All acid reagents should be neutralized with an alkaline rinse and vise versa.
- ❖ Unknown stains should be treated with simple methods of cleaning, if no reaction then milder reagents can be used followed by stronger ones.

It must be strongly emphasized that owing to the variety of fibres used in modem materials and the unknown qualities of some stains, stain removal is a highly skilled job, and should not be undertaken lightly.

Soft Furnishings

It is a term used to represent different furnishing material made from different type of fibers and it includes curtains, cushion covers, loose covers bed spreads. The ^mishing materials contribute greatly to the appearance of any room or place by bringing color, pattern and texture to it. Some furnishings provide protection and some in addition give warmth and comfort as each is subjected to some amount of wear and tear, it follows that the fabrics or fibers from which the furnishings are made must be suitable for the purpose.

Cushions

Cushions are used to increase the comfort of chairs and sofas and bring colour, pattern and texfure to the rooms and areas. They may be shaped to fit the chair and sofa forming the seat and the back or they may be used loose as scattered cushions. Cushions may be therefore of all shapes and sizes filled with feather, foam, plastic, cotton, rubber etc and it may be covered with various materials. The covering materials should be matching or contrasting with materials of the chair and sofas. They require constant attention because they are often removed from their original position and feather ones becomes easily squashed, untidily and unsightly.

Care And Cleaning:

1. Shake and beat to tidy frequently.
2. Repair when necessary.
3. Brush and clean regularly.
4. Remove covers, wash or dry clean as required.

Bed Spreads

Bedspreads are used to cover the bed during the day and are folded and put away during night: The colour and pattern must be matching or contrasting with the colour of the curtains or carpets of the room. The bedspread is frequently sat on so care has to be taken during selection of the material that it does not crease or fold easily. Cotton and satin are the best and most commonly used material for bedspreads.

Care And Cleaning:

1. Dust them frequently.
2. Give for washing and dry-cleaning frequently.

Curtains

Curtains are used to give privacy to any room or area where windows may be overlooked to darken the room when necessary and also bring character and atmosphere to a room by their line, colour, pattern and texture. Any ^mishing material can be used for the purpose. Moreover the size and position of the windows and the characteristic of the room will decide the weight, colour and pattern of the fabric. The fabric should be chosen keeping in mind its resistance to fading and abrasions soiling and flame resistance.

Different Types of Curtain Hanging System Are as Follows
Suspend from the pelment

DIFFERENT TYPES OF CURTAIN HANGING SYSTEM ARE AS FOLLOWS

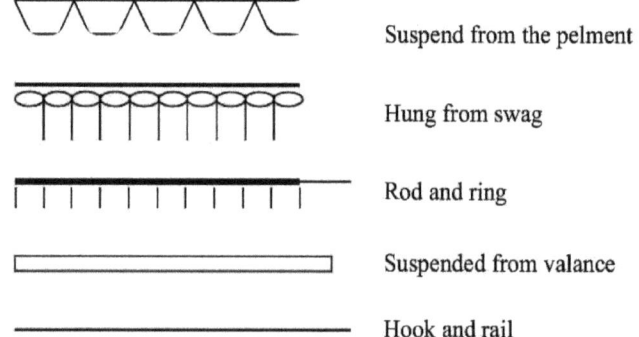

Hook And Rail

Pelmets and valances are decorating heading fixed on the top of the curtain to hide the suspension.

The valance is made of frilled or pleated material and hangs from a valance rail.

A swag is a draped finish to hide the curtain heading and is frequently with a tail.

The life expectancy of the fabric is related to its amount of exposure to sunlight and airborne soiling. Fibres such as glass fibre, terylene, acrylic, rayon blends and bright nylon can withstand sunlight well airborne soiling and acid can do great damage to cotton, so there should be a thorough ma: itenance program. Generally curtains are laundered in hotel laundry itself. Curtains need to be suspended from the horizontal rod or a transverse track, which may be made of metal, wood or plastic. The width may be as same as that of the window or may be extended either sides of the window frame.

Care And Cleaning:

1. Keep track and rod free from dust by using a feather flick.

2. Shake often to remove dust and send for repairs when needed.

3. Reverse the position of the curtain regularly so that no part of it is continuously exposed to the sunlight.

Loose Covers

Loose covers are detachable, fitted over upholstery, chairs, etc. They can give a clear and fresh appearance to a room or a place but they are easily soiled and damaged by continuous use. They are used to mainly cover shabbiness and also to protect the original upholstery. They may reach almost down to the floor level; and can be pleated or gathered patterned or may be tailored and fixed around the chair. Closely woven fabrics are to be preferred for loose covers e.g. chintz.

Care And Cleaning:

1. Shake and tidy it frequently.
2. Brush or suction clean regularly.
3. Attend to any repairs.
4. May be laundered or dry-cleaned as required.

Net, sheer or glass curtains are made of translucent fabrics, frequently polyester net, which soften and diffuse the light as it passes through them. They are held by rod or stretched plastic coated wire through the top hem passes; a drop rod is particularly useful for long net curtains, so that they can be lowered and changed easily. Net curtains, becomes soiled easily and require frequent change.

Blinds

Venetian blinds are sometimes used in place of net curtains where windows can be overlooked and they can give protection from the sum to fabrics, paintings and objects d'art. Venetian blinds, need constant care and cleaning, cut off a great deal of light if attached to the window head even when raised. Many blinds of the roller type made of vinyl or similar coated material are available; they may be brightly colored and patterned.

Care & Cleaning:

1. Attend to badly hanging blinds.
2. Dust or wipe frequently.
3. Wash with warm water and synthetic detergent as often as required.

Venetian Blinds

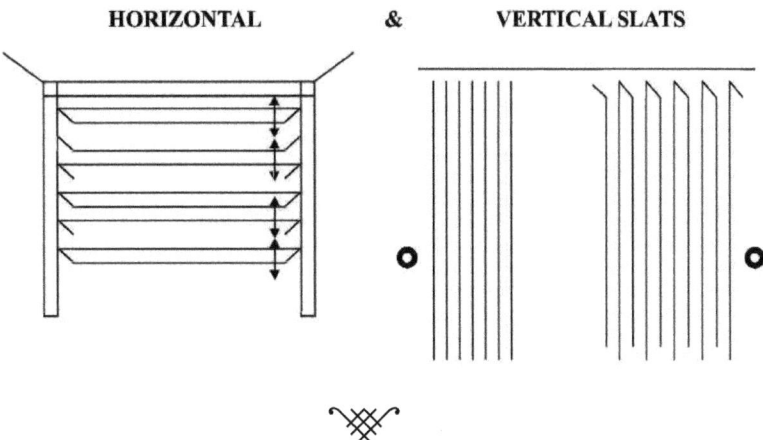

Pest Control

Insects and pests are of nuisance value and are dangerous at times creeping," crawling, flying creatures. They affect man and animals and the food supply of man and also the property.

Broadly They May Be Divided into Three Groups

1. Those that bite and infect the blood stream creating particular disease. They are mainly varieties of mosquitoes, bed bugs and certain types of flies.

2. Those that contaminate the food-stuff such as flies, ants, cockroaches, spiders etc.

3. Those that destroy the property, different types of ants, white ants, types of spiders, cockroaches, cloth moth, silver fish etc. These destroy books, cloths, wooden surface and furniture.

Moth

Cloth and house moths are of a pale buff colour (dull bluish gray) and are often seen flying between June to October. They are relatively small and mainly live for longer than a month. The materials, which are attacked by moths, are fur, skin, wool, feather etc. Those that are immune are rubber, man made and vegetable fibres. While feeding on these materials the moth form small holes n the articles and damage occurs frequently during storage, because of warmth darkness and lack of disturbance. It is advisable that the articles to be stored should be cleaned (washed, vacuumed or dusted) protected by a moth deterrent and inspected frequently. Commonly used moth deterrents are naphthalene, camphor tablets and paradichlorobenzene, while nsecticides containing pyrethrum is used to kill the pests. Materials maybe treated by a chemical process to render them immune from moth. Heat treatment or fumigation can also kill moths (temp. 60°C) together with moth eggs.

Carpet Beetles

Carpet beetles are 2-4 mm long like small mottled brown gray and cream lady- birds. Their larvae are small, covered in brown hair and tend to roll up when disturbed. Carpet beetles are now the major textile pests and do more damage than moths. The damage consists of fairly well defined round holes along the seams of fabrics where the larvae have bitten through the threads. Frequent vacuum cleaning of fluff and debris from storage, cupboards, carpets and upholstery is the main means of control. Insect killing powder may be sprayed at the affected areas to get rid of these insects.

Wood Beetles

These beetles can be likened to the moths and carpet beetles. Many pieces of wood have exit holes and these insects are found these holes. Small piles of bore dust are found beneath these holes if the insects are present there. The treatment involves applying shellac, varnish, lacquer or polish, which can act as a deterrent. To kill woodworms the exit holes should be sprayed, brushed or injected several times with one of the proprietary oil, soluble woodworm fluids e.g. Rentokil, Cuprinol. There are other treatments such as heat and fumigation processes with poisonous gas but these have disadvantages do not prevent re-infestation and their use is best left to experts. A badly infested piece of wood is better brunt.

Fleas

These insects are frequently associated with dirt. They abound in un-hygienic conditions and their entry into clean places maybe entirely accidental. There are many different kinds of fleas and each has a preference for one kind of host e.g. human, cat, dog, vermin's and any of these hosts can introduce fleas into an establishment. Fleas bite their hosts and causing annoyance, and in the humans large red itching spots appear on the skin. They can cover considerable distances because of their jumping power. They like darkness and warmth and are capable of laying a large number of eggs mostly in the cracks of the floor. Spraying with insecticides is a suitable way of getting rid of them.

Bed Bugs

Bed bugs may be found in second hand fomiture, bedding and books or in any wooden. or cane furniture. Bed bugs are about 5 mm long and 3mm wide, reddish brown in colour and are able to survive without food for many months. Their bite causes considerable irritation and may result in large red patches with swelling in some people and they give off a very foul smell. These can be removed by spraying with suitable liquid insecticides (tick-20) or by heat treatment or fumigation, which is normally carried out by experts.

Silver Fish

These are wingless- insects silver gray in colour and about 1 cm long. The young ones closely resemble the adults and both are rounded in front and tapered towards the rear. Silver fish require a moist place in which they live and are found in basements, around pipes, drains, sinks etc. They leave their hiding place in search of food of cellulose nature. They feed on starchy food and are often found behind wallpaper, books, and in cotton cloths which are starched. Daily cleaning of cupboards and surroundings concerned may prevent their growth; and insecticide powder may be sprinkled wherever silver fish has been seen.

Cockroaches

It is the filthiest pest and gives off a foul smell. Cockroaches may go undetected. These are more likely to be found in the kitchen, restaurants and accommodation areas. Cockroaches do not necessarily need human food and will survive on whitewash, hair, and books if no other food is available. Cockroaches are difficult to eradicate but a residual insecticide e.g. chlorodicone in raw liver base maybe used in cracks and crevices and holes.

House Fly

It is one of the filthiest of pests and is found all over the world. It has a hairy body, three pairs of legs, each having a pad with glandular hairs. Secretions from these pads enable dirt and germs to stick to it, which is later, transferred to food. A single fly can carry 280,00,000 bacteria in its alimentary canal and 50,00,000 bacteria on its body and feet. They are attracted to food and food wastes. Aerosol sprays are useful in getting an area rid of flies.

Fruit Fly

These are seasonal, coloured and smaller than the housefly. They are most attracted to overripe and decaying fruit. These pests are not attracted to sewage and other wastes; hence transmit less number of microorganisms.

Their larvae eat their way through different fruits and spoil them. Control measures include checking of fruits for infestation and getting rid of decaying fruits.

Rats & Mice

These are more likely to be found in kitchen and dining areas than in bedrooms, Scraps of foods, candles, soap etc attract them. Hygienic storage and disposal of food and all kinds of waste are important to prevent an infestation. Rats and mice may be destroyed by poison.

Wood Rot (Dry Rot)

This is the term used for the decay of timber by a fungus, which grows and lives in the wood and reduces it finally to a crumbling state. Hence it is called dry rot. It nearly always starts in damp, unventilated places, behind wood paneling, and spreads by sending out thin root like structure, which creep over the surface. Having ascertained and cured the cause of the dampness all rotten wood must be cut away 30-60 cm beyond the infected area and burnt at once and never stored.

Wet Rot

This is the name given to fungal decay in amber under severe damp conditions. It is often found in cellar with leakages and is the reason why it is called as cellar fungus. It may be found in any place where there is some sort of leakage. The fungus causes severe darkening of wood, which, breaks up into rectangular pieces on drying the treatment for it is as same as the dry rot.

Ants

These common but annoying pests are known to mechanically transmit diseases from excrement to food. Ants cause immense wastage of food by eating some of it, thus making the food unfit for human consumption. They are known to destroy crops and also eat into wrappers. These are called social pests as because they exist in groups or colonies and live and work together.

Stored Grain Insects

This group include : flour beetle, rice weevil, granary weevil, the Indian-meal moth, saw-toothed grain beetle, lesser grain borer, & grain moth.

These insects are like beetles with long snout and lay eggs in each hole. The grub or larva burrows into the grain and cats away a part of the grain. The rest of the contaminated grain is low in flavor, taste, hygienic quality & acceptability. Tiny holes in the grain along with powdery substances are the signs of the infestations.

Firebrats attack bakery products. They prefer warm and dry places for breeding, and like sweet and starchy food.

Waste Disposal

The hygienic disposal of waste materials is extremely important in the control of most pests. The accumulation of food waste and greasy or starchy paper may attract insects and pests. The waste should be kept in tightly covered bins, which should be removed by house porter to the main waste collection point outside the building from where they will be removed by the local municipal authority. Liquid wastes from sinks, basins, lavatory basins, w.c.pans etc. should be taken by a proper system of pipeline.

Flower Arrangement

Flower Arrangements contribute greatly to the atmosphere since they provide beauty, colour, as well as an air of luxury. Flower Arrangements are done in the Hotels because of the following reasons:-

   a. Creating ambience and decor

   Religious reasons

   Amenities for VIP Guests

   Personalized services

   To fit empty, unattractive spaces - i.e. to act as a camouflage

   Special functions

Most hotels do not have a specialized person doing this job - and if they do, it is generally a contract service. Large hotels have a Horticulturist who looks after the entire gardening as well as a florist who supplies and arranges flowers. In smaller hotels, it is often a part of the duties of the Executive Housekeeper or the Assistant Housekeeper in charge.

The Areas where Slower Arrangements are Done in The Hotel, are Mainly as Follows:

   a. F&B Outlets (Restaurants, Bars, Buffets) - Flowers are given in bud vases on the tables, on the side boards, on the bar counters, etc.

Banquet / Function Halls - Flowers are provided at the entrances, as centerpieces relevant to the function. May be suspended from the ceiling or strung up on walls or as a backdrop.

Main entrance (Lobby, Lounge) - Flowers are provided as Landscapes, centerpieces, Niches, etc.

Flowers are provided on the Reception Counters

Flowers are provided in all the Rooms

Flowers are provided in all the Executive Offices

Levels of Placement

It is evident that the placement of flower arrangements can be categorized into three different and distinct levels as follows :

- *Low Level (On the floor up to 8")* : This type of arrangement is found in landscapes. driftwood, large decorative vases, etc.

- *Eye Level (18" to 4 ft.)* : This type of arrangement is found on coffee table, dressing table, sideboards, dining table, top of T.V. cabinet, alcoves and niches, etc.

- *High Level (5 ft. and above)* : This type of arrangement is found on pelmets, top of wardrobes, etc.. Even, they can be suspended from the ceiling.

Equipments used in Flower Arrangement : Like any other art or craft, Flower arrangement requires good equipments. It is essential to store all equipments in one place ready for use when required. They are discussed below :

- **Shears:** They are of two types - the normal scissor type and the double-spring scissor type having a spring between blades so that less effort is necessary. They must be sharp to prevent cutting plant material with a jagged edge.

- **Buckets:** An adequate supply is required to store plant materials while arranging, and ensure that they are not crushed and suffocated by all being placed in one container.

- **Pinholders:** They are of various shapes and sizes to meet all requirements and are fit for flat containers. They are commonly referred to as Stemholders. The Japanese term is Kenzun.

Basically, one should look for the following:

- Close, sharp points so that it is easy to impale stems on the holder
- A weighted base, so that it does not topple over with the weight of the stems
- Non-rusting material, since it is submerged in water for a long period of time.
- **Chicken Wire**: It is also commonly known as Wire Mesh. It should be fairly pliable, but not too thin. It is crumpled and packed into the mouth of a tall vase, where a stem holder is of no avail. A combination of the needle point holder and wire mesh can also be used.
- **Oasis**: It is a synthetic substance, cellular in nature able to hold water. It may be used to impale stems, but cannot be reused - and is therefore expensive. It is also called Foam. Oasis is generally of two types - Green Foam is used for fresh arrangements, and Brown Foam is used for dry arrangements.
- **Beeswax**: It is used to anchor the pinholder to the container and prevent it from shifting while arranging flowers. Waterproof plasticine, rubber pinholder bases, or even a pad of newspaper are equally good substitutes.
- **Stem Supporters**: Florist's tape, florist's wire, toothpicks, pins, and rubber bands can be used. Professional tape and wire are available in varying shades of green and brown, so that they can be camouflaged.
- **Accessories**: An accessory can be anything - from a lid to a figurine, to a few leaves, rocks, pebbles, stones, ribbon, etc. It is used for adding variations to the flower arrangement, or to camouflage the pinholder.
- **Water Sprinkler:** Water is sprayed to keep plant materials fresh.
- **Containers**: There is a wide variety, so that it can be chosen to match with the available materials, and at the same time, with the place where the arrangement is to be placed.

Points to remember to ensure that plant materials last longer : The points to be kept in mind for ensuring longer life of plant materials are as follows :

- **When to cut**: All plant materials should be cut either early in the morning or late in the evening - when the rate of transpiration is at its lowest.

- **Immediate immersion**: Plant materials once cut, should be placed immediately in water to prevent wilting from setting in.

- **Hardening**: Plant material should be allowed to stand in water 8" deep upto their necks for 6 to 8 hours before arranging - ensuring absorption of water which can be stored for sometime in the stem.

- **Cutting under water**: Whether first cut, or bought from the florist, stems should be cut under the water so as to prevent air bubbles forming within the stem which blocks the water supply causing the flowers to wilt. Put water in the container whilst arranging.

- **How to cut**: Use a sharp cutting instrument and cut diagonally across the stem to have a clean cut providing the maximum area for water absorption.

- **Searing**: Stems which emit a milky sap when cut, should either be held over a flame or placed in boiling water for a few seconds to prevent the life-giving sap from draining off.

- **Shearing lower half of stems** : Leaves and thorns that are unnecessary, should be removed, especially if submerged - as they create a tangled appearance, increase transpiration and decay causing early wilting and unpleasant odour.

- All receptacles should be clean and free from detergent.

- Ensure that the arrangement is placed away from direct draughts or sunlight.

- Ensure that the water level is adequate, and maintain it. Use a water sprinkler to keep the air fresh.

- Flower arrangements lasts longer by addition of sugar, aspirin.

- **Styles of Flower Arrangement** : Leading artists in the field of flower arrangement, like any other artists in any medium, prefer one style to another. On the basis of definite characteristics, flower arrangements are broadly divided into the followings :

- **Western / Traditional Style** : They are stylish arrangements, displaying mass grouping of flowers and foliages of many varieties. Generally, they tend to have some symmetry.

- **Japanese Style** : Ikebana compositions are popular because of the beauty of lines and symbolic significance. These are generally sober and simple. Ikebana uses three radical elements / groups known as Subject (Heaven), Secondary (Man), and Tertiary (Earth). Japanese call them as Soe, Shin, and Hikae respectively.

Compositions in Moribana style are made in low containers, and contain groups of plant material representing natural landscape scenery.

Nageire composition adheres to the fundamental principle of Ikebana - where arrangements are done in tall vases.

Morimono is the arrangement done with fruits.

- **Free Style:** Fusion of Western and Japanese style resulted in this new style, free from stiffness of rules and traditional forms.

- **Abstract Style:** In this style of flower arrangement, the design reflects the designer's own feeling with regard to the subject matter interpreted. It is based on structural designs or geometrical patterns.

- **Principles of Flower Arrangement** : The basic principles of art are also applicable to the art of flower arrangement. The principles are discussed as follows :

- **Design:** All arrangements should have a design; that is the structural pattern of the arrangement which determines the shape, size, and suitability of the various a component parts and their relationship to each other. In order to create a good design, certain fundamental principles need to be followed. These are :

❖ The stems should all flow from a central point, avoiding cross stems.

❖ The local centre should be under the tallest point.

❖ The flowers used should not be monotonous.

❖ The height, width, and depth are required to be proportionate.

❖ The shape ought to be clearly defined.

- **Scaling:** Materials should be chosen that relate to each other and to the background. To achieve the correct scaling, there are a number of points to be borne in mind. They are as follows :

❖ We should avoid using together very different types of materials.

❖ We ought to put really huge flowers in a large low container rather than in a tall and narrow one.

❖ No flower should be more than one-third of the size of the container.

❖ If we use a round vase, we should use a round base.

❖ If we have a given space to fill, we should only fill it two-third and use the surrounding space to set off the arrangement.

❖ A tall, narrow space may suggest an arrangement four times the height of a tall container - but if this is done, the arrangement should be very airy-fairy at the top.

❖ The height of the material should be approximately one-and-a-half times the height of the container (or the width of the container if it is long and low).

- **Balance:** Balance is shown in the way in which materials are grouped in a design. The different types of balance are :

Symmetrical Balance- This occurs where the material is so arranged that if you draw an imaginary line through the centre of the arrangement, you would have a visually equal distribution of material on each side of the line.

Asymmetrical Balance- This is where the material is so placed that high and light materials appears to be on one side of the imaginary line flowing in towards the axis, is balanced by larger, shorter material flowing away from the axis on to the other side of the line.

Balance by Placement- It means that the arrangement is placed to one side of a long base.

❖ ***Balance by Accessory*** - It means that anything from a figurine to leaves may he used - usually on the weakest side, i.e., the side that has the least weight in Terms of plant material.

Do not put an asymmetrical arrangement against a symmetrical background.

- **Focal Point:** It is usually under the tallest point and provides the core or heart of the design on which to focus attention. It is the central area from which the flowers and foliages appear to emerge.

- **Rhythm:** This is the feeling of notion created by using curved lines and graduating sizes on different degrees of opening of the flowers so that they lead towards the centre and on again. We should be aware of flower stepping (placing one flower immediately above another). We should avoid placing flowers in a straight line.

- **Emphasis:** It means to emphasize some special area of the arrangement. And in order to give it special prominence, group the materials by using strong contrast, e.g. : use dark leaves to accentuate light colours. In achieving emphasis, it is necessary to avoid monotony in flower forms.

- **Harmony:** In the finished arrangement as a whole, the material used, the container, and any accessories should harmonize into one overall framework.

- **Distinction:** This is the most important asset. Either the arrangement has it, or does not. It is achieved by the followings :

❖ The use of unusual material or an unusual container.

❖ The use of some unusual method of emphasis.

❖ Skilful colour combination.

❖ Perfect finish.

❖ A good contrast has built up a strong design.

Names of Some Flowers Commonly Used in Hotels	
Chrysanthemums	Camasean
Tulip	Poppies
Lily	Iris
Sweet Peas	Roses
Daisy	Lotus
Orchid	Daffodil
Tuberose	Anthorium
Dahlia	Lilacs
Philodilphus	Weigelia

Hydiangeas	Lupius
Anchusa	Boconia
Heliohopes	Minosa
Anenones	Hypericum

Interior Decoration

In today's world Interior decoration has assumed great importance, there are various aspects of interior decoration such as colour texture, pattern, lighting, heating, ventilation etc. Probably there is no department in a hotel more concerned with interiors and their design and furnishings than the professional housekeeper and the housekeeping department. Yet few housekeepers today are actually involved in creating the initial plan and visual impact of a room. That in itself is a full time occupation requiring talent as well as special training. The housekeeper, however, is likely to be very much involved in selection of items for replacement when the components of the interior becomes worn or too soiled to save.

What is Colour

To the scientist it is reflected light which, viewed through a prism, breaks - into visible spectrum. The colours that we see all around us are either imparted to surface by dyes or pigments or are the natural colours of objects. The colour of a surface absorbs all of the spectral colours in the light rays that strike it, except the colours you see. The colour you see is reflected back to your eyes. A surface that absorbs all of the colours in the light rays appears black. Therefore the controlling factor in determining what colour we see is light. Colour is one of the most important aspect of interior decoration and play an important role as colour can increase or decrease the size of the room, add to the length of the room, evoke (bring out] certain feelings to a room. The hotel lobby is supposed to be inviting. The rest rooms are supposed to be colourful hence cool colours must be hygienic and appetizing.

Colours Acquire Three Main Types.

1. Primary colour
2. Secondary colour
3. Tertiary colour

I. Primary Colour :

Which are the very basic colours. These are red, blue, and yellow. For example yellow, sky blue and red earth.

II. Secondary Colour :

Are the mix of two primary colours, example, red combines with yellow to give orange, yellow and blue gives green, blue and red gives violet.

III. Tertiary Colour :

Are combination of one primary colour and one secondary colour. Example red and orange gives russet.

Terms Related To Colour

Value - the lightness or darkness of a colour.

Shades - darker side of a colour

Tints - lighter side of the colour

Chroma - the intensity of purity of a colour e.g. yellow is full colour.

Hue - the colour itself e.g. red, blue, green, etc.

Weight - this is the subjective term for lightness.

Colours may vary according to their specific qualities or names (hue), according to their lightness or darkness (value), or according to their brightness or dullness (intensity). Hue, value and intensity may be described as the three properties or dimensions of colour.

Hue is simply the colour quality that has been given a certain name for identification. Although the words, 'colour' and 'hue' can often be used interchangeably 'colour' is more general term than 'hue'. Hue is a specific term referring to definite identifiable colours.

Value is the lightness or darkness of a colour. The basic colours of the colour wheel can be lightened to the pale tints or darkened to shades by mixing them with black or white. The use of a dark colour against a light colour, or a light colour against a dark colour is called 'contrast'. Dark and light value of the same colour used together also creates contrast. Some colour contrast is essential for good colour distribution, but when the contrast is extremely sharp, the lightness of one colour area will emphasize and exaggerate the darkness of the other and vice versa.

Intensity sometimes is also called chroma - it is the brightness or dullness of a colour. A bright colour is said to be at full intensity and may be described as strong, rich, forceful, brilliant, vivid, and sharp. If the intensity is offensive, it may be called gaudy, garish or flashy. A colour that is not bright is said to be 'toned down', and terms used to describe it may range from such adjectives as subdued or softened to such adjectives as dull, weak or drab. Intensity of a colour is reduced without changing it's value by mixing gray of the same value with the colour, or by mixing in some or the colour that, on the colour wheel is directly opposite the colour to be toned down.

There are various colour schemes, which may be followed, all relating to the colour wheel.
1. Monochromatic Colour Scheme:
This colour scheme makes use of one particular colour in different shades and tints, example, to use in different shades in a room one could have sky blue for the ceiling, navy blue for the walls and a Roselle blue for the floor.

2. Dichromatic Colour Scheme:
This scheme is similar to the first except here two colours are used in different shades and tints.

3. Complementary Colour Scheme:
Here exactly opposite colours of the colour wheel are used (example, red would make use of the exact complement of green). One in a bright tone for small areas and the other in grayed tones for larger areas. They should be used with a neutral colour.

4. Split Complementary Colour Scheme :

One would pick a particular colour on the colour wheel and then use the colours adjacent/either sides to its complement contrast. For example, if yellow were picked then it would be used along with red violet and blue violet.

5. Analogous Colour Scheme :

This scheme makes use of a particular colour on the colour wheel and colour immediately adjacent/side by side to this colour. For example, green, yellow green and blue green.

6. Triad Colour Scheme :

Under this scheme three colours from the colour wheel could be chosen but all three colours should be equi-distant from each other. In other words, it uses 3 primary, 3 secondary or 3 tertiary together. Under this colour scheme one colour should. dominate the other two always. For example, red, yellow and blue is used, and blue is the dominant colour.

Colour Can Also Alter The Apparent Size of a Room:

Reds, yellows browns and darker shades are warmer. These colours when used on an end wall would shorten the apparent length of the room or if applied on the ceiling would lessen the height of the wall.

- Cool colours, pale greens, blues, and other lighter shades are cooling and tend to make a small room look larger.

- Reds, oranges and yellows are warm and stimulating.

- Pastel shades are cooler and more restful.

- Green is cool and has a soothing and pleasing effect.

- Pale blue is fresh and cool but dark blue can be depressing if used in large areas.

- Purple has richness, while brown and other darker colours give an impression of comfort.

- White can appear hygienic and cold.

- Light colours reflect light while dark colours absorb light.

- Colours can be affected by the amount of light falling on them (curtains look darker at day & light at night when light falls on them), the type of surface (rough surfaces cast small shadows thus appearing darker than smooth glossy ones), the surrounding colours (strong colours may distort other colours)

Black, White, Grey and Cream Are Neutral Colours

When choosing a colour scheme, it is necessary to consider the type of building and the customers or the clientele who use it. The character of the building is also important and the features it already has. The amount of light coming into the rooms for instance will affect what colours and patterns you choose.

Many Colours Have a Similar Effect on People.

- Reds, oranges and yellows are warm and stimulating.
- Pastel shades are cooler and more restful.
- Green is cool and has a soothing, pleasing effect.
- Pale blue is fresh and cool but dark blue can be depressing if used in large areas.
- Purple has richness.
- Browns and other dark colours give the impression of comfort.
- White can appear hygienic and cold.

Pattern

Colour is used in conjunction with pattern and adds interest to decorative schemes.

1. Too much patter is disturbing to the eye and may create a busy room.
2. Large patterns can be over powering and small patterns may be lost in a large area.
3. Vertical stripes make the eye look upwards and make a room higher and narrower.
4. Horizontal lines make a room look lower and wider.
5. Pattern should be used with restraint. Too much is disturbing to the eye.

It is possible to introduce more than one pattern in a scheme but they should be different in character. For example, a striped and floral pattern in which one pattern should be dominant.

Pattern can be used to alter the apparent size of a room *To give height to the room.*

1. Remove or camouflage any horizontals.
2. Use striped wallpaper or one with a vertical pattern.
3. Pale ceiling and light coloured carpet.
4. Furniture should be low.

To Reduce The Height of The Room.

1. Paint the ceiling down onto the walls with a dark colour.
2. The carpet should match the ceiling drawing both together.
3. Introduce a lot of furniture.

To Increase The Size of The Room.

1. Break cluttering the wall and room with too many pictures and furniture.
2. Pale and cool colours give an illusion of space.
3. Marble ceramic, chrome (silver coating like for bathroom tap coating etc) and glass all give an illusion of space.

4. Wallpaper and paint can match the curtains. This adds continuity.

To Reduce The Size of The Room

1. Break up the wall with pictures.

2. Create a focal point, which attracts eyes towards and away from the vastness in the room.

3. Use rags and Durries (floor mats) to break the monotony of the floor.

4. Large furniture may be used.

To Reduce The Length of Narrow Long Room

1. Have the wall painted in darker colour than the rest of the room.

2. Bookshelves along with wall add width.

3. Ceiling of light colours.

This matters a great deal; in any scheme it may vary from cold, shiny, smooth surfaces of glass to the warmer, rougher surfaces of cloth and paper coverings. It is always usual to plan from the largest to the smallest areas. Thus, floors, walls and ceilings are considered first, curtains come next (upholstery) and smaller areas are considered last.

In a hotel maintenance programmes, wall coverings may be renewed every 2 to 3 years. Soft furnishings every 4 to 5 years and complete change of decoration and refurnishing changing everything in the room, depending on the type of hotel. Refurbishing is done every 8 to 10 years.

Floorings

Often out last other furnishings, so most of the decorative schemes should be planned to fit in with the existing floor. Carpets are used to give warmth, provide insulation, and give a luxurious feel, to have a sense of completeness. Carpet squares and rugs tend to break up the monotony at a cold floor and help to reduce space. Texture with floorings can very, a very rough material and a very smooth material such as marble or granite.

A patterned carpet should have a design in keeping with the size, style, function and the atmosphere of the room. Plain carpets are suitable for heavily decorated rooms and vice versa.

Wall Coverings

Varies from paint, wallpaper, fab ic wall coverings, plastics, glass etc. They form the background for any schemes. Mirrors break up the walls and tend to add more space to a room. Using full-length mirrors, ceramic tiles, stained glass on walls gives a general feeling of space. Mirrors help to double the size of the room by giving a reflection. However too much light in the room might be a source of danger to the short sighted.

Curtains

Curtains are often the most expensive item of soft furnishing. They should enhance the floor and wall coverings and complement the rest of the furniture and furnishings. Besides contributing to the decor they have a number of other uses. They insulate a room against noise and cold. They are often used to cut out light during the day, especially in hotels where people are sleeping in the daytime (especially in airport hotels). Some furnishings are damaged by too much sunlight, and many people find sunlight uncomfortable - so curtains can be used to shade a room. Net curtains can stop a room being overlooked, especially in a built up area. If the windows are large, curtains may become a form of an entire wall of a room. Curtain hanging in folds adds a bit of rough texture to the rooms. They can change the features of the rooms so also the lighting. Texture in its own way plays an important role for the decoration of a room and all of the furnishings should be used in union with texture. Man-made fabrics probably does not exist that is not resistant in one way or other to something - soil, abrasion, fire, water, sunlight, wrinkling, creasing, and even odours.

Windows

It is the lifeline to the outside world. It should always be attractive and eye appealing. No drapery design or colour in the world can compensate for dirty windows. The curtains / window coverings are obviously part of the decor, but also the view from the window. It the view is unattractive, it can be obscured by net curtains or blinds or by dark glass, which allows light to enter but obscures the view. If there is a blank wall in front of the window, it can be painted - either white to reflect the light into the room, or with an attractive mural. Plants or flowerpots could be hung on the blanket wall. Curtains can frame an attractive view from the window. Other decorative finishes on windows can be as follows :

1. Pelmets

A pelmet is a curtain heading used to hide the curtain tracks or rods. They are made of wood or hardboard, which can be painted or papered to match the decor or covered in the same material as the curtains.

2. Blinds

Blinds are used where it is difficult to hang curtains or to hide a view. These reduce heat loss in winter and keep rooms' cooler in summer, while still allowing diffused light into the room.

3. Roller blinds

These are available in a variety of fabrics and almost anything, although no fabric can be made resistant to everything. These coated fabrics are impregnated with invisible chemical finishes that affect neither the fabrics colour nor its texture.

Stain repellents are undoubtedly the most popular. Fabrics treated with fluoro- chemicals resist oil, water and soil stains. When something spills, the liquid does not seep into the fabric, it remains on the surface and therefore can be blotted (never rubbed) with a dry cloth or towel. As for soil and dust, they collect on top of the fabric surface and only have to be brushed off. Most stain-resistant fabrics last through five launderings or dry cleaning before having to be re-treated.

Silicones are responsible for a fabrics heat resistance. Among their outstanding virtues is the ability to withstand temperatures up to 500°F. Draperies in public areas must be treated to be flame-resistant. Most curtains need to be lined, with the exception of those materials, which have interwoven lining, backing or insulation material. The life of the curtains is prolonged by having linings since they are protected from the damaging effect of the sun's rays. Lining material is usually of mercerized cotton that withstands the effect of the sun's rays. Lining provides better heat insulation. Air trapped between the curtain and the lining proves to be a bad conductor of heat and the extra weight given to the curtain is protection against draughts. The curtains usually hang better when lined and lined curtains exclude more exterior light. From the exterior of the building, lined curtains give a uniformity of appearance, however linings do increase the initial cost of outlay on material, and lined curtains are more expensive to make up. Unless linings are detachable there may be uneven shrinkage between the lining and the curtain.

4. Glass curtains

Glass curtains cover the glass of the window assuring privacy, but are thin enough to admit light and air. They may be used alone or in combination with draperies.

Pinoleums

These are slatted blinds, made from wood or quill woven together with cotton are suitable for garden rooms or when an area or a room needs to be screened from viewing. They give an oriental effect.

Venetian blinds

These are made of slats of metal, wood, or plastic slotted on cords which operate their opening or closing. Another set of cords raises and lowers the blind. The amount of light room is adjusted by the slant of the slats. They are difficult to clean. They tend to collect dust and dirt.

Vertical blinds

These are like Venetian blinds hung vertically. By altering the angle of the slats more or less light is allowed to enter. The slats are about 10cms wide, 80 care should be taken to see that curtains are hung far enough from the blinds to allow for the slats to be opened.

Draperies

These are also called over curtains or heavy curtains, and are generally made of heavy material, tailored to fit the particular window. They are usually lined and weighted at the bottom. There are 3 ways by which curtains can be drawn :

> ➢ A cord attached to the rollers in such a way that if the cord is pulled both curtains arc drawn.

> ➢ A pole attached to the top of each curtain is used to draw the curtains.

> ➢ Electronically, which draws curtains by pressing a button remote from the window.

1. Curtain headings

Using different kinds of tape makes the heading of the curtain. The tape is sewn to the top of the curtain, and the cords pulled to make the gatherings, pleating, etc. the ends of the cord should then be neatly secured.

2. Gathering

A gathered heading is often hidden under a pelmet. The tape should be placed about 1.5 cm from the top of the curtain. The curtain width required is 1.5 times the length of the track.

Assessing The Amount of Material Required:

Plain fabrics require the length from the top of the track to 1.25 cm above the windowsill plus turnings. OR 15 cm below the windowsills plus turnings. OR 2.5 cm above the floor and turnings.

Patterned fabrics require extra material depending upon the pattern. Allow an additional pattern to repeat for every width of curtain after the first, e.g. if five widths are required then four pattern repeats are needed. At least 20 cm should be allowed for turnings, headings and hems. The width of the curtain should allow for overlap at the side of the window and at least 15 cm at the centre. The tracks should take care of this, so the length of the track is usually taken as a guide.

The choosing factor of fabrics depends on the amount of daily abuse it will take including excessive exposure to sunlight, humidity, soil, frequent handling or mishandling by guests and employees, how much vacuuming they require, etc.

Furniture:
Should Perform The Following Functions.

1. It is functional and ergonomically designed. (It means any person of any height weight can use it) height of the door roof.

2. It blends in with the rest of the decoration.

3. It does not lose space in a small room.

4. Wood used in furniture has a warm appearance and is regarded as neutral. Timber looks expensive and if used has to be cleaned appropriately. Loose covers may be used using hooks and eyes, zips, touch and close fasteners to attach them. Furniture should be used in conjunction with the wall coverings and should have an appeal to create the required atmosphere. Furniture used in conjunction with artificial lights help to enhance that particular feature.

Furniture covers a wide range of items, which are in constant use; therefore it should retain its overall appearance. Furniture choosing should depend on the following needs:

D Practical design and appropriate size.

D Comfortable to use.

D Sturdy to with stand considerable wear and tear.

D Easy to clean and maintain

D Pricing should be within the budget of the establishment.

Furniture once purchased should fit for it's purpose and meet the requirements of the guest, housekeeper and the management. Therefore the following points must be kept in mind when considering buying furniture :

1. The type of guest staying and the standards of accommodation, this specifies the type of hotel, the furniture is chosen for and it's star rating.

2. Atmosphere to be achieved, e.g. modem or olden day theme so as to give the correct degree of comfort.

3. Shape and size of the articles in relation to the human body (this is called science of ergonomics which means the study of people in relation to their work environment) e.g. shelves are more serviceable than drawers in a bedroom, built-in furniture can save floor space.

4. Durability of an article/furniture as it is likely to be handled by a large no. of people.

5. Versatility and movablity e.g. furniture should be movable type in case of twin or double bedroom type so as to be let out for small functions like luncheons, exhibitions, conferences and then set back to normal later.

6. Ease of cleaning, e.g. heavy furniture could have castors, shelves instead of drawers, drawers with wipe easy surfaces rather than lined, etc.

7. Standardization - all furniture bought could be of standard measurements so as to be moved from room to room as and when required.

Cane, Wicker And Bamboo

These are the names given to the items of furniture made from thick grasses (bamboo), palms (cane), and willow shoots (wicker). They have similar characteristics to timber products but are generally woven or plaited into chairs, tables, baskets, etc. They are easily damaged if they are not used or stored carefully. Regular cleaning is necessary to avoid a building of inaccessible dust, dirt and grease. Cleaning involves brushing or vacuum cleaning each day and wiping approximately once a week with a solution of warm water and washing soda or a solution made up of 5 ml borax and 50ml of water. Both methods should be followed by rinsing in a cold saline solution (15gm of salt in 1 litre of water) to help stiffen the strands. It should be allowed to dry naturally and over wetting should therefore be avoided. Oil or wax polishes may be applied, if desired, to those, which are varnished or painted gloss. Polish should not be used on items used with food.

Protecting Wood Surfaces

Unprotected wood will absorb moisture, which causes the grains to swell and so create gaps into which dirt and germs can fall and become trapped when it dries. Liquids such as coffee and wine, leaves stains on the surface, which is difficult to remove and scratching is difficult to avoid particularly on floors. The following are the most frequently found methods of protection and may be referred to as wood finished.

Cellulose Lacquer

This is fairly durable matt or gloss finish, applied mainly to solid timber furniture during manufacture. Which should be dusted and wiped with a damp cloth. Then dried with a soft one. Cream or spray polish may be applied to give a glass finish. Heat, water or solvents may cause damage to it.

French Polish

This is used on small decorative items of furniture only as it is easily damaged by heat, water and solvents. Deterioration is caused by light and the atmosphere in general. French polishing is produced by rubbing the solid wooden surface with a solution of shellac (dark red resin) and methylated spirit. It should be polished up well, working in the way of the grain, while dusting should be done on daily basis. If desired a cream, liquid or paste polish may be applied occasionally to remove light soiling and improve the gloss.

Oil

Solid wooden furniture can be given a matt protective finish by rubbing the surface with a mixture of oil (usually linseed oil) and resin. This process gives very little protection although it will help to reduce the absorption or water. Daily dusting is essential as the matt finish does little to repel dust. Marks can be removed by lightly rubbing with very fine steel wool. About twice a year the surface should be rubbed with a mixture of equal quantities of turpentine and raw linseed oil. Proprietary polishes should be avoided.

Paint

This is very widely used on furniture, window frames, door surrounds, skirtings, staircases, etc. unlike most other finishes it can be very colourful. Gloss paint is tougher then matt or silk and will with stand more frequent washing. All painted wood should be dusted daily and wiped with a synthetic detergent solution or solvent each week. Spray or cream polishes can be used to retain the shine on gloss surfaces. Although paint is easily damaged by heat, alkalis and abrasives, it is easy and inexpensive to renew.

Resin

Natural and synthetic resins such as polyesters, melamine's and polyurethanes are used extensively on wooden furniture window frames, door surrounds, skirtings, floors and staircases. The finish may be very glossy or matt and is frequently applied to furniture made from chipboard. Resin is extremely tough, it will resist heat, water, solvents and abrasives but once damaged by scratching or chipping it is very difficult to repair, Dust should be removed daily and cream or spray polish used on the gloss surfaces after damp wiping. Matt surfaces should be rubbed up occasionally using a mixture of 500 ml of turpentine, 100ml of boiled linseed oil and 500ml of vinegar

WAX(Bees)

This is applied to solid wood furniture or floors. The degree of protection depends on the of wax which are applied and the efficiency with which it is rubbed in. This will also affect the degree of gloss. It provides a very attractive finish exposing the pattern of the wood, but it is easily damaged by heat, water and solvents. Waxed surfaces should be dusted daily, cleaned each week with cream or liquid polish. And when considered necessary rubbed with another coat of wax, which should be allowed to dry before rubbing up well.

Floor Finishes

Floors are functional and decorative and cover the vast area, which is walked on in any building. They undergo a lot of wear and tear and it is upon the maintenance, cleanliness and beauty of the floor that, part of the star category depends upon. It is the clearest way to measure the standard of a hotel or establishment.

In the olden days without much furniture the floor itself had multifaceted use of all activities. Even now the greatest care must be taken for maintaining a clean floor. The choice of the floor depends upon various factors mainly the utility or purpose of the room or area. The joint between the wall and floor should be hulled or rounded to facilitate cleaning and there must be a skirting going up at least 6" of the wall with extended flooring also for better cleanliness. In case the room has drainage the entire floor must be sloping slightly and very evenly towards the point of drainage outlet, which must be kept properly, wired against insects.

The finish of the floor may depend upon the appearance required, the type of comfort desired, the durability, and quality of the material, whether it is easy to maintain and upkeep whether it is safe and lastly whether it is within the budget.

What is a Sub-Floor?

The effective life of most flooring will depend on how they are laid initially and on their subsequent care and cleaning. Many properties of a flooring may be enhanced or ruined by the base i.e. the sub-floor, on which the flooring is laid.

Sub-floor is made of concrete, but in older and smaller buildings it consists of soft wood boards, at least 10 cm wide nailed to wooden joints. In large modem buildings the sub floor is often made of concrete, but in older smaller buildings it consists of soft wood boards nailed to wooden joints.

Any of the following floor finishes may be used on the top of a suitable floor. Granolithic, terrazzo and other cementitious finishes laid in the form of small blocks. Bitumastic finishes, ceramic tiled floorings, wood, semi hard finished - thermoplastic, vinyl, rubber, linoleum, cork. Carpets are normally regarded as floor coverings rather than floor finishes.

Whereas, concrete sub-floors, have the advantage of being solid and fire retardant. However a risk of rising damp is always there.

Floor Finishes will only in rare cases be chosen solely for luxury and normally consideration should be given to

    a. Appearance, colour, design, cold, warm, etc.

    b. Amount of traffic to which they will be subjected.

    c. Resistance to spills - Water, grease, food, acid, etc.

    d. Ease of cleaning in relation to the type and amount of spoiling.

e. Sound and heat insulation.

f. The nature and condition of the sub floor.

What is a Seal?

A seal is applied to clean, dry floor and gives a non-absorbent, semi permanent gloss or finish, which will wear in time.

Before the floor can be re-scaled, any remaining seal has to be stripped off, wind this can be done in the case of wood and cork floorings by sanding out, in other cases a chemical stripper has to be used. In order to preserve the real a polish should be applied to pealed floorings.

What is a Polish?

Polishes are either spirit or water based. Spirit based floor polishes may be paste or liquid and require buffing when dry to produce a shine; water based polishes and liquid and dry to a shiny surface, which in some cases can be improved by buffing and in others cannot.

Types of Floorings Hard Wood Floor *Wood*

Wood finishes of good quality are among the most beautiful floorings, provided the variety of the wood and the size of the unit are chosen for effect. These floorings, which are to be mainly uncovered and subjected to a good deal of wear, must be of hard woods.

Strip Wood Flooring

Strip wood flooring consists of lengths of narrow stripe (under 4 inches wide) of hard wood of good appearance, example maple. The boards are fixed to jousts or to timber insets in concrete, and this construction, together with the length of the strip, gives the floor its resilience, and makes it very suitable for bathroom floors. A spring floor has springs under the joists to increase resilience.

Wood Block Floomng

Wood block flooring consists of rectangular blocks (example 9in. x 3in. or 12in. x 2in.) laid in an adhesive on a level concrete base. The blocks are generally laid to form a patter and may be of oak, teak, jarran, missandu, etc. and are chosen for their durability rather than their appearance when used in linen rooms, store rooms and staff halls.

Parquet Flooring

Parquet flooring in appearance resembles a wood block flooring in that it also consists of rectangular pieces of wood (9in. x 3in. or 12in x 2in.). However, the blocks are very much thinner (less than 3/8 in. thick), and are pinned and glued to wooden sub floor, often in a herringbone pattern. Parquet is used in foyers and lounges in conjunction with rugs. A cheaper parquet flooring may only have a veneer of good quality wood on the surface and so forms a much less hardwearing floor.

Wood Mosaics

Wood mosaics are generally made up in panels, i.e. 18in. square formed of 4^ min. squares in basket pattern, laced with paper or backed with felt or aluminum according to the manufacture. They are laid in adhesive, either on concrete or as an overlay on an existing floor.

Advantages:

1. Wood can be of various colours and grains.

2. When used as strip or parquet floorings, and if well cared for, they have a good appearance.

3. They are hard wearing repairs are not usually frequent.

4. The surfaces can be sanded down and new ones exposed.

5. Wood is a poor conductor of heat and therefore a good insulator.

Disadvantages:

1. They are rather noisy.

2. They are inflammable and susceptible to dry pot.

3. They get scratched and will splinter with the dragging of heavy articles.

4. Unless sealed, they are absorbent and cleaning is laborious and expensive.

5. The initial cost is comparatively high.

Care And Cleaning:

1. Clean regularly.

2. Attend to loose blocks and splinters.

3. Resurface by sanding when necessary.

These are the designs used for laying out the floor that must be of best quality, well seasoned, durable, pest resistant timber, laid on damp free, well-ventilated sub floors.

Tiles or Laid in-Situ Hard Floors Asphalt/Bitumastic Flooring

In this type of floor a type of asphalt rolled on to a solid sub-floor, in a hot plastic state. It is normally black, red or brown, but may have other colors rolled in giving a matted surface effect. This kind of flooring softens with heat and dents with heavy weights and is harmed with spirit, oil and acids but the initial cost is low. It is used in bathrooms, and to protect other floor finishes from rising damp.

Advantages:

1. Coved edges facilitate cleaning.

2. It is not affected by water and may have a drain incorporated.

3. It is durable.

4. It is vermin proof, impervious to dry rot and non-slip.

5. Cleaning is easy.

6. The initial cost is low.

Disadvantages:

1. It has poor appearance.
2. It dents with heavy weights and softens with heat.
3. It is harmed by spirit, oil and acids.

Care and Cleaning:

1. Clean regularly.
2. Use special floor paint to restore old colour when necessary.

Resin Flooring

These consist of synthetic resins, usually epoxy, polyester or polyurethane with appropriate hardeners. Vinyl or marble chippings may be included to give a decorative look. Resin flooring may be laid in situ. Mainly this kind of flooring is used in kitchen, canteens and other areas where food is handled because it is unaffected by any kind of food spillage:

Granolithic Flooring

It is a hard floor finish of grated granite chips set in cement. It is laid in plastic state on solid sub floor. It is used for basement, corridors, storeroom, stair-ways and laundries.

Advantages:

1. Removal pre-cast slabs can be made to cover service pipes for ease of maintenance.
2. Coved edges facilitate cleaning.
3. They are not affected by water and may have a drain incorporated.
4. They are durable.
5. They are vermin proof, impervious to dry rot and fire resistant.
6. Cleaning is relatively easy.
7. The cost of granolithic is low whereas terrazzo is higher.

Disadvantages:

1. They are hard and noisy.
2. They are cold in appearance.
3. Cracks may appear.
4. Granolithic will chip, especially an stairs; with terrazzo the marble chippings may become loose.

Care And Cleaning:

1. Clean regularly.
2. Attend cracks and loose clippings.

Terrazzo Flooring

It is also a hard floor finish consisting of a mixture of marble and other decorative chipping set in fine cement, which can be colored. Is laid in-situ as as pro-cast tiles. Is harmed by alkalis and acid. The application of self-polishing emulsions can help to prevent slipperiness and is used in cloak-rooms, staircases and kitchens. Marble is a special form of rock mainly found in Italy, and may be white, black, green or brown in colour and when used for flooring is normally laid in slab form and is very expensive. Terrazzo, being only chippings of marble is much cheaper. The application of self-polishing emulsions can help prevent slipperiness and terrazzo is used in foyer, cloakrooms and kitchens.

Advantages

1. Removal pro-cast slabs can be made to cover service pipes for casa of maintenance. Coved edges facilitate cleaning.
2. They are not affected by water and may have a drain incorporated.
3. They are durable.
4. They are vermin proof, impervious to dry rot and fire resistant.
5. Cleaning is relatively easy.
6. The cost of terrazzo is higher than that of granolithic.

Disadvantages:

1. They are hard and noisy.
2. Terrazzo is slippery when wet.
3. They are cold in appearance.
4. Cracks may appear.
5. Terrazzo the marble chippings may become loose.
6. Terrazzo is adversely affected by acids and strong alkalis.

Care And Cleaning:

1. Clean regularly.
2. Avoid strong alkalis on terrazzo.
3. Attend cracks and loose clippings.

Marble Flooring

It is a special kind of rock mainly found in Italy and in India, Rajas than and Madhya Pradesh. It is available in green, brown, black and white. Marble floorings are laid in slab form. Some marble has small cavities in it, which offer slip resistance but allow dust and dirt to accumulate. Other stone floorings are sand stone, quartzite and slate.

Magnesite Flooring

It consists of wood flour and others fillers mixed with burnt magnesite and laid "in situ" or in the form of small blocks. This finish is extremely porous and washing should be avoided whenever possible. It is harmed by water, most chemicals and coarse abrasive. It is moderately warm in appearance and the initial cost is low.

Advantages:

1. It is moderately warm.
2. It has good appearance.
3. Cleaning is relatively easy.
4. The initial cost is low.

Disadvantages:

1. It is hard and rather noisy.
2. There is little choice of colour.
3. It is slippery when polished.
4. It is harmed by water, acids, alkalis and abrasives.

Cleaning and Care:

1. Clean regularly.
2. Avoid frequent washing.

Ceramics Tiles

It is a clayware available in a variety of qualities, colour and sizes. Quarry tiles are made from a natural type of clay, often of several blends, and are fired under pressure to make them hard and durable and less absorbent.

Advantages

1.	Removable pre-cast slabs can be made to cover service pipes for case of maintenance.
2.	Coved edges facilitate cleaning.
3.	They are not affected by water and may have a drain incorporated.
4.	Many qualities, colours and sizes are available.
5.	Ridged and abrasive surfaced tiles are available which are less slippery.
6.	They are not affected by acids, alkalis or grease.
7.	They are durable; repairs are not very frequent and one loose tile may be reset or replaced.
8.	They are vermin proof, impervious to dry rot and fire resistant.
9.	Cleaning is relatively easy.
	Disadvantages
1.	They are hard and noisy.
2.	They are cold in appearance.
3.	They are slippery when wet or greasy.
4.	They may crack or break with heavy weights.

5.	Marks are difficult to remove if left.
6.	The initial cost is average.
Care And Cleaning	
1.	Clean regularly
2.	Attend to loose and broken tiles.

Semi Hard/ Resilient Floors

They are also available in tile/sheet form/and sometimes, PVC floors are laid in situ, proved over the prepared surface in a thick viscous liquid.

Cork tiles are made from granulated cork, moulded into blocks, which are subjected to pressure and high temperature. During this process the natural resins bind the granules, and the blocks are then cut into tiles of the required size and the required thickness, usually % in. V2 cm. Variations in the brown colour of the tiles 'result from the different amounts of pressure and heat to which the blocks are subjected. Owing to their absorbent nature, they are normally sealed and/or polished. They can be used in offices, corridors, bathrooms and as surrounds to carpets.

Advantages:

1. It has a warm appearance.

2. It is quick and non-slip.

3. It is possible to sand down and expose a new surface.

4. If sealed, cleaning is easy.

Disadvantages:

1. Unless sealed, it is absorbent and pot easily cleaned.

2. Granules become loosened and can be lost.

3. It bums.

Rubber Flooring

These are obtainable in tile and sheet form. During the manufacturing process, rubber with filling materials and pigments is VULCANIZED (heated out of contact with air) to give hard finish to make it durable and colorful. It is soft, quiet and resilient. Spirit, grease, sunlight, alkalis and coarse abrasives harm it. They should be laid in a suitable adhesive to a smooth sub floor, and may be left unprotected or polished with a water-based polish. They are used in bars, entrance halls, bathrooms, etc. Rubber can be used for an infinite variety of mats and mattings and are found in places where protection is required for the floor beneath. The door mats, mats in front of service lifts and hosing on stairs may therefore be made of rubber.

Advantages:

1. It is warm and comfortable to walk on.

2. It has good appearance.

3. A variety of colours are available.

4. It is durable.

5. It is non-absorbent and second only to carpet for sound absorption.

Disadvantages:

1. It is slippery when wet.

2. It is harmed by spirit, grease, sunlight and coarse abrasives.

3. It marks badly, especially with rubber heels.

4. The initial cost is high.

Care And Cleaning:

1. Clean regularly.

2. Use water based and not spirit based polish.

Linoleum

This type consists of a mixture of cork in powdered form, resin, linseed oil and pigments for colour, put in a foundation of jute and canvas and subjected to heat and pressure. The product is passed through polishing rollers and further heated to make it non-absorbent. It is possible to obtain factory sealed linoleum.

The thickness of the surface layer varies with the quality, and may be for heavy duty, 4-6 mm thick and for less heavy duty, 2-4 mm thick. In good quality linoleum the colour and pattern are inlaid, example, right through to the backing, whereas in cheap quantities it may only be printed on the surface and so wears off. Linoleum may be bought in rolls usually 2 yards wide, or in tiles. The tiles are always stuck down while the rolls may be stuck or laid loosely. In sheet form linoleum is liable to stretch, and unless stuck down, requires trimming after 2-3 weeks before pinning. Linoleum may be sealed and/or polished and is used in many places, for example, linen rooms, staff bedrooms, offices, corridors, bathrooms, canteens, etc.

Cork carpet has much greater proportion of cork than ordinary linoleum, and the cork granules are larger which makes it softer and quieter to thread.

Advantages:

1. There are many colours and designs.

2. It can be laid on any sub floor provided this is dry, smooth and even.

3. If well laid and stuck down, it resists moisture.

4. It is durable.

5. It may be patched or a tile removed and replaced.

Disadvantages:

1. It can be slippery if over polished.

2. It is harmed by alkalis and coarse abrasives.

3. Indentations occur with heavy furniture.

4. Broken castors may tear the surface.

Care and cleaning:

1. Clean regularly.

2. Avoid scrubbing, use of alkalis and coarse abrasives

Thermoplastic Flooring

The floor tiles are made from a variety of asphaltic binders with inert fillers and pigment. They are rigid tiles usually 9 inches square shape and laid on a smooth rigid surface, set as closely together as possible with an approved adhesive. These are non-porous, but strong alkalis will remove their surface rendering them porous. They are also harmed by grease and spirit. They are laid in a warm, pliable state (thermoplastic) but harden on cooling and may be carried up the wall to form a small coved skirting. They may be polished with a water-based polish, and are used in bathrooms, cloakrooms, corridors, offices etc.

Advantages:

1. A great variety of colours are available.

2. They are cold in appearance.

3. Cleaning is relatively easy.

Disadvantages :

1. They are hard and tend to be noisy.

2. Some are cold in appearance.

3. They are slippery when wet.

4. They are harmed-by-spirit, grease - and coarse abrasives.

5. They dent with heavy weights and soften with heat.

6. Scratchesofecourt with grit and sharp edges.

7. They mark -badly^tdspeOidlly- withgrubber-heelss. menus, and heating habits, hat has been going on for hundreds of years still continues. Changes

Care And Cleaning:

your reactions to culinary traditions.

1. Clean Regularly.

, TT na. forces can be seen at. work throughout the history of cooking. One

. se wa er <bs]ed<andnno|ospirJStPasedpoish', and instead to emphasize th<

Replace loose or brokfen-tilesi as -soon- ast-possible invent, to highlight d

\/T\Tvi t?t accent on fancier, more complicated presentations and pr V'RINGi d and healthy; they continually refresh and renew the art of eookina

It is also made of PVC and similar synthetic resins, inert fillers and pigments. The greater the amount <of vinyl in the < flooring We -g^atef mistMc^ t^ -welt grease, scratching and indentation to the point of load. Under this type comes vinyl asbestos in which the fillers include short fibred asbestos (obtainable only in tile form), flexible vinyl in plasticizers are added to make it flexible (obtainable only in shoot form O and are usually used in different places like bathrooms, corridors. canteens, bedrooms, offices and hospitals. It is available in di'es or sheet form when it is sometimes mounted on canvas or some other suitable backing material. There are coved skirtings available and the sheet material may be used in bathrooms, cloakrooms, corridors, canteens and offices.

Advantages:

1. They are relatively non-slip.

2. They have great resistance to wear, especially the flexible type.

3. They are generally grease and oil resistant.

4. They are resistant to acids and alkalis.

5. They have a greater resistance to point loads than the thermoplastic tiles.

6. They are not easily scratched.

7. They are easily washed and polished.

Disadvantages:

1. They are affected by cigarette bums, especially the flexible vinyl floorings.

Care and Cleaning:

1. Clean Regularly

Each of these materials has their advantages and disadvantages. According to the type of flooring the cleaning must be done regularly in a methodical way. To make the maintenance easy, most of the floor softer cleaning and drying are sprayed and sealed with a special type of transparent resin containing chemical which gives the top a smooth, shiny, glossy surface, which is easy to clean. The scaling has to be done by experts and repeated after intervals. When the seal becomes cracked or chipped. Before re-scaling certain chemicals are used to clean away the old scaling and then again on the clean dry surface the process is repeated.

Hardwearing floors of kitchen, workshop, pantry etc. require hard, durable, washable floors. The semi-hard floors may get a depression by heavy weight though they are warmer, comfortable and colourful than the hard floors. They are used in corridors, library, linen room, offices and other places of less wear and tear.

Some of the polishes used for floors are solvent-based polish, which should not be used on semi-hard floors. Water based wax pc lishes are better for semi-hard floors. Polymer type of water emulsion may be chosen for a wider variety. The floor stripping-agent has to be chosen with care.

Wall And Wall Coverings

Walls are supporting the roof of any building and the inlets und outlets leading to the room and out are positioned on the wall. It gives lighting and ventilation into the room and for the safety of the inhabitants the inlets and outlets, i.e. the doors, windows, skylight, ventilators are properly guarded against burglars and undesirable admittance. Sometimes fly and mosquito/proofing and screening is done. Some of the walls are made of special type of glass to frame the scenery outdoors, and give a good view to the room and becomes part of the decor.

For wall cupboard, shelves and built in furniture, the planning of the wall has to be of a special type and planned during the construction.

Certain areas near the airport etc. may have greater sound pollution. To avoid that, a special type of wall is built in two layers keeping a gap in between to make it more sound resistant. The bricks used for the wall-may be of various types and sometimes according to the interior decor a good quality of brick is used with only "pain ng" and no cement covering. Plastered walls may have vai aus types of finishes. Before applying any of them the wall has to be prepared well i.e. it has to be clean, smooth, dry and damp proof.

Following are some of the common varieties of wall finishes used :

- **Paint**

Paint is used extensively as a decorative wall finish, but it is also used to preserve and protect structural surfaces.

- **White Washing**

Special type of lime is soaked in water with blue and glue and applied on the wall which has been prepared in thin layers of at least three coats one after the other had dried. This is also known as line wash. It is disinfecting and cheapest method of finishing.

- **Emulsion Paint**

Are water-thinned but are based on dispersions of synthetic resins (polyvinyl acetate) which dry to tough, washable and wear resistant films. Emulsion paints are available in a wide range of colors and various degrees of sheen from Matt to semi-gloss or silk finish, but then silk finishes are not recommended on bumpy walls and ceilings where a high level of light reflection can be unpleasant.

- **Alkyd Paint**

Alkyd paints are based on synthetic resin combined with a vegetable oil, such as linseed oil.

Alkyd paints are generally easier to apply and have better durability and wearing properties then the older types. Alkyd paints are available as gloss, silk and flat finishes.

- **Multicolour Paints**

These paints are usually dispersions of cellulose colours in water. Each colour is present in a "blobs" or "spots". Usually this type of paint must be spray-applied. Corridors, staircases, cloakrooms are the ideal places for this kind of paint.

Texture or plastic paints are usually plaster-based and are intended to give a textured effect on the surface. The texture is obtained by working over the material after application and, while it is still wet, using combs, palette knives etc.

- **Microporous Paints**

These paints have a rubberized base, which give little gloss but offers elasticity, allowing movement when the surface expands or contracts.

- **Distempering**

It is parallel to lime wash except that the special distemper powder containing pigments and building agents are dissolved into a solution and applied in the similar way with a finer brush.

- **Mural or Wall Painting**

A portion of the wall in a strategic place may be specially treated for painting scenery as in a canvas specially textures may also be given and according to the choice of the artist and interior decorator a befitting scene is painted. Such walls should have special lighting system to attract eyes and show it clearly.

- **Glass or Mirrors**

Glass can be used in the form of decorative tiles, sometimes in the form of mosaics. Colored opaque glass sheets or tiles may be used as a wall covering in the hotel bathrooms. Glass as a wall covering is often used in the form of mirror tiles to reflect light and form the wall itself. Mirrors are used not only for utility but to introduce grandeur and space into the room. The framing may be of different types, wood and metal carving, but must be kept spotlessly clean, A glass-less mirror is available now which has the advantage of not misting up or shattering and is about one-fifth of the weight of a conventional mirror.

- **Wall Papering**

Wall-papers may vary in length and width. The price varies enormously. Wall - paper may be smooth or have textured effect. The pattern of wall paper may be floral, geometric abstract, striped etc. The choice of wall-paper, depend on the aspect, height, size and use of the room. May be of various types. These days plastic coated washable wallpapers are also available. They may come in different colors and design and color and depicting a scene. Usually they are purchased in rolls one side of which is glued. This is moistened and attached on to the prepared wall with a roller presser, to avoid any air bubble.

0 Wallpaper have a warmer appearance 0 Are not normally applied on new walls.

0 Offer some sound insulation.

0 Become soiled, scratched and torn with abrasion.

0 Patterned and textured paper-cover blemishes.

Various Types of Wallpaper Are :

- Ordinary surface printed papers
- Spongeable papers : specially treated during manufacture to withstand water.
- Anaglypta: which has an embossed or raised pattern. It is white and normally painted over.
- Wood chip papers which have inter-layered chips of wood, it is cream in colour.
- Oatmeal papers, where texture is produced by the inter-laying of wood dust, chopped Straw or similar material during manufacture.
- Flock papers, which are treated with adhesive to which silk, wool, cotton or synthetic fibres stick to give a raised pile
- Wood grain papers: Photographic reproduction of various wood grains waxed during manufacture.
- Metallic papers Printed with gold and other metallic powders.
- Paper- backed hessians, which give a rough textured effect and are available in different colours.
- Paper backed felts.
- Paper backed woven grasses or similar materials in beautiful natural colours.
- Paper-backed wools, with fine or course strands of wool in natural colours or bright dyes laid parallel fashion on a paper backing.
- Other paper-becked mate ials, including silks, linen, suede, and veneers of cork and wood.
- Lincrusta; a paper-backed textured composition, frequently simulating wood paneling.

Surface Board. Melamine Is The Resin In This Kind, And May Simulate Wood Paneling or Fabrics, E.G. Formica, Etc.

Plastic Wall Covering

It is very hard wearing and can afford some sound insulation and is also easily cleaned. They are obtainable in variety of sizes, with a great price range. As they are non-porous there is a greater tendency for the growth of moulds so the adhesives should contain fungicides or fungicidal wash may be given to the wall before hanging the plastic wall covering.

The Main Types of Plastic Wall Covering Are:

Paper-backed vinyl-where the vinyl may have the appearance of almost any material, eg. silk, tweed, hessian, cork, grass-paper, wood, stone or brick.

Fabric-backed vinyl - Similar in appearance to the above and even more durable.

Vinyl flock papers. Plastic wall tiles - Intimating ceramic tiles.

Laminated plastic - As a veneer

Expanded Polystyrene - In sheet or tile form, used on walls to give heat and sound solution and to eliminate condensation. It can be with emulsion paint.

Fabric Wall Covering

It is possible to cover the wall with any fabric and its durability will depend on the fibre and weave used in its manufacture. Fabrics chosen should be liable to sag buckle or stretch when hung permanently on a wall and should not collect excess dust and dirt. Wild silk and other fabrics may be padded for heat and sound insulation and put on the wall. Tapestry may be used on the wall i.e. a woven fabric when used on the wall usually depicts a scene and hangs loosely on the wall.

Wood Panelling

Woods used for paneling are usually hard, well seasoned and a decorative appearance, and they may cover the wall completely or form a dado. Wood panelling may be solid or veneered. Wood, veneers may be stuck to paper, giving a similar effect of solid wood at much less cost and maintenance. Wood paneling may be found in such places as entrance halls, staircases, assembly halls, board-rooms and restaurants.

Wall Carpets

They are usually silk, beautifully designed wall hanging, which should be cleaned periodically to maintain its beauty.

Matting

Grass, cane; jute, coconut fibre etc. used. Leather and animal skins are used for soundproofing.

Metal Wall Coverings

Metals may be used for their decorative and their hygienic qualities. Metals such as copper and anodized aluminum and decorative and may be used for effect in such areas as bars, where bottles and metals may give a special effect.

Carpets

Carpets are used-extensively in all types of establishments because of:

> Their appearance - resistance to wear and tear.

> Warmth and comfort

> Safety factor

> Sound insulation

A good carpet should keep its colour, not flatten unduly with heavy furniture and with stand the expected wear and tear of traffic and spillages. In general, carpets consists of a backing o foundation and a surface pile which may be cut or uncut. This is normally made from jute or cotton threads. Wool has been the main fibre for many years because:

> It has resilience (pliability)

> It can with stand abrasion (wear & tear)

> It feels warm and gives comfort

> It does not soil or ignite easily/readily

> It retains it's appearance well if properly maintained

Now days, due to the varying properties of fibres, carpets are made with blended fibres so as to get the best qualities. Some examples are:

a. Wool/Nylon (80/20)

b. Acrylic / Rayon (50/50)

c. Wool / Evlan / Nylon (45/40/15)

Carpet Construction
The key factors that help in assessing carpets include :
a. **Construction-** it refers to:

> The type of surface, usually called the pile or the face yams.

> How these yams are anchored to the backing.

> The type of backings

b. **Pile density-** this refers to the number of yams (yam is the fibre used in the making of fabrics, it could be made from animal, vegetable or man-made/synthetic fibres). DENSITY = 36 X

Face Weight: Pile Height

The 36 indicates the number of inches, that is one yard, the face weight is the number of tufts. So, 1/8 gauge means that there are eight tufts across the inch. Pitch is a density indicator for woven carpets. It refers to the number of warp or lengthwise yams in a 27-inch width of carpet.

c. **Pile height-** this refers to the height of the yams, the smaller the height, the stronger the carpet, and vice versa. The heavier the carpet, the better it will withstand heavy traffic.

d. **Fibres-** this refers to the threads obtained for the making of a carpet. Threads can be obtained from vegetable, animal, of man-made sources like for example :

> Vegetable fibre - cotton, jute, sisal, hemp, coconut choir, etc.

> Animal fibre - wool, silk, camel, etc.

> Synthetic/man-made fibre - nylon, rayon, terycotton, polyester, etc.

a. **Resilience -** this refers to how quickly the yarn springs back after being compressed. If the carpets are not resilient enough, it will become permanently crushed in certain areas and show a fast wearing walk pattern.

b. **Backing -** this refers to the material to which the yams are attached. Carpets have a primary backing, which is the actual underside of the carpeting, and usually a secondary backing, which is bonded on for additional strength.

Manufacture of Carpets

Manufacturer of carpets	**Woven**	**Wiltons Carpets -** These can be made in both plain and patterned varieties. The patter is controlled by a special device (a jacquard) on the loom and this enables one coloured thread at a time to be drawn up as pile, while the remaining threads, 'deads' are hidden in the backing of the carpet. It is unusual for there to be more than 5 colours because more would mean a great deal of wastage of pile yams carried along the backing. They have a firm, smooth back with streaks of colour in it where the particular threads are not required as surface piles. The pile is cut and close, often made from wool/nylon (80/20), it may vary in length, even in the same carpet, which results in a textured appearance.
		Plain wilton carpets are made on a similar loom to the patterned, but without jacquard, and extra jute threads, known as stuffers, fill the back of the carpet instead of the hidden threads, 'deads'.

		Brussels Carpets - Brussels and cord carpets are variations of the wilton weave in which the pile is uncut, i.e. looped. Brussels is an uncut patterned wilton and cord is an uncut plain wilton. The latter was originally made from hair cord, i.e. made from a mixture of hair fibres from horses, goats or cows, but it now frequently has rayon or cotton added, which makes it not so hardwearing but is cheaper. Brussels carpets are more hard wearing then wilton carpets; because looped or uncut pile carpets give 5-10% more wear than cut pile carpets but lack the softness/ resilience as in the case of cut pile carpets.
		Axministers Carpets - these carpets are woven in such a way that the pile is almost entirely on the surface and the backing has a distinctive rib, no dead threads are carried in the backing and the pile is longer and less close than in wilton, Types of axminister carpets are spool (it can have unlimited no. of colours in the design), gripper (it can accommodate only 8 no. of colours), and chenille (is French for caterpillar, in this case the pile is produced first as a long strip rather like a furry caterpillar, and during weaving of the actual carpet, the catcher thread attaches these strips of pile to the backing. The result is a soft, thick carpet with unlimited colours and designs).
		Oriental Carpets - these are hand woven from the middle & far east. The pile may be of wool, silk or a mixture of these and is made by the individual worker knotting lengths of yam to the cotton warp threads of the handloom. Examples of oriental carpets are Persian (these are rugs made as tapestry wall & floor coverings), Indian (these were made from coarser, longer pile than other carpets), Chinese (they have a close silky pile with a well-defined pattern).
		Tufted Carpets - these are produced by a Non-woven much faster and cheaper process than weaving. 100% synthetic fibres and blends with wool are used in the making of these carpets. The pile yam is inserted into a pre-woven backing by a long row of needles and a loop is formed. This may be left uncut or cut. Mixtures of high and low piles, cut and looped areas may be found in the same carpet. The pile is firmly held to the backing material by an application of natural/synthetic rubber adhesive, on top of this a secondary backing of hessian is added to give the carpet body and to prevent stretching and buckling.
		Pile Bonded Carpets - these have a pile of nylon or polypropylene, which is struck: into PVC backing. The dense pile has a firm anchorage and the carpets do not fray, seams can be bonded and the carpet can be stuck to the floor.

		Needle Punched Carpets - these are resin impregnated or heat-treated materials used in sheet or tile form. A thick web of nylon, polypropylene, acrylic or polyester fibres used as 100%, or as blends, is fed into the needling sector of the machine. By the reciprocating movement of several rows of barbed needles, which penetrate the web, the fibres are entangled and consolidated. Often a supporting fabric (a scrim of polypropylene or jute) is fed along with the web into the needling machine and the fibres are pushed through the fabric, giving dimensional stability. The needled product is then heat treated or impregnated with a resin, compressed and finally dried. Coarse denier fibres are used for needle-punched products used for sports facilities.
		Electrostatically Flocked Carpets - these are produced by projecting electrically charged fibres downwards into an adhesive-coated backing material. Straight nylon fibres are locked by molecular bonding into a glass fibre reinforced vinyl backing. The 'nylon 66' fibres are round, smooth, non-hollow and closely packed, hardwearing, easy to clean and quick to dry. The vinyl base is completely waterproof and the carpet is anti-static under normal conditions. These carpets may be used in wet areas like cloakrooms, canteens, entrances, waiting rooms, etc. Flotex tiles have an extra heavy-duty backing, which ensures that they stay flat and are suitable for loose laying. They are anti-static.

Various Methods of Fixing Carpets

- ❖ Glued - the carpet may be stuck to the sub-floor.
- ❖ Tackless Gripper - steel pins protrude out from the plywood, or metal strips fixed to the floor or stairs and hold the carpet in place.
- ❖ Turn & Tack - the edge of the carpet is turned under and tacked through the double surface thus lifting the carpet is difficult.
- ❖ Sunken - the carpet is laid in a sunken area, the edges of which are covered with brass or wood as for sunken front door mats.
- ❖ Pin & Socket / Press Studs / Touch & Close Fasteners - these methods are especially suitable where a carpet needs lifting frequently, e.g. banqueting rooms cleared for dancing.

Cleaning of Carpets is Necessary in Order to :

- ❖ Remove dirt, grit and other soiling.
- ❖ Remove stains as soon as possible.
- ❖ Prevent damage by moths and carpet beetles.
- ❖ Retain the original appearance of the carpet as long as possible

Cleaning of Carpets

Daily Cleaning of Carpets:

This would remove superficial dust and crumbs by the use of a carpet sweeper. Grit and other soiling, which has gone into the pile, is removed by suction (using a vacuum cleaner).

Special Cleaning of Carpets:

During special cleaning, the edges of the carpets are cleaned using a damp duster, carpet brush or a vacuum cleaner. Cleaning is done in all 4 directions of the fibres so as to remove maximum dirt and grit from within the piles.

Periodic Cleaning of Carpets:

This involves deep cleaning of the carpets and after thorough vacuum cleaning one of the following methods, may be used:

Shampooing Hot Water Extraction Dry Foam Extraction

When shampooing, the detergent solution is released from a tank on the rotary scrubbing machine and the surface of the carpet is slightly scrubbed, and then left to dry. Finally the loosened soiling and detergent residue is picked up by suction.

The Following Points Must be Observed:

- The detergent used should be one, which dries to a powder so that a sticky residue is not left on the carpet.
- Excess water should be avoided so that the backing of the carpet does not become too wet.
- Each stroke of the brushes should overlap the previous one.
- No metal, e.g. castors or legs of furniture should come in contact with the damp carpet.
- Walking and replacement of furniture on the damp carpet should be avoided.

Hot water extraction machines are expensive machines with no rotary action. Hot water and the detergent are 'shot' into the carpet with high pressure spay nozzles. The dirt is flushed to the surface and the soiled water is picked up by the suction action of the machine. There is a tank for the hot detergent solution and another for the soiled water. The advantage of this machine over the rotary shampooing machine is that drying time is cut to a minimum.

In dry foam extraction, the cylindrical brush type machine lays down a moist foam, brushes it in and immediately extracts the soil-laden foam with a built-in vacuum head located behind the power brush.

Different Types of Machines Used For Cleaning Carpets :

- Carpet sweepers - suitable for level carpets with a low pile height.
- Electric brooms - gets into smaller places and under beds.
- Upright vacuum cleaner
- Shampooing machine
- Hot water extraction machine

❖ Dry foam extraction machine

Advantages of Carpets:

a. Carpets add to the decorative appearance of the room.

b. They can give a luxurious appearance and feel.

c. They are warm and may keep out draughts.

d. They are quiet and afford some sound insulation.

e. They are non-slip.

f. Carpet squares and rugs break up a floor surface and can be turned around, fitted carpets make a room look larger and there is only one floor surface to clean.

g. Patterned carpets do not show stains as much as plain ones.

Disadvantages of Carpets:

a. The surface holds dirt, so careful cleaning is necessary.

b. They are cut by grit and sharp castors and some are burned or melted by cigaretto ends.

c. They may be attacked by moth, if made of wool.

d. Shading can occur. E Fitted carpets show definite areas of wear.

e. Plain carpets show stains readily and stains can be difficult to remove.

f. A large pattern for a fitted carpet is extravagant because of the need to match the pattern.

g. Initial cost of good carpet is high.

Lighting

Daylight

Only about 10% of normal daylight enters a room. In spite of this it is brighter than artificial light. Colours look different in daylight and in artificial light. Daylight varies in intensity and colour throughout the day. Most building needs additional artificial light even during the hours of daylight.

Advantages of Daylight Light:

a. It costs nothing except the cost of providing windows.

b. It is natural.

c. Because it varies according to the time of the day, it is soothing and kinder to the human eye, and possibly causes less fatigue than a constant uniform artificial light.

Disadvantages of Daylight:

a. The variation in the strength of daylight can change the mood or atmosphere of the environment.

b. Brilliant sunshine fades some colours and rots some materials.

c. The heat from the sun rays can cause discomfort.

d. Daylight varies with the aspect of the windows and furnishings should be selected accordingly.

The hotel is an institution important to everyone traveling as it performs the basic function of providing food and comfortable accommodation to the traveler whether on business or holiday. Lighting plays a very important part in the comfort and safety of the occupants of the building.

Good lighting should be in harmony with the function in the area of which it is intended. Lighting is a means to end and the end is to light up the area in the most decorative, practical and efficient way. It is a well-known fact that without light, they have no visual significance, unless there is no As light rays strike a surface, they are either absorbed or reflected. The colour and Texture of the substance upon which the light rays full determine the reflective qualities.

A Good Lighting Design is Realized if:

- All spaces (entry; transition, work areas and exist) are properly composed in a clear of importance and purpose.
- Make it possible to see quickly without strain.
- The lighting mood is consistent with the function and design of each space. It is pleasing to the eye.
- It promotes productivity.

- ❖ Eliminates hazards.
- ❖ It is readily maintainable.
- ❖ It is energy effective.
- ❖ It has fully utilized the potential of daylight when it is available.

Light levels are measured in lumens and lux. The amount of light given out by a light source is measured in lumens, but some of this light is lost, as it becomes absorbed by mist, dirty fittings, coloured shades, dark coloured furnishings, and distance. All these factors mean that the amount of usable light which reaches the working surface is often very different from that which leaves the light source. Therefore a lumen is a unit for measuring the quantity of light emitted at the source, and lux is the measure of requirement for a fire certificate.

Light is a form of energy that enables the eye to see. It can be natural from the sun or artificial from the lamps. Lighting plays an important role in creating the right atmosphere with in an area. It should be decorative and functional. The amount of light required in an area depends on the function of the area and the colours used in furnishing and floor coverings.

The Effect of Lighting on Interior Decoration Are :

- ❖ Dark colour absorb light.
- ❖ Light colours reflect light.
- ❖ It can reveal features of construction.
- ❖ Create impression of space.
- ❖ Conceal space by areas in shadows.
- ❖ High light pictures, statues, floral decorations etc.
- ❖ Gives background to furnishings.
- ❖ It can dramatize colour and texture.

To Satisfy the Guest And The Management, Light Fittings Should be :

1. Well positioned.
2. Emit light in the direction required and the right quantity of light should be emitted.
3. Pleasant to look at whether lit or unlit.
4. Well made, durable, mechanically sound and electrically safe.
5. Not prone to over heating.
6. Easily cleanable.

Plays key role in creating the right atmosphere in a room. I should be decorative and functional. It should contribute to the character and the atmosphere of a room and be adequate for general lighting and bright illumination.

Types of Lighting

1. Direct
2. Indirect
3. Defused
4. Semi indirect lighting
5. General lighting
1. Reflected lighting
2. Spot lighting
3. Directional lighting

1. Direct lighting does not require any shade. It is suitable for giving complete illumination. The light is thrown on to the ceilings and walls from where it is reflected.

2. In Direct has a partial shade.

3. Defused lighting breaks up the light when passed through glass.

4. Semi indirect has some light passing through a diffusing bowl and some is a mix of 2 and 3, giving not a very bright feature to the room. Examples of lighting include tube lights, compact fluorescent bulbs, wall shades, lampshades, bed fights, night-lights, and-angle posed lamps, down lighters and up lighters.

Methods of Lightings:

Architectural lighting-cove, comice, soffit, luminous, spot lighting

Non-Architectural lighting-ceiling and wall fixtures, portable lamps, chandeliers etc.

Various Areas Require Different Types of Lightings:

1. Valance lighting - a horizontal fluorescent tube is placed behind a valance board casting upward light which reflects off the ceiling and then down that shines on the drapery, thus producing both direct (downward light) and indirect (up ward light) lighting.

2. Cove lighting - it consists of placing a continuous series of fluorescent tubes in a grove or trough placed on one or more walls of a room about 12 inches from the ceiling. This enables the light to be thrown on the ceiling and then in the room.

3. Comice lighting - a comice is installed at the ceiling and directs the light downwards only. It can give a dramatic effect on drapery, wall coverings and pictures also emphasizing on ceiling height.

4. Soffit lighting this refers to the underside panel of a built in light source.

5. Entrance halls should be bright and be able to attract the attention of the guests especially at the lobby and reception desk. Therefore chandeliers and comice lighting would be suitable in which the light is reflected from the ceiling

6. Luminous or recessed, used primarily for kitchens, utility areas and bathrooms.

7. Mirrors on the ceiling reflect light and gives an impression of greater height.

8. Various F&B outlets will cater to a definite clientele and therefore the type & intensity of lighting will vary. E.g. a cafeteria requires a quick turnover therefore their should be high degree of illumination especially at the food counter and tables - fluorescent lamps, pendent fittings or panel lights may be used. In a restaurant - subdued lighting is more usual, through table lamps or candles may also be used. Higher general lighting can be used for public functions in banquet halls and luncheons etc.

9. Staircases should be will lit to prevent accidents therefore lights should be set into the stair itself or along the wall. Two-way switches should be used as it can be operated from 2 places.

10. Guest rooms and bedrooms do not require general lighting but there should be adequate light in different parts of a room like a bed side lamp, dressing table light, corridor passage lights, etc. two-way switches can be used so as to work from door and bed.

11. Bathrooms should have vapor proof fittings, the position of the light by the mirror should be such that the face is lit adequately. The switches should be preferably outside wall of the bathroom area.

Factors to consider when planning a lighting system :

The following areas require the following amount of lighting :

Reception - 300 lux

Halls - 150 lux

Stairs - 100 lux

Landings -150 lux

Dining rooms - 100 lux

Food preparation areas - 150-200 lux

Bedrooms - 50 100 lux

Reading lamps - 150 lux

Bathroom - 100 lux

Mirror - 150 lux

Writing tables - 300 lux

General overall lighting - 50 lux

Lighting contributes a great % [a major %] to the interior, decor of the room. Now a days low energy bulbs and low voltage bulbs are being used to decorate corridors, elevators etc. where heavy lighting is not required at all times.

Fillings and Shades

Many electric lamps particularly filament ones are needed to be concealed. Filament lamps are ones in which, once the bulb gets fused, it has to be replaced. It cannot be used again and again. Lamps generally provide soft lighting. Shades used could be of glass, plastics, fabrics or even metal. Some of these materials tend to fade, discolour air become ruined by the heat. Shades and fittings should be used in conjunction with the interior decor. It should also be pleasing to look at whether lit or unlit. Shades may be dusted or suction cleaned.

To Satisfy The Guest The Management of Light Fittings Should Be

1. Well positioned.

2. Emit light in the direction and quantity required.

3. Pleasant to look at whether lit or unlit.

4. Well made, durable, mechanically sound and electrically safe.

5. Not prone to over heating.

6. (7) Easily replaceable and cleaned.

Lighting May be Used in Interior Decoration For:

1. Revealing the structure of the room.

2. Creating space.

3. Acting as focal point.

4. Accentuate (enhancing) colour and texture.

5. High lighting pictures, statues, floral decorations etc.

6. Giving a background.

7. Dramatizing colour and texture.

Heating and Ventilation

The comfort of the human body is dependant on its being surrounded by moving air of a suitable temperature, humidity and is important that the conditions should be produced with the minimum amount of cost and inconvenience. An individual requires the following suitable conditions - a temperature between 15-20°C, relative humidity between 40-60%, and not less than $2.800m^3$ of fresh air per person.

Recommended Standards of Warmth are :

Lounges Bed room General offices Public areas Bathroom and toilets

20 to 21 degrees centigrade

13 to 16 degrees centigrade

20 degrees centigrade

13 o 18 degrees centigrade

18 degrees centigrade

In most of the hotel areas ventilation is a must for common odours to evaporate. Bedroom and lounges are ventilated naturally by the use of windows, but bathrooms, cloakrooms, store rooms, kitchen etc require some mechanical means to introduce fresh air and extract stale air.

Extractors help promote fresh air in the rooms.

In most establishments there is some form of central heating and cooling, which includes fuels like oil, coal, gas, steam etc. All these cause pollution. The occupants of a room contribute continuously to the temperature and humidity of the room. Where there are a large number of people, several changes of air per hour may be necessary. In these circumstances, the department of health recommends the number of changes per hour of air as follows :

20 to 60 per hour

6 and 2 per hour

5 to 10 (depends on climate)

In modem establishments the A/c plants are installed in such a manner that it provides for minimum pollution. Ventilation and heating in any hotel assumes drastic proportions,

1. Kitchen
2. Bathroom and cloak room
3. Bedrooms

Especially when furniture and other equipment (electrical) are involved, example, computers not being kept in a cool environment may result in subsequent breakages. Extreme humidity in bedrooms may result in wooden furniture having the problems of white ants and termites, ultimately resulting in crumbing of the furniture.

Hotels generally have strict norms for humidity control, and as a result of this, most of the equipment is rendered free from effect of extreme heat, cold. Heating and ventilation though not the most important, play a very important role in the look of general surroundings. A large number of plants in a room will automatically flush up stale air in the room. Ventilation helps promote a sense of work atmosphere, efficiency, productivity. Ventilation in keeping with hotel requirements should be properly followed, in all service areas, to ensure first class service to the guest.

Energy Saving

Space heating accounts for 45% of total energy spent in an establishment, half of which is lost by transmission through - walls, windows, roof, flooring of the building, etc. Therefore energy may be saved by taking precautions like :

- Using thick curtains/drape curtains.
- Using well-fitted carpets as they produce extra warmth and insulation.
- Close fitting doors and windows in the guest rooms and entrance lobbies.
- Sealing the edges of the windows.
- Putting reflective materials behind the radiators.
- Use of thermostats on radiators.
- Controlling the temperature of domestic hot water, i.e. 40-45°C for bathrooms and 60°C for kitchens.

- ❖ Encouraging the use of showers.
- ❖ Use of spray taps in cloakrooms as less water is used than in the case of normal flow taps.
- ❖ Good maintenance of taps, heating and dish washing equipments so that no wastage of energy takes place.

Planning And Organizing

People involved during the construction of the housekeeping department:

1. Sales and marketing Manager.
2. Chief Engineer.
3. General Manager.
4. Resident Manager.
5. Director of F&B.
6. Executive housekeeper, Front office, etc.

Points, which are considered in selection of material to facilitate ease of movement, cleaning, personnel required, cost of cleaning.

Areas to be considered for the layout are lobbies, guest rooms, restaurant, conference halls, swimming pools, back areas, back office, locker rooms.

Storage areas like floor pantries, room service pantries and storage space for maintenance department.

The landscaping of the property is undertaken by the horticulture department.

Planning And Organizing The Housekeeping Department

An executive, housekeeper may be involved in a soon to open operation in which, Department planning has yet to be undertaken. This will give the manager the opportunity to influence how a department will be set up.

The Housekeeper is normally appointed only a few weeks before opening. It is necessary for him/her to set priorities i.e. planning, organizing and staffing functions are of first importance, then the design systems, establishment of procedures, determination of supply and equipment needs and reporting and coordinating relationships must be considered.

Identifying Housekeeping Responsibilities

The work that must actually be accomplished needs to be identified as soon as possible. After obtaining a set of working architect's drawings of the rooms portion of the hotel and related areas (which allows the housekeeper to study the physical layout of the facility), he/she should make, regular tours of the property and prepare a 'Division of work document' which states the scope of cleaning the property will require. This should be presented to the executive committee (top policy making body comprising of GM, Resident Manager, Director F&B, Controller, Director Sales and Marketing. Chief Engineer, Director of Personnel, Security Director) with recommendations as to who should be responsible for cleaning and maintaining each area. The executive committee (or GM in smaller hotels) will assign area on a copy of the floor plan blue print, by showing boundary lines, so that no overlapping occurs and no area is left unassigned.

Most housekeeping departments are responsible for the following areas: guest rooms, corridors, public areas, pool and patio areas, management offices, storage areas, linen rooms, laundry rooms, locker rooms, banquet areas, exercise rooms, hotel operated shops, etc. If housekeeping is expected to clean a certain area other than these, such as kitchens, then budgetary compensation and personnel must be provided and charged to the department receiving the service.

During the frequent tours of the property, one should also learn the location of the various storerooms and service areas. Joint tours are recommended so that department heads can reuse with one another about the use of space such as housekeeping needs floor linen rooms, the chief engineer will need storage space, F & B requires service pantries, etc.

Area Inventory Lists

The first step in planning is developing Area Inventory Lists. These lists will show in detail all of the items within the areas, which will need housekeeping's attention.

Prequency Schedules

Frequency schedules indicate how often items an area inventory list must be cleaned and inspected. Items cleaned daily or weekly are made as part of a routine cleaning schedule and incorporated into standard work procedures. Items which are cleaned bi-weekly, monthly or according to some other cycle are inspected daily or weekly but are part of a general (spring) cleaning program which are scheduled on a calendar. The housekeeper should coordinate spring cleaning for periods of low occupancy.

Performance Standards

Productivity standards determine the quantity of work to be performed by employees. They determine the time required to perform tasks according to performance standards. Quality and quantity must always be balanced and neither be sacrificed for the other. The Executive Housekeeper should always seek methods for increasing efficiency and productivity while maintaining performance standards.

Inventory Levels

To ensure that employees have the necessary equipment and supplies to do their jobs, the Executive Housekeeper should maintain and control two types of the inventories within the department.

Recycled inventories include items that are used for long periods replaced only when they wear out or fail to meet the needs of the staff. Example linen, maid carts, vacuum cleaners. The number of recycled items required in inventory for daily operations is called

Non-recycled inventories are consumed and exhausted during routine activities and are replaced often, example cleaning products and guestroom amenities. A purchase order system for non-recycled inventory establishes a par number of items based on minimum and maximum. Excess stock takes up space and ties up too much of the property's cash

Budget

Housekeeping is not a revenue generating department, the executive housekeeper's primary responsibility for achieving financial goal is to control the department's expenses.

The Budget Process

- The operating budget outlines the financial goals of a hotel.

- The purpose of the operating budget is to relate operational costs to the years expected revenues.

- The yearly operating budget is broken down into budgets for each month of the fiscal (financial) year.

- In addition, each dept. prepares its own monthly budget. These budgets serve as a guide for how dept. will achieve its expected contribution to the property's financial goals.

Essentially Budget is a Plan. It Projects Both:

- The revenue the hotel anticipates during the period covered by the budget.
- The expenses required to generate the anticipated revenue.

'A budget is a plan by which resources required to generate revenues are allocated'.

The ex. Housekeeper's responsibilities in budgetary process are in two fold:

- The ex. Housekeeper is involved in the planning process that leads to the formulation of the budget. This informs the rooms' division manager and G.M. what expenses H.K. will incur in light of forecasted room sales.

- The budget represents an operational plan for the year. The ex. housekeeper ensures that dept's actual expenses are in line with budgeted costs and with the actual occupancy level.

As a plan a budget is not 'set in stone'. It may need to be adjusted in light of unforeseen circumstances.

If occupancy level exceeds expectation, then increased expenses need to be planned for, and incorporated into a revised budget. Their effect on the overall plan needs to be assessed as well.

As a plan budget is also a guide. It provides managers with the standards by which they can measure the success of operation.

By comparing actual expense with allocated amount, the ex housekeeper can track the efficiency of housekeeping operations and monitor the dept.'s ability to keep the expenses within the prescribed limits.

Types of Budget

Two types of budgets are used in managing a hotel's financial resources:

- Capital budget and Operating budget.
- Categorized by types of expenditure-

Capital budget- A capital budget plans for the expenditure of company assets for item costing 25,000 or more. For e.g. furniture, fixture, equipments etc. are capital expenditure. Capital budget in H.K. may include Room attendant's cart, vacuum cleaner, pile lifter etc.

Operating budget- Operating budget forecasts revenue and expenses associated with the routine operation of the hotel during a certain period. Operating expenditure are those costs the hotel incurs in order to generate revenue in the normal course of doing business. In housekeeping the most expensive operational cost is salary and wages. The cost of non-recycled items, such a cleaning and guest supplies are also considered operational cost.

Pre-opening budget- These force the planning necessary for the smooth opening of new property/hotel. These budget allocate resources for opening parties advertising, generation of initial goodwill, liaison, and PR. Pre-opening budget also include the initial cost of employee salaries, wages, as well as purchasing supplies, crockery, cutlery, linen, etc.

Types of Budget	Inclusions
Capital Budget	Furniture, fixture, equipment
Operating Budget	Non Recycled Items
Pre- Opening Budget	Supplies, crockery, cutlery.

Categorized By Department Involved-

Based on department involved budget may be categorized into master budget or department budget.

Master budget- These represent the forecasted targets set for the whole organization and incorporate all incomes and expenditures estimated for the organization.

Department budget- Each dept (FnB Maintenance, housekeeping and front office etc) of the hotel forwards a budget for its estimated expense and revenue to the financial controller. Rooms' division budget is in this case a combined budget of the front office and housekeeping dept.

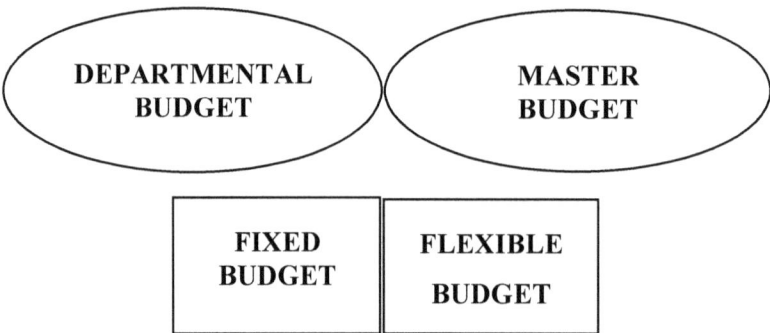

Categorized by Flexibility of Expenditure-

- **Fixed budget-** These budget remain unchanged over a period of time and are not related to the level of revenues. Such budgets include budget for advertising and administration.

- **Flexible budget-** These budgets pre- determine expenditure based on the revenue expected and differ with different volumes of sale.

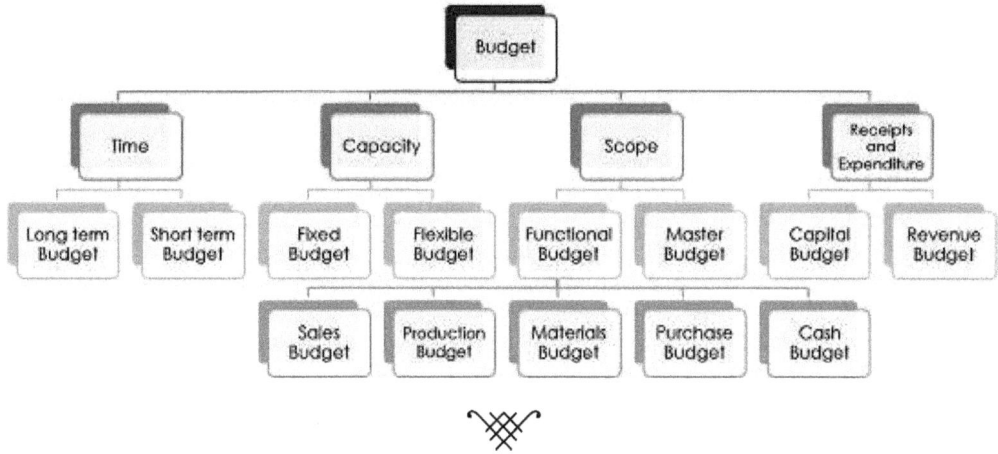

Emergencies And Dealing with Them

Emergencies are unpredictable combination of circumstances that call for immediate and enlightened action. It can often be anticipated but seldom foreseen.

The 2 important aspects of emergencies, are that they are unpredictable and uncontrollable. Both these factors produce unwanted and unanticipated side effects, since reactions to emergencies by guests and at times employees, are equally unanticipated and unwanted. It is therefore imperative that there be advance planning and safety precautions in combating all types of emergencies.

Safely is the term used when discussing disasters, fire prevention and protection, protection devices and commissions that provide for freedom from injury.

In order to maintain a safe premise, the management must be ready to cope with 5 types of emergencies.

a. Fire iv. Death of a guest / employee - suicide, etc.

b. Bomb threats v. Civil disturbances - riots

c. Natural disasters - floods, storms.

Bomb Threats

Bomb threats could be done in three ways :

i. Telephonically ii. Written iii. Orally

If a telephonic threat is received, then

Telephone Operator	Inform the Gm
➢ **Remain Calm**	
❖ Note the time.	Notify police, security and maintenance
❖ Get another employee to monitor the call so as to duplicate information.	Record chronologically actions and events
❖ Pay attention to message background and noise.	Discuss with police to determine partial or complete evacuation. Complete telephone threat checklist.
❖ Try to keep the caller on line as long as possible.	Decide about localized or general search. Based on information received take action
❖ Try to get following information ▪ Expected explosion time ▪ Location ▪ Type of explosive	

- How to recognize
- What will it set off?
- What would influence him to change tactics? (What are his demands?)

If a written note is received, then the receiver should read it very carefully, calmly and try to keep all fingerprints on it. It should then be handed over to security and the GM should be informed. The GM in turn informs the police, who decide whether the hotel should be evacuated or not.

If an oral threat is received, then detain the person who brought the message, inform the GM, who in cum informs the police. If the person has left the hotel, tack him down or get his physical description or car number, etc.

Natural Disasters - Flood *Prevention:*
- Identify low lying areas
- Life jackets
- Shift important equipment to higher floors
- Make the place water tight using sandbags at doors.

The Following Equipment Should be Kept at Hand:
- Supply of containers for cb 'nking water.
- Battery operated radio wi ti spare battery, flash lights.
- Bags for sand bagging.
- Fully stocked first aid kit.
- Rope for landing down objects.

Responsibilities of The Management:
General Manager
- Monitor radio, T. V. for information update.
- Follow progress of preparation in hotel.
- Determine how many employees are needed and willing lo remain.
- Maintain contact with claims adjustment organization (Insurance).

Engineer
- Hotel vehicle io be kept ready.
- Move tools and equipment to higher floors.
- Disconnect power to lower levels.

Housekeeping
- Move furniture and supplies to higher levels.
- Fill tubs / sinks with water.

F&B Management
- Contact guests - explain weather conditions and emergency preparations.
- Offer guests opportunities to decide whether they should stay or leave.

Death of Guest/Employee

The front office should inform the CM. security officer and call for the hotel doctor. An alarm is to be raised or guests informed of the fact. The room must not be touched, cleaned without permission and must be scaled until all police formalities are over. People known to the deceased are coolacted through addresses entered on the registration card. If the guest is at foreigner the embassy should be informed.

If an employee dies on duty, the procedure followed is the same. A report is done on the death, i.e. whether accidental, etc. and the relatives are informed.

Inform the Lobby Manager und Executive Housekeeper Seal of the area (DND displayed)

Nobody allowed inside, nothing to be removed. Do not clean up until permission is granted.

Notify local police, hotel doctor, next of kin (Indian), embassy (foreigner)

Body removed through the service entrance with permission of police, Room thoroughly conduct witnessed inventory of cleaned and fumigated, deceased's belongings and store securely.

Obtain receipts from local authorities and from individuals claiming the deceased's belongings

Fire

Fires are either minor or major. In either case, they cause panle which increases the situation and at times even cause death.

The hotel follows certain policies for fire. Resically they are 3, one for the hotel, one for the employees and one for the guest. In the hotel we find fire alarms, fire escapes and fire extinguishers. For the employee fire fighting training, fire drills. For the geust, (booklets).

Hotel Fire Fighting Team

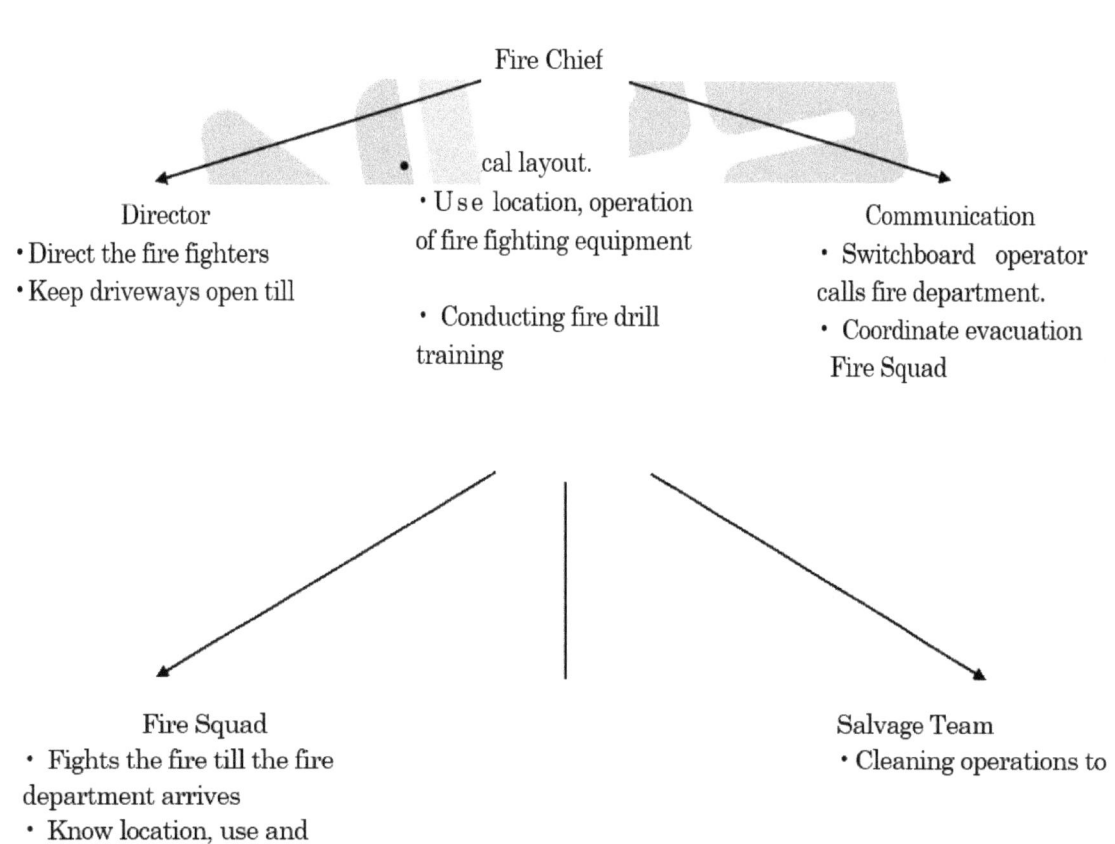

Environmentally Friendly Processes

The reduce, reuse, recycle, credo of the environmental movement is playing a growing role in lodging operations. Concern for the environment is on the minds of many travelers, and mom properties do not want to risk alienating guests with policies that show a callous disregard for the environment. There are various ways of exhibiting environmentally sound cleaning practices like:

- Rethinking cleaning practices to find ways to reduce chemical, water, energy and paper usage.

- Reviewing the contents of cleaning chemicals to make sure that they are biodegradable and environmentally safe.

- Buying exclusively from vendors who also promote environmentally friendly products

- Finding outlets for reuse of consumable supplies.

- Creating training programs for staff like showing them films, or providing them with information packages.

- Helping guests to be aware of the use of environmentally friendly methods of cleanliness like re-using bath and bed linen during the stay of a single guest, asking the guest to place empty recycled cans and bottles on top of the minibar/dresser and the room attendant would do the needful. Tent cards or door hangers could also be provided to the quest's explaining to them the hotel's environmental programs.

The housekeeping department will have the maximum changes within if the hotel opts for environmentally friendly practices. Therefore the executive housekeeper should ensure that going 'green' retains a low budgetary investment and no risk to staff and guests as well as prove the best to save our natural resources.

The following methods could prove fruitful is incorporated into the hotel's operating systems:

Conservation

- Giving guests the option of not having towels and linen changed daily.

- Use fluorescent bulbs which last longer and reduces energy usage.

- Using all bath, hair and skin care products in permanent wall dispensers.

Waste Reduction

- Ideally nothing should be discarded.

- Usage of refill containers.

- Use of cloth bags instead of paper.

- If paper is used, it should be recycled.

- Providing guests with glasses instead of plastic.
- Old furniture and mattresses should be given away during staff auctioning or to charity.

Water/Energy Conservation

- Reset the rooms air conditioning or heating, to minimal in vacant rooms.
- Leave on only one lamp at turndown service.
- Disconnect fridges and minibars in vacant rooms.
- Close faucets tightly and report any leakage.
- Do not iron linen, fold immediately after drying crease remains.
- Avoid letting water run until it is hot.
- Wash only full loads of laundry.
- Turn off the lights in the back of the house when work is completed.
- Turn off the lights in areas not in use during the day especially.

Recycling

- Cans, bottles, newspapers, etc should be recycled therefore instruction should be given to staff and guests to segregate them after use. Storage of all glass, aluminum and papers should be done separately.
- They should not attract pests and vermin therefore storage of these should be for a minimum time period.

Glossary

A	
Acrylic **Antimicrobial treatment**	Synthetic material used in making fabric or moulded transparent fixtures.
Acoustics	Carpet treatment in which a solution is applied to the carpet to kill bacteria and fungi and the odours they cause.
Amenity	Sound absorption quality of certain materials, usually on the walls, ceilings or floors.
Alkalies	A service or item offered to guests or placed in guest rooms for convenience or comfort at no extra cost. Laundry chemicals that help detergents lather better and keep stains suspended in the wash water after they have been loosened and lifted from the fabric. They also help in neutralizing acidic stains and making detergents more effective.
Antichlor	Laundry chemicals that are sometimes used at the rinse point in the wash cycle to ensure that all the chlorine in the bleach has been removed
Acute hazard	Something that could cause immediate harm. e.g. a chemical that could cause bums on contact with skin is an acute hazard. Scheduling staff to work hours different from the regular work hours.
Area inventory list	A list of all items within a particular area that need cleaning or attention of housekeeping personnel.

B	
Back of the house	The functional areas of the hotel in which employees have little or no guest contact
Box Springs BCF	Type of bed springs fastened to a wood frame. Bulk Continuous fibre that are used to construct non-woven or tufted carpets.
Bleach	It is a chemical It is a chemical used generally in the laundry for whitening of fabrics and also for disinfection and stain removal. There are two types of bleach : oxidizing bleach and reducing bleach.
Break	This is a point in the laundry wash cycle at which a high alkaline soil-loosening product is added. The break cycle is usually at medium temperature and at low

	water level.
Builders	Builders or alkalies are laundry chemicals that are often added to detergents to soften water and to remove oils and grease.
C	
Cross Training	Teaching employees to fulfill the requirements of more than one position.
Capital Budget	A detailed plan for the acquisition of equipments, land, buildings and other fixed assets.
Capital Expenditure	Items that are very expensive and are not used up in the normal course of operation and that, which has a lifespan that exceeds one year. Something that could cause harm over a long period. Items with tops and sides such as bureaus and desks.
Chronic Hazard Case goods	Intensive or specialized cleaning undertaken in guest rooms or Public Areas. Often conducted according to a special schedule or on a special project basis.
D	
Deep Cleaning	A department or property programme that influences employees to encourage friends or acquaintances to apply for a position.
Delustered	A process in which mangers seek outside applicants to fill open position. A key, which opens all guest room doors even when they are double lock.
E	
Employee referral programme	Carpet treatment in which a solution is applied to make the carpet resistant to static electricity.
External recruiting	The functional areas of the hotel in which employees have extensive guest contact.
Emergency key	A schedule that indicates how often each item on an area inventory list needs to be maintained.
Electrostatic dissipation	Positions that must be filled regardless of the volume of business. A training model used to implement an on-the-job training programme
F	
Front of the house	The four steps are prepare, present, practice and follow-up.
Frequency schedule **Fixed Staff Positions Four-**	These are laundry chemicals that keep fabrics looking new and colours clothes to their original shade. These chemicals are often pre-mixed with detergents. They are also called optical brighteners.

step training	
Flatwork ironers	These are used for ironing flats. These press by rolling over the material. Some ironers also fold the articles automatically
Flushes	Steps in the wash cycle that dissolve and dilute water-soluble Sails to reduce the soil load for the upcoming suds step. Items are generally flushed at medium temp & at high water level.
Flame Spread Index	A scale that measures how quickly a flame will spread across the materials exposed finished surface.
Fill or Weft Yams	Yams running the width of the fabric.
Flat Bed Spring	Bed spring made of metal slats linked with helical hooks.
Face	The pile of the carpet.
Face fibres Face weight	Yams that form the pile of the carpet. The measure of a carpets pile equal to the weight of the face fibres in lsg yard of the carpet.
G	
Guest Room Key	A key that opens a single guest room door if it is not double lock.
H	
Hard floor	A flooring which is hard and non resilient. Types of hard floors include terrazzo, ceramic tiles, natural stones, wood etc.
Homogeneous colour	Colour that permeates the entire layers of vinyl flooring so that the colour does not wear of with use. Hot cold-water extraction A deep cleaning method of carpet in which a machine sprays a detergent and water solution into the carpet and vacuums up the solution and the soil.
Helical hooks Hand caddy	Small coils with hooks on both ends. A portable container for storing and transporting cleaning supplies carried by the room attendants. Openings in washing machines through which detergents can be poured.
Hoppers	Also called ports Hazard communication standard. The total number of each type of linen that is needed to outfit all guestrooms one time. This is also referred to as one par of linen.
HazComm Standard House setup Housekeeping	A report that housekeeping department prepares that indicate the current housekeeping status of each room based on physical check.

status	
Incentive programme	A programme offering special recognition and rewards, to employees based on their ability and exceptional performance beyond the paycheck.
Internal recruiting	A process in which managers recmit candidates from within a department or property.
Inventory	Stocks of merchandise, operating supplies and other items held for future use in a hospitality operation
Issuing Innerspring mattress	The process of distributing inventory items from the store room to authorized individuals by the use of formal requisition. Mattress in which springs are sandwiched between layers of padding.
Job safety analysis	A detailed report that lists every job performed by all housekeeping employees. Each task is further broken down into a list of steps; these steps are accompanied by tips and instructions on how to perform each step safely.
Job analysis	Determining what knowledge each position needs, what tasks each position needs to perform, and the standards at which the employees must perform the task.
Job breakdown	A form that details how the technical duties of the job should be performed
Job knowledge	Information that an employee must understand in order to perform his or her task
Job list	A list identifying all the key duties of a job in the order of their importance.
Job description	A detailed list identifying all the key duties of a job as well as reporting relationships, additional responsibilities, working conditions and any necessary equipments and materials.
K	
	The process of reducing guest and property theft and other security related incidents by carefully monitoring and tracking the use of keys in a hotel
Leased employees Lead-time quantity	Employees which a leasing agency hires and leases to business. The number of purchased units consumed between the time that a supply order is placed and the time that the order is actually received
Linen room	An area in an hospitality operation where the entire linen of the hotel is stored, issued, exchanged and controlled
M	
Modacrylic Metal coil	

springs Mitering	
	Acrylic fibre that is less resistant to stains and abrasions.
	Bed springs in which metal coils provide support and resiliency. A method of contouring a sheet or blanket to fit the corners of the mattress in a smooth and neat manner. It is also referred to as envelope fold or square corners.
Mildewcides Master key	Laundry chemicals added to the wash cycle to prevent the growth of bacteria and fungus on linen.
MSDS	A key which opens all guest room doors which are not double locked.
	Material safety data sheet-A form that is supplied by chemical manufacturers containing information about a chemical
Maximum quantity	The greatest number of purchase units that should be in stock at any time.
Minimum quantity	The fewest number of purchase units that should be in stock any given time.
Motivation	Stimulating a person's interest in a particular job, project, subject so that the individual is challenged to be continuousl attentive, observant, concerned and committed.
Mid-market service	A modest but sufficient level of service which appeals to the largest segment of traveling public.
N	
Non-recycled inventories	Those items in stock that are consumed or used up during the course of routine housekeeping operations; it includes cleaning supplies, small equipments, guest supplies and amenities.
Networking	Developing personal connections with friends, acquaintances, colleagues, associates, teachers, counselors and others
	Not having pores thus is non absorbing.
Nonporous NRC scale	Noise Reduction Coefficient; a scale that designates the amount of sound a material absorbs.
Napery	Table linen.
O	
Occasional table OSHA	A small end table.
Operating budget	Occupational Safety and Health Act; a broad set of rules that protects workers in all trades and professions from a variety of unsafe working conditions.
Operating	A detailed plan for generating revenue and incurring expenses for each

expenditure	department within the hospitality operation.
Organization chart	Costs incurred in order to generate revenue in the normal course of doing business.
Occupancy Report	A schematic representation of relationships between positions within an organization showing where each position fits into the overall organization and illustrating the divisions of responsibility and lined of authority. A report prepared by each shift in the housekeeping department showing the actual status of rooms after a physical check.
P	
Preventive maintenance	A systematic approach to maintenance in which situations are identified and corrected on a regular basis to control cost and to keep larger problems from occurring.
Par number	A multiple of the standard quantity of a particular inventory item that represents the quantity of the item that must be on hand to support daily and routine housekeeping operations.
Performance standard	A required level of performance that establishes the quality of work that must be done.
Productivity standard	an acceptable amount of work that must be done within a specific t'me frame according to an established performance standard.
Performance appraisal Par	The process by which an employee is periodically evaluated by his or her manager to access job performance and to discuss steps the employee can take to improve job skill and performance. The standard quantity of a particular inventory item must be on hand to support daily and routine housekeeping operations.
Perpetual inventory systems	An inventory system in which receipts and issues are recorded as they occur. This system provides readily available information on inventory levels and cost of sales.
Proforma income statement	A report that predicts the result of current or future operation, Including revenues earned and expense incurred in generating the revenues for the period covered by the statement.
PH scale	A scale that measure the acidity or alkalinity of a substance; according to the scale a pH of 7 is neutral; acid has values of less than 7 to 0; and alkalis have value from 7 to 14. A polyester and a cotton blend.
Polycotton Ports	Openings into washing machines through which detergents can be poured; also called hoppers.
Permanent assembly	In lamps when the base and the light sockets are fused together to prevent loosening.

Porous Plain weave	A material having pores and which is also absorbent. A type of weave of weave in which filled yams are alternately woven under and over the warp yams.
Pile	Consists of fibres or yearns the form raised loops that can be cut or sheared.
Pile distortion	Pace fiber condition such as twisting, piling, flaring or matting caused, by heavy traffic or improper cleaning methods.
Primary backing	The part of the carpet to which face fibres are attached and which holds this fibres in place.

R

Resihent floor	A type of floor that reduces noise and is considered easier to stand and walk on than hard floors, Types of resilient floors include vinyl, rubber, linoleum etc.
Rotary floor machine	Floor care equipment that accommodates both brushes and pads to perform both carpet shampooing and floor burnishing, scrubbing, buffing etc.
Room attendant's cart	Floor care equipment that accommodates both brushes and pads to perform both carpet shampooing and floor burnishing, scrubbing, buffing etc.
Room inspection	A detailed process in which guest rooms are systematically checked for cleanliness and maintenance needs.
Room status report	A report that allows the housekeeping department to identify the occupancy of a hotel's rooms
Recycled inventories	Those items in stock that have relatively limited useful lives, but are used over and over in housekeeping operations. They include linen, uniforms, equipments and guest loan items
Recruitment	Activities related to the upkeep of the property that are initiated through a formal work order or similar document.

S

Scheduled maintenance Support center	An operating division or department which does not generate direct revenue, but plays a supporting role to the hotel's revenue centers. Support centers include housekeeping, accounting, engineering etc. A process in which the appropriate number of employees are assigned to fulfill necessary duties and positions each workday. A system used to establish the number of labour hours needed. The number of purchase units that must always be in hand for smooth operation in the event of emergencies, spoilage, unexpected delays in delivery or other situations. Conditions in which people are safe from injury, hurt or loss.
Scheduling	The prevention of theft, fire and other emergency situations.

Staffing guide Safety stock	A committee consisting of key management personnel and selected employees that develops and monitors a property's security plans and programmes
Sizing Sour	Laundry chemicals used to stiffen polyester blends. Mild acids used to neutralize residual alkalinity in fabrics after washing and rinsing.
Steam cabinet Steam tunnel	A box in which articles are hung and steamed to remove wrinkles. A laundry equipment that moves articles on hangers through a tunnel, steaming them and removing the wrinkles as they move through.
Surfactants Spline Satin weave	These are chemicals present in detergents that aid in soil removal. Thin wood slat used to attach panels to a wall or ceiling. A type of weave in which the warp threads interlace with filling threads to produce a smooth faced fabric.
Solid mattress Secondary backing	Mattress stuffed with hair, cotton, coir or a similar material. The part of a carpet that is laminated to the primary backing to provide additional stability and more secure installation.
Shading	A carpet condition that occurs when the pile is brushed in two different directions so that dark and light areas appear.
Staple fibres	Fibres approximately seven to ten inches long that are twisted together into long strands.
T	
Tufted carpets	Tunnel washer
Thread count Ticking Twill weave Turndown service	Number of warp and weft yarns per square inch of the fabric. A sturdy fabric used to cover mattresses and springs.
Tunnel washer	Type of weave in which a diagonal yarn pattern emerges. A special service provided by the housekeeping department in the evening in which a room attendant gives the turndown service to the bed, restocks supplies and tidies up the room. A long sequential laundry machine that operates continuously processing each stage of the wash or rinse cycle and extracting in another section of the machine.

	V
Vitreous china	A material from which bathroom fixtures are made.
Variable staff positions	Positions that are filled in relation to change in hotel occupancy

	W
Wi-fi	Wireless fidelity - An amenity provided nowadays by hotels. The technology enables guests to access a wide range of information, applications and computing resources without having to worry about connectivity issues.
Work Study	An analysis of the tasks, the equipments and the time taken to do a specific job. This is an important tool for determining standard operating procedure.
World class service	A level of service, which stresses the personal attention given to the guest. Hotels offering world class service provide upscale restaurant and lounge, exclusive decor, concierge service and various other services. Floor care equipment used to pick up spills or to pick up rinse water that is used during carpet or floor cleaning.
Wet vacuum Wicking	A carpet condition that occur when the backing of the carpet becomes wet; and the face yam draw the moisture and the colour of the backing to the carpet surface.

www.ingramcontent.com/pod-product-compliance
Lightning Source LLC
LaVergne TN
LVHW070530070526
838199LV00075B/6743